THE ROMANCE OF THE STATE

The essays in this book explore the scope, limits, and fate of some
key concepts in the mainstream culture of politics that have come
to structure India's public life.

This brilliant and provocative book reveals Nandy's astonishing range of
interests, his ability to discover invisible dimensions in everyday concepts
and events, and his profound imagination and concern for the future of
democratic politics. These powerful alternative readings of the vital issues
facing Indian politics will seal Nandy's image as the most important
commentator on Indian society and politics of this generation.

The Romance of the State

And the Fate of Dissent in the Tropics

Ashis Nandy

OXFORD
UNIVERSITY PRESS

OXFORD
UNIVERSITY PRESS

Oxford University Press is a department of the University of Oxford.
It furthers the University's objective of excellence in research, scholarship,
and education by publishing worldwide. Oxford is a registered trademark of
Oxford University Press in the UK and in certain other countries

Published in India by
Oxford University Press
22 Workspace, 2nd Floor, 1/22 Asaf Ali Road, New Delhi 110 002

First Edition published in 2003
Oxford India Paperbacks 2007
18th impression 2024

ISBN-13: 978-0-19-569333-1
ISBN-10: 0-19-569333-7

Typeset in Giovanni 10/12
by Eleven Arts, Keshav Puram, Delhi 110035
Printed in India by Manipal Technologies Limited, Manipal

To the memory of Kamala Nandy, who walked out of this world to make me aware that an age was over

Contents

Preface   ix

PART ONE

The State: The Fate of a Concept   1

Culture, State and the Rediscovery of Indian Politics   15

PART TWO

An Anti-Secularist Manifesto   34

The Twilight of Certitudes: Secularism, Hindu
    Nationalism and Other Masks of Deculturation   61

History's Forgotten Doubles   83

State, History, and Exile in South Asian Politics:
    Modernity and the Landscape of Clandestine
    and Incommunicable Selves   110

Terrorism—Indian Style: The Birth of a Political Issue
    in a Populist Democracy   132

PART THREE

Culture, Voice, and Development: A Primer for the
    Unsuspecting   151

Development and Violence   171

The Scope and Limits of Dissent: India's First Modern
    Environmentalist and His Critique of the DVC   182

Index   208

Preface

D uring the last three decades I have worked intermittently on the culture of Indian politics. This is a strange, ill-defined area stretching across the borders of political sociology and cultural psychology where political cultures shape the fate—the birth, growth, decline, death and after-life—of traditions. Work in this area has taught me that in an open society, however imperfect the openness, politics can be an instrument of collective creativity. For politics is nothing less than a means of redefining a society's selfhood by renegotiating the distribution of power and the legitimacy of existing centres of power in different domains of life.

This connection with the redefinition of self explains why political choices at the ground level, contrary to the belief of hard-nosed political analysts, tend to be moral choices. Even when the morality underlying them is exploited by politicians driven by a pure theory of self-interest, even when that morality finds itself hitched to causes that are sectional or xenophobic. Those who want to intervene in real-life politics cannot ignore that moral frame. Hence the constant efforts of practitioners of the art of politics to justify, honestly or hypocritically, their most expropriatory and sadistic projects in languages that pay respect to the social and cultural values of their society. Political hypocrisy is the homage that *realpolitik* pays to the popular culture of politics in a plebiscitary democracy. That is the lesson we should have learnt from twentieth-century applications of nineteenth-century social theories which, in their romantic enthusiasm for the apparent certitudes of modern science, mounted a vain search for a fully value-neutral—read amoral—social knowledge. Such attempts to actualize our visions through scientized social interventions explain a significant proportion of the violence and exploitation to which the twentieth century has been witness.

This tacit moral substratum of politics explains why, in some phases of a country's life, when the political class becomes unusually venal, violent and Machiavellian, the structure of power comes to depend not merely on social hierarchies like class and caste, but also on the dominant ideology of public life. That ideology provides the moral veneer to mainstream political activity, which would otherwise seem to follow the law of a Hobbesian jungle. More important, this dominant ideology of public life marks out a place for, and partially legitimizes, ethical transgressions as sad but unavoidable temporary compromises that have to be made for a larger good. When such a culture of politics crystallizes in a country, knowledge becomes the key to power not in the popular sense that knowledge is power, but in the odd sense that it is mainly through cognitive categories that dominance is produced, sustained, legitimized and, as sometimes happens, subverted. This collection of essays reflects the growing awareness of that alternative route to, and justification for, the fuzzy subdiscipline called the politics of knowledge.

Most of these essays were written in the 1980s and 1990s, some as parts of a psychological biography of the Indian state that never got written. I gave up the enterprise halfway, not so much because I had had my say on the subject—my recent work shows that the subject has, if anything, grown on me—but because I got tired of dealing with the darker side of public life. State-formation and nation-building are everywhere something of a criminal enterprise and delving into them can be tiresome after a point. The beautiful prose, the laudable sentiments, and the languages of rationality and science that cover up the enterprise deserve sustained analysis, but I decided I was probably not the right person for the job.

The best I could do was explore the scope, limits and fate of some key concepts in the mainstream culture of politics that have come to structure India's public life. These concepts constitute the dominant public ideology of the Indian state and ground this ideology within the consciousness of the expanding middle classes in the country. The concepts I have in mind range from concrete concerns such as 'secularism' and 'development' to more abstract ones such as 'dissent' and 'history'. This collection of essays is thus a companion to my other book, *The Savage Freud and Other Essays on Possible and Retrievable Selves* (New Delhi:

Oxford University Press, 1995). Both are premised on Theodor Adorno's almost casual proposal that political analysis is closer to the truth when it subverts the interests of the class from which it emanates. I hope Asian and African intellectuals living in post-colonial societies, haunted by and simultaneously fighting the ghosts from their colonial pasts and the dreams of progress their parents dreamt, will find some resonance in the problems raised here.

There is one other caveat. The standard historical, philosophical and social-scientific scholarship on the state offers little scope to those obstinate Asians and Africans who see the post-seventeenth-century concept of the state as less than perennial. Almost the entire body of European socialist thought has not merely bypassed nonwestern experiences with the state but has been dismissive of it. Even Bakunin and Kropotkin, though deeply suspicious of the modern state, are undeterred by their total ignorance of the non-West and summarily steamroll all nonwestern traditions of the state into a unified concept of the state so as to critique it.

The essays in this book, though mostly inquiries into the culture of the Indian state, suggest tangentially the directions in which to move for a cultural and psychological biography of the state. In no system can there be a perfect accord between the institutions of state and the myths and fantasies that get organized around the idea of the state. In post-colonial societies the gap between the two is not only more pronounced but also less predictable. These societies cannot take a merely instrumental view of the institutions of the modern state or, for that matter, of modernity. Yet they suspect that they live in a world in which the space available for their precolonial and noncolonial traditions is limited. They have to simultaneously live in a number of cultures and epochs and with a variety of political technologies of survival. Once the idea of historical stages and the triumphalism of the European Enlightenment are jettisoned, one may open up for these societies creative possibilities unimagined by existing scholarship on the state.

The essays assembled here, by the very nature of this enterprise, are products of three influences, none of them respectable. First, my illiteracy in formal political theory which has made me open to non-academic intellectuals such as Henry David Thoreau, William Blake and Mohandas Karamchand Gandhi. Second, my admiration for the obduracy of those who refuse to accept the intellectual constructions of the European Enlightenment as the last word in social ingenuity and political creativity. And third, my occasional flirtation with human-rights activism which has convinced me that the modern nation-state, when transplanted into the Third World, can outperform any old-style Oriental despotism in matters of authoritarianism and organized violence.

The idea of a moderate state—of a state that was neither over-burdened with the responsibility of engineering all aspects of its citizens' lives nor seeking to extend the Midas touch of the market and global capital into every corner of every society—was not unknown to all societies at all times. While such moderate states may not have been great successes and may not have survived, neither can the modern nation-state system, claim to be the greatest success story of all times. The question of its survival as an arrangement of political communities, too, remains to be finally decided. The essays in this book explore the vicissitudes of the idea of the modern state under different cultural and psychological conditions.

All this is only a long-winded way of claiming that there is scope for new theories located outside the mainstream academic discourse on the state that will be more clearly geared to serve the purposes of the non-state actors and movements in Asia and Africa. These theories will be in simultaneous dialogue with popular expectations from the state and vague public memories of the pre-modern states in the region and may not be too keen to engage formal academic works on the contemporary state.

Earlier versions of some of the essays have been published in various places. 'The State: The Fate of a Concept' first appeared in Wolfgang Sachs (ed.), *The Development Dictionary* (London: Zed, 1992); 'Culture, State and the Rediscovery of Indian Politics', was delivered as the Rajiv Bambawale Lecture at the Indian Institute of Technology, New Delhi; 'An Anti-Secularist Manifesto' and 'Terrorism—Indian Style' were published in *Seminar*; 'The Twilight of Certitudes' in its earlier incarnations in *Alternatives* and *Postcolonial Studies*. 'State, History and Exile' was presented at the Macalester International Roundtable and published in Ahmed Samatar (ed.), *The Divided Self: Identity and Globalization* (St. Paul: Macalester College, 1997). 'History's Forgotten Double' is a revised version of the Opening Address at the World History Conference at the Wesleyan University, 1994, and published in *History and Theory* 1995 (Theme Issue 34); 'Culture, Voice, and Development' was written for a Japanese volume, Yoshikaju Sakamoto (ed.), *The Changing Structure of World Politics* (Tokyo: Iwanami Shoten, 1991); 'Development and Violence' was first written for Charles Strozier and

Michael Flynn (ed.), *Trauma and Community: Essays in Honour of Robert J. Lifton* (New York: Rowman and Littlefield, 1996); and 'The Scope and Limits of Dissent' was first presented in a conference on the Greening of Economics at Bellagio, 2–6 August 1993.

These essays owe much to discussions with and criticisms from friends, colleagues, and enemies all over the world. I should especially mention Giri Deshingkar, Ziauddin Sardar, Philip Pomper, Stephen and Frédérique Marglin, Jyoti Ananthu, Wolfgang Sachs, T.N. Madan, Vijay Pratap, Bhikhu Parekh, Tariq Banuri, Veena Das, R.B.J. Walker, and Vinay Lal. This collection also gives me a chance to acknowledge my immense debts to three persons who have shaped my understanding of the empirical realities of Indian politics for about three decades but whose influence, because of the nature of my concerns, has never been obvious—Dhirubhai Sheth, James Manor and Bashiruddin Ahmed. I am grateful to Ruchi Pant for supplying and processing some of the data used in the paper on Kapil Bhattacharjee and to Tilottama Bhattacharjee, Radium Bhattacharjee-Dalwadi, Pradyumna and Sutapa Bhattacharjee for biographical details of the life of Kapil Bhattacharjee and for making available to me some of his unpublished works.

A couple of these essays have been mauled by time, especially since they were direct responses to live public issues, written as conversations with movements and activist friends. I have included them because they also are a record of what I have learnt by trying to decipher the often-unacknowledged theoretical assumptions that inform the environmental, peace, human rights and other forms of political activism of friends too numerous to be listed. I may disagree with them on many issues, but I am sure the next generation will be as beholden to them as I for making the earth a less uninhabitable, violent and expropriatory place.

New Delhi
2002

PART ONE

The State: The Fate of a Concept

The growing interest in the nature of the state represents the revival of a major intellectual concern of the 1950s and 1960s: state- and nation-building in old societies turned new nations. However, the current interest in the state has a different tonal quality to it, for during the last three decades the world has witnessed a major change in the context in which studies of the state are conducted.

The 1950s and 1960s were a period of optimism. It was widely believed in the modern world, and in modern centres of the nonmodern world, that every society had to pass through clear-cut historical stages and finally conform to the prevalent model of a proper nation-state—exactly as every economy had to go through fixed stages of growth to attain the beatitude of development. It was also believed that while passing through these inescapable stages, each society had to restructure its culture, shed its retrogressive bits, and cultivate those cultural traits that were compatible with the needs of a modern nation-state.

Two forces seem to have changed that easy, progressivist view of the relationship between culture and the state. First, a huge majority of southern societies have failed to walk successfully the arduous path of 'progress'—laid out so considerately by the dominant school of post-World War II social sciences—and they have failed to develop into viable nation-states along the lines prescribed by post-seventeenth-century Europe. The state in these societies often looks today like some kind of specialized coercive apparatus or private business venture. Second, culture in these societies has shown more resilience than expected by the learned and the knowledgeable. When pitted against the needs and rationales of the state, it is often the state that has given way to culture. This resilience of culture, also expressed in the spirited resurgence of ethnic self-awareness in many societies, seems to show that what was once possible within small tribes and minorities is no longer possible within larger cultural entities without arousing stiff resistance. Cultures can no longer be bulldozed by the global forces of modernity. Increasingly, cultures are refusing to sing their swansongs and bow out of the world stage to enter the textbooks of history. Indeed, cultures have now begun to return, like Freud's unconscious, to haunt the modern system of nation-states.

It is against this background that the recent vicissitudes of the idea or construction of the state in the dominant culture of global politics must be explored.

What we have learnt to call the state is actually the modern nation-state. It became a serious presence in the European landscape only after the treaty of Westphalia in 1648. Though a contractual element between an apparatus of power and the general public had already entered civic space by the thirteenth century in parts of Europe, the treaty of Westphalia gave formal institutional status to the emerging concept of a state in Europe. But even then the concept would never have attained the power it later did if the French Revolution had not underwritten it by linking the state, or statehood, with nationalism.

With the spread of republicanism in Europe after the French Revolution severe doubts grew among European élites about the sustainability of long-term legitimacy within the emerging non-monarchical states. Nationalism came in handy at this point and was systematically promoted as the alternative basis for such legitimacy. The Weberian charisma previously concentrated in the person of the monarch—supposedly mediating between sacred and secular orders—was now distributed among the population, though not equally of course. Given the loss of this centralized monarchical charisma, a less specific, impersonal nationalism was seen as the best guarantor of the stability of the state.

This insecurity in the élite, for which nationalism was supposed to be the cure, persisted in the culture of the nation-state. From the very beginning, nation-building—a polite term for the cultural and ideological homogenization of a country's population—became one of the stated or implicit goals of the modern state. Some early nation-states, for instance, even proscribed trade unions for a while. And, of course, there was always some godforsaken minority or other that these states could exclude. Such minorities had a place only in the few fragmented nations where the construction of the past was dominantly plural and could not easily be built on a romanticized imperial memory.

The concept of the state that emerged from this experience had some distinguishing features. Among other things, the new concept assumed a closer fit between the realities of ethnicity, nation and state; it gave a more central role to the state in the society than the *ancien régime* had done; and it redefined the state as the harbinger and main instrument of social change, which in the European context meant being the trigger for and protector of modern institutions associated with industrial capitalism. These newly-assumed functions naturally made the modern nation-state suspicious of all cultural differences, not on the grounds of racial or ethnic prejudice, but on the grounds that such differences intervened between the 'liberated' individual and the republican state and interfered with the more professional aspects of statecraft.

Even more important, thanks to the new institutional ordering that went with the new concept of the state and the expansion of colonial empires—which had already become globally visible—within a short time the concept of a nation-state not only marginalized all other concepts of the state in Europe but also began to enter the interstices of public consciousness all over Asia, South America and Africa.

The increasing dominance and spreading hegemony of this idea had two consequences. First, under the influence of the concept of the nation-state, the state was increasingly seen in a more idealized form—as an impartial, secular arbiter among different classes, ethnicities and interests. Most states did not live up to the image, but few disowned it. Some even negotiated the transparent gap between principles and practice the hard way. For instance, some of them went democratic but propounded clear-cut structural limits on democracy. In England, in the eighteenth and nineteenth centuries, a line was drawn between democracy and freedom, and the popular as well as élite ideology of the state came to include the belief that freedom sometimes needed to be protected from democracy, if necessary by curbing the participation of the lower classes and women in politics. Likewise, some states managed to become more tolerant of ethnicity only after ghettoizing or driving out problematic minorities. What France did to the Huguenots or Poland to the Jews before they learnt to be more tolerant, others states like the United States or Australia did less conspicuously, but as ruthlessly, to their aboriginal and black minorities.

The second pay-off was that each nation-state began to see itself as a repository of specific cultural values even though, in reality, each sought to equate these values with a territorial concept of nationality that militated against the broader meaning of culture as inherently not confinable within territorial boundaries. Occasionally, states vied with one another to emerge as the upholder of particular cultural values. England and France both spoke on behalf of European civilization, even whilst they wet to war with each other and when both declared war in the twentieth century against Germany, they claimed again to be the defenders of European civilization. Nazi Germany in turn tried hard to become a symbol of European civilization, albeit in a somewhat idiosyncratic fashion, and to some of the best minds of the twentieth century—Ezra Pound, Knut Hamsun, Martin Heidegger—the Nazi claim did not seem particularly exaggerated.

In the beginning, the new concept of the state in Europe and its corresponding institutional arrangements had to contend with other, surviving concepts and structures of the state that differed from and were antagonistic to the new concept. These contending concepts and structures often went with culturally distinctive expectations and demands from the state. British colonialism, for instance, though it was perfectly at home with the concept of the nation-state in Britain, operated in India within the broad cultural framework of the Mughal empire which had preceded it. This it did explicitly and self-consciously during the early decades of the Raj, and more tacitly and partly unwittingly roughly till World War I.[1] During the first sixty-five years of British rule it is doubtful that the new ruling circles in India had an operational concept of a 'civilizing mission' on their part. They certainly did not have a programme of state-directed social change and resisted, in virtually every instance, Indian attempts to introduce major social reforms in the country. As for its secular commitment at that time, it suffices to say that the British-Indian state not merely proscribed Christian missionary activities, but even participated in religious festivals and running some Hindu temples, and claimed a part of the donations made to the temples on those grounds.

Despite these early compromises, gradually the concept of the nation-state did manage to disparage and corner all the other surviving notions of the state outside the West as so many instances of medievalism and primitivism. The process was strengthened when, in one society after another, indigenous intellectuals and political activists confronting the

[1]See, for instance, Bernard S. Cohn, 'The Command of Language and the Language of Command', in Ranajit Guha (ed.), *Subaltern Studies* (New Delhi: Oxford University Press, 1985), Vol. 4, pp. 276–329; and 'Representing Authority in Victorian England', in Eric Hobsbawm and Terence Ranger (ed.), *The Invention of Tradition* (Cambridge: Cambridge University Press, 1983), pp. 165–209; Radhika Singha, *A Despotism of Law: Crime and Justice in Early Colonial India* (Delhi: Oxford University Press, 1998).

colonial power found in the idea of the nation-state *the* clue to the West's economic success and political dominance. The idea of a native nation-state, thus, was increasingly seen as the cure-all for the ills of the Third World. Rarely did anyone think of an indigenous modern state as a contradiction in terms. Indeed no other idea, except perhaps the twin notions of modern science and development, was accepted so uncritically by the élites of ancient and continuous civilizations like China and India. Even modern science and development became, for the Afro-Asian élite, the responsibility precisely of the nation-state and two new *raisons d'etat*. It is possible to argue that the story of the modernization of Asia that began in the nineteenth-century is actually the story of the internalization and enculturation of the idea of the modern state by individuals as diverse as Rammohun Roy (1772–1833), Sun Yat-Sen (1866–1925) and Kemal Ataturk (1881–1938).

As a result today, in most of the world any reference to a state usually means the modern nation-state. All political arrangements and all state systems are now judged by the extent to which they serve the needs of—or conform to—the idea of the nation-state.[2] Even the various modes of defiance against the state are usually informed by this standardized concept of it. Karl Marx (1818–83), while he spoke of the state withering away, had in mind a nation-state which had first to be captured by a dedicated vanguard fully versed in the intricacies of a modern—read 'western'—polity.[3] And when the likes of Mikhail Bakunin (1814–76)

[2]The standard historical, philosophical, and social-scientific scholarship on the state also offers little scope to those savages in the southern world who want to see the modern, post-seventeenth century concept of the state as less than perennial. Nevertheless, studies exploring the historical (and therefore possibly transient) character of the state are helpful, like E. Morgan, *Inventing the People: The Rise of Popular Sovereignty in England and America* (New York: Norton, 1988).

[3]Despite their anti-state rhetoric, the anarchist and Marxist traditions have nothing but their touching faith in the European concept of the state to offer to non-Europeans. In fact after reading Marx, one fears that the prophet would be seriously annoyed if European-style states were not first established in the southern world, before they wither away as a consequence of revolutionary activism. For elements of a fundamental critique of the idea of the state, therefore, one is sometimes better off studying rather conservative thinkers like M. Oakeshott, 'The Character of a Modern European State', in his *On Human Conduct*, (Oxford: Clarendon Press, 1975), or the young radical of his time, W. von Humboldt, *Limits to State Action* (Cambridge: Cambridge University Press, 1969; first written in 1792). More relevant for the southern world could be the insights of non-academic intellectuals like Henry David Thoreau, *The Selected Works of Thoreau* (Boston: Houghton Mifflin, 1975), or M.K. Gandhi, *Hind Swaraj*, in *Collected Works of Mahatma Gandhi*, (Delhi: Government of India, 1963), Vol. 4, pp. 81–103.

and Piotr Kropotkin (1842–1921) spoke of the ills of the state, they invariably had in mind the western nation-state. The anarchists were as ignorant as the Marxists were contemptuous of the very different kinds of state that lesser mortals in the savage world had lived or experimented with.

It is only now, forty-five years after World War II, that some social analysts have again begun to take seriously the growing inability of the nation-state to serve the needs of civil society in large parts of the world. As I have already pointed out, there *were* critics of the state in nineteenth century Europe. Some, like Marx, expected the state to wither away after playing its role in history, some like Leo Tolstoy (1828–1910) found it a moral abomination which had to be kept in strict check, and some like George Sorel (1847–1922) and Kropotkin thought the state could be done away with straightaway. But they were all, without exception, severely Eurocentric. They showed little knowledge of or respect for the diverse traditions of conceptualizing the state in other parts of the world. Whatever feeble accommodation of diversity there was consisted primarily in theorizing a vague idea of the nonwestern state which was later formalized by scholars like Karl Wittforgel as 'Oriental despotism' and by Max Weber as 'the pre-modern state'.

Predictably, this mythical premodern state propagated by the better-known European scholars looked remarkably like a primitive Afro-Asian version of the *ancien régime*. It was mythical because it analytically steam-rollered the diverse pasts of the non-West, collapsing them into a single ideal type, which (as in Weber) instead of increasing an understanding of these societies, diminished it. After all, this was primarily an effort to make manageable diverse nonwestern pasts by incorporating them into a more familiar western past. Later, this process of incorporation was scientifically sanctioned and institutionalized through Weberian political sociology, particularly its post-World War II Parsonian version which dominated the behavioural persuasion in western political science till the 1970s.[4]

[4]Satish Arora, 'Pre-Empted Future? Notes on Theories of Political Development', in Rajni Kothari (ed.), *State and Nation Building*, (New Delhi: Allied Publishers, 1976), pp. 23–66. For a more recent attempt to locate such critiques in the overall culture of the globally-dominant knowledge system, see Tariq Banuri, 'Modernization and Its Discontents: A Cultural Perspective on Theories of Development', in Frédérique Apffel-Marglin and Stephen Marglin (ed.), *Dominating Knowledge: Development, Culture and Resistance*, (Oxford: Clarendon Press, 1990), pp. 73–101; and Chai-Anan Samudavanija, The Three-Dimensional

Not that everyone during the last three centuries has dutifully jumped on the bandwagon of the modern state. But they are the exceptions. And these exceptions have been systematically neutralized by the dominant culture of knowledge. Given the overall spirit of post-Enlightenment Europe, it has been easy to re-read intellectuals such as William Blake (1757–1827), Henry David Thoreau (1817–62) and John Ruskin (1819–1900) either as incurable romantic visionaries or as grand eccentrics. They are respected as poets, critics and moral exemplars, but not as thinkers who have something to say about public life and the fate of civil society the world over. It has gone against these intellectuals that they sensed the growing links between the state, organized nationalism, mega-science and an urban–industrial society—and especially the consequent marginalization of some of the older, less totalist conceptions of the state. Industrialism and scientism have, since the late eighteenth century, been the ruling ideologies in Europe. Anyone even slightly critical of the urban–industrial and technocratic future of humankind is seen as outside the bounds of normality and sanity.

This hegemony of the idea of the modern nation-state has created a political paradox in debates on the state today. Newer critics find the concept of the modern state looking more and more tired and unreal, and unable to cope with the new problems and threats to human survival. Yet, in the meanwhile, the concept has acquired immense institutional power and a wide base within global mass culture. It has become an axiomatic part of conventional wisdom or common sense. This paradox has ensured that organized political power cannot easily be mobilized, even in the southern world, to resist the pathologies of the modern state. Either the resistance has to come from the fringes of the polity, or it has to legitimize itself in the language of the mainstream. Vested interests which have grown up around the idea of the modern state, thus, define not merely the mainstream but also most of the popular concepts and forms of dissent.

The results are plain. In society after society, in the name of protecting or helping the state, rulers have begun to extract new kinds of economic and political surplus from the ruled and have unleashed on resisting citizens new forms of violence. Simultaneously, in society after society, for the sake of the state, a growing proportion of citizens is willing to tolerate that violence as a sacrifice they must make as patriotic citizens

State', paper presented at the International Conference on Political Institutions in the Third World in the Process of Adjustment and Modernization, Berlin, 4–7 July 1989, mimeo.

for future generations of their compatriots. Even those deeply suspicious of the state's dominant role in the economy are perfectly willing to trust it when it comes to national security and international relations. Even as the idea of the nation-state loses a part of its gloss—as in West Europe in the 1980s and 1990s—it strengthens its hold on the imagination of many in the Third World who see in it one of the few instruments available to ensure progress and equality within the global system. That the state is also a means of ensuring First World standards of living for those who have control or access to it in the Third World, is, of course, seen as an unfortunate and incidental by-product.

What explains this anomalous relationship between the state and society in large parts of the world? The answer differs from society to society but there are some common threads.

First, the idea of the nation-state entered most southern societies through the colonial connection, riding piggyback on the concept of the white man's burden. That experience was internalized. When, after decolonization, indigenous élites acquired control over the state apparatus, they quickly learnt to seek legitimacy in a native version of the civilizing mission and sought to establish a similar colonial relationship between the state and society.[5]

They found excellent justification for this in the various theories of modernization floating around in the post-World War II world. Payments once made to colonial regimes for their civilizing mission were now demanded by those controlling the indigenous state as agents of modernization and guarantors of national security. They were not called payments though. They were called sacrifices for the future of one's country and they invariably came more from those who had less access to—or facility in—handling modern institutions. Even authoritarian regimes in the Third World have systematically justified themselves thus. From Ferdinand Marcos to Lee Kuan Yew, from Ayub Khan during the second period of military rule in Pakistan to Indira Gandhi during the Emergency in India, not to speak of sundry despots in South America and Africa, it has been the same story. None of these worthies ever bothered to justify themselves as guardians of civil rights or democracy, though all of them were indirect beneficiaries or products of movements for self-rule and democratic rights in the colonial period. At most, they justified themselves as public benefactors removing roadblocks to a future

[5]See, 'Culture, State, and the Rediscovery of Indian Politics', pp. 16–33.

democracy which the citizens in their societies would one day come to deserve. That is, if the citizens got themselves properly educated in the intricacies of modern social and economic institutions.

A second common thread in the relationship between the state and society is the direct link which the modern state has established with mega-technology on the one hand, and doctrines of national security and development on the other. These links have become more and more conspicuous to the victims of state violence, thanks to consistent attacks by many states in the Third World on their citizens in the name of development and national security, and the systematic export of violence and authoritarianism by some western states, both liberal capitalist and socialist, during the past 150 years.[6]

These elements in the ideology of the state have come under criticism because, apart from becoming justifications for new kinds of violence, they have become conceptually hollow in real life. Let me give one or two examples. The changing nature of modern technology has ensured that the state can provide security primarily only to itself, not its citizens.[7] If there were to be a nuclear war between India and China for example, and Nepal maintained its traditional neutrality, that neutrality could no longer guarantee the personal security of a single Nepali citizen. For good or ill, our hypothetical average Nepali citizen must look for security elsewhere. The modern state can always ask the citizen to make sacrifices in the name of security; but it cannot always deliver that security.

Likewise, even spectacular state-controlled development in a society is no guarantor of the development of that society, however paradoxical this may sound. There are a number of states in the world where development means only the development of the state itself or, at most, the state sector. In fact, in a number of cases the development of the state has been the best predictor of the underdevelopment of society.[8] Some

---

[6]On the intimate connection between the state and the coercive might of science, see for instance Shiv Visvanathan, 'From the Annals of a Laboratory State', in Ashis Nandy (ed.), *Science, Hegemony and Violence: A Requiem for Modernity* (Tokyo: The United Nations University and New Delhi: Oxford University Press, 1988), pp. 257–88; and Claude Alvares, *Science, Development and Violence: The Twilight of Modernity* (Delhi: Oxford University Press, 1992).

[7]See for instance, Giri Deshingkar, 'People's Security Versus National Security', *Seminar*, December 1982, (280), pp. 28–30.

[8]There is a closely associated category of such states—Herb Feith calls them repressive-developmentalist regimes—which we are not considering here; in them, the state's role as the ultimate development agency legitimizes its authoritarian nature and repressive policies. See Herb Feith, 'Repressive-Developmentalist regimes in Asia: Old Strengths,

scholars have, consequently, defined development as the slogan by which the state mobilizes resources internally and externally and then eats them up itself, instead of allowing them to reach the bottom and peripheries of society.[9] There is enough evidence that the nation-state, when transplanted into the southern world, can out-perform any oriental despotism in authoritarianism and organized violence.

National security and development are only two of the major elements in the ideology of the modern state. Two others are that it represents the principle of scientific rationality (which rationalizes, in Freud's sense of the term, all actions of the state that in turn seeks to rationalize, this time in Max Weber's sense of the term, the society it lords over); and the state as a means of secularizing society.

The state as the epitome of scientific rationality and the chief secularizing agent have also come under attack in recent times. The modern state has established such a close relationship with modern science and technology that it has now become the major source of attack on all nonmodern systems of knowledge. In the politics of knowledge today, nobody can imagine one without the other. Reportedly, more than 95 per cent of all scientific research in the world is now applied research and of this 95 per cent, roughly two-third is military research sponsored by the state. Almost the entire coercive power of the modern state now comes from mega-science and mega-technology, and developing the state today means primarily equipping it with greater coercive might with the help of modern science and technology. Once again, the brunt of this attack on the plurality of knowledge is felt more in the former Second

New Vulnerabilities', paper presented at the conference of the World Order Models Project, New York, June 1979, and published in Christian Conference of Asia, *Escape From Domination: A Consultation Report on Patterns of Domination and People's Movements in Asia* (Tokyo: April 1980).

[9] See for instance, in the context of Africa, Afsaneh Eghbal, 'L'etat contre L'ethnicite— Un Nouvelle Arme: Le Development Exclusion', *IFDA Dossier*, July-August 1983, pp. 17–29, and Richard Falk, 'A World Order Perspective on Authoritarianism', (New York: World Order Models Project, 1978), mimeo.

In the southern countries the main *raison d'etre* of the state has been development. For an influential critique of development as a process and an ideology, see Gustavo Esteva, 'Regenerating People's Space', in *Alternatives*, 1987, 12(1), pp. 125–52, and what probably are the two most comprehensive analyses of the fate of the development idea from Arturo Escobar, Power and Visibility: The Invention and Management of Development in the Third World, Ph.D. dissertation, University of California, Berkeley, 1987; and Tariq Banuri, 'Development and the Politics of Knowledge: A Critical Interpretation of the Social Role of Modernization Theories in Development', in Apffel-Marglin and Marglin, *Dominating Knowledge*, pp. 29–72. See also 'Culture, Voice and Development' pp. 151–70.

and Third Worlds. There are institutional checks in the First World against the use of certain kinds of force against citizens. These checks hardly existed in the Second World before its collapse and are often subverted in the Third World with the help of the First World.[10]

As for that other major ideological pillar of the modern state, secularism, instead of leading to greater tolerance of ethnic diversity, state-sponsored secularism has often only managed to secularize ethnic conflicts and bring them within the purview of the state. In the process electoral politics organized around the state has worsened the relationship between communities and ensured, in the name of progress, the destruction of hundreds of lifestyles and life-support systems that traditionally sustained cultural diversity in different parts of the world.[11]

The various kinds of traditional state systems that in times past used to be spread all over the world were often violent and authoritarian. But one thing they did not—or could not—do. They did not try to enter all areas of human life and they did not set up total systems for social and political engineering based on a theory of inexorable historical laws. Such states neither had the technological wherewithal nor, in most cases, the philosophical hubris to mount any such ambitious effort. As a result, citizens, even when victims of state violence, had a few escape routes. The state, too, knowing that its writ did not run beyond a point, had to learn to live with human diversity, if not on ideological grounds, at least on grounds of *realpolitik* and pragmatic considerations.

Under the dispensation of the modern nation-state, similar escape routes can be kept open only when the polity is fully democratic. Otherwise, the state's control over a citizen's rights and freedom becomes much more total. With the help of modern technology, management systems and information control, such a state can successfully plug the escape routes that used to be available to the citizen of pre-modern or nonmodern societies.[12]

[10]See Alvares, *Science, Development and Violence*.

[11]This process has been described in some detail in Ashis Nandy, Shikha Trivedi, Achyut Yagnik and Shail Mayaram, *Creating a Nationality: The Ramjanmabhumi Movement and Fear of the Self* (New Delhi: Oxford University Press, 1995). See also, Vandana Shiva, *The Violence of Green Revolution*, (Penang: Third World Network and London: Zed books, 1991); Tariq Banuri and Durre Sameen Ahmed, 'Official Nationalism, Ethnic Politics, and Collective Violence: Karachi in the 1980s', presented at the UN University-WIDER Conference on Ethnicity, Karachi, 14–18 January 1989, mimeo; Ashis Nandy, 'The Politics of Secularism and the Rediscovery of Religious Tolerance', *Alternatives*, 1988, 13(3), pp. 177–94; and Ashis Nandy 'The Political Culture of the Indian State', *Daedalus*, 118, Fall 1989, pp. 1–26.

[12]Rabindranath Tagore, *Nationalism* (Madras: Macmillan, 1985). This is a collection

It is easy to identify many of the problems with the prevalent idea of the state. It is less easy, when dealing with a social organization as fundamental as the state, to foretell its future or guess what forms may ultimately emerge in its place. Some scattered nonmodern or postmodern concepts of state have, however, begun to emerge in response to the crisis of the nation-state in our times. For while it is an open question what forms the postmodern state will take, there is little doubt that the dominant concept of the state will be drastically altered. If not in response to intellectual doubts and criticism, at least in response to the larger processes of democratization and globalization going on all over the world. Of these, globalization is a much studied process these days, even though the crisis of the modern state springs primarily from the contradiction that has arisen between it and the demands for democratization of the world of knowledge and restoration of the dignity of peoples peripheralized during the last two hundred years.

First, there have emerged the concepts of multi-national, multi-ethnic and multicultural states as correctives to the standard idea of the unitary nation-state. In the past, bureaucratic socialist states like the USSR or Yugoslavia used to prefer the first concept; western liberal societies like the United States and Britain the latter two. None of the three has been an unmixed blessing and the strains have begun to show. The concept of the multi-national state has not helped China or the Soviet Union to avoid ethnic politics and strife; that of the multi-ethnic or multi-cultural state has not helped Britain, France or Canada to live in peace with their minorities. Ethnic and religious strife was not unknown earlier either, but the modern state seems keen to prove that its claim to greater tolerance of diversity in these two sectors is a triumph of hope over experience.

Second, noticing how the concept of the nation-state seeks to pummel major civilizations into shape, some have tried to redefine the state. At least one scholar has pleaded for the use of the concept of a civilizational state in large countries such as India.[13] *Prima facie*, the concept seems to presume an overlap of geographical, cultural and state boundaries that may be impossible to obtain in reality. In the case of India, it does not seem to account adequately for the political status of independent

---

of lectures delivered in the 1930s in Japan and India. Often maudlin and unbearably purple, it remains the first, and an impressive, critique of the modern state on the ground of its totalism. Predictably, the lectures were not particularly popular in Japan and India.

[13]Ravinder Kumar, 'Nation-State or Civilizational State?' (New Delhi: Nehru Memorial Museum and Library, 1989), Occasional Papers, mimeo.

Hindu monarchical states like Nepal. Nor does it adequately explain the cultural status of states such as Thailand, Indonesia, Bangladesh, Pakistan and Sri Lanka, separated from India not by civilizational but by political boundaries.

Third, there have been others to whom the concept of a moderate or civil state promises some respite, if not a remedy.[14] It is possible, they feel, to recover the liberal, pace-setting role of the state through detailed monitoring of it by those politically active outside the state sector, in areas such as environment, peace, human rights, feminism, alternative sciences and technologies. In this fashion, the enrichment of civil society and reform of the state will bring about a redefinition of its scope. Though this is the way resistance against state-initiated violence has crystallized in many societies, one wonders if the modern nation-state has retained enough flexibility to allow for such monitoring. Especially given the consensus most modern states have now built among large sections of the middle classes and the media against the idea of diversity and in favour of professional expertise. Both these kinds of consensus allow the nation-state democratically to marginalize grassroots initiatives of various kinds, especially if they do not happen to be politically or ideologically correct.

Finally, there has been a re-emergence of anarchism of various hues. In the West, this response is usually anaemic and defensive, and survives camouflaged in some forms of environmentalism and alternative-science movements. When directly political, such anarchism somehow conveys the impression of being a form of eccentricity or esoterica. In the Third World, it occasionally has some political clout, thanks to the fact that the anti-imperialist movements, *in practice*, often had to operate from outside the state sector. Probably the best instance is the 'anarchism' associated with the name of Mohandas Karamchand Gandhi.[15] Many Indian Gandhians are still trying to live down that heritage and convert Gandhism into a non-threatening, official voluntarism acting as an adjunct of the Indian state. But Gandhi, nearly forty years after his death, has obviously retained some nuisance value and at least some young Gandhians have

[14]Rajni Kothari, 'Crisis of the Moderate State and Decline of Democracy', in Peter Lyon and James Manor (ed.), *Transfer and Transformation: Political Institutions in the New Commonwealth: Essays in Honour of W.H. Morris-Jones* (Leicester: Leicester University Press, 1983); and D.L. Sheth, 'Grassroots Stirrings and the Future of Politics', *Alternatives*, March 1983, 9(1), pp. 1–24.

[15]For example, Gandhi, *Hind Swaraj*, pp. 81–208.

come closer to those for whom the return to a revised form of a culturally-rooted, less monolithic, 'softer', nonmodern minimal state holds the most promise.

None of these dissenting new approaches, however, as yet pose a serious threat to the dominant culture of the state, despite the widespread awareness that there is something rotten in the state of the state. None of the alternatives mentioned here has captured the imagination of the public, except over short stretches of time. On the other hand, given the mounting problems with the dominant model of the state, these fringe dissenters do not look as insane as they once did. It is possible that in the future they may develop into more formidable enemies of public order and conventional political rationality.

In the meanwhile, the dissenters can perhaps console themselves that no system becomes morally acceptable merely because human imagination has failed to produce an alternative to it at a given point in time.

Culture, State and the Rediscovery of Indian Politics

A society can understand the relationship between its culture and its state in two ways. The first way is to look for the means by which culture can be made to contribute to the sustenance and growth of the state. The state here is seen as operating according to certain fixed, universal, sociological rules. Elements of the culture that help strengthen the state are seen as good; elements of the culture that do not help the proper functioning of the state or hinder its growth are seen as defective. A mature society, in this view, sheds or actively eliminates these defective elements, to improve both the functioning of the state and the quality of the culture.

The second way of looking at the relationship between culture and the state is to do so from the standpoint of the culture. This approach may regard the state as a protector, an internal critic or a thermostat for the culture but not as the ultimate pacesetter for the society's way of life. The state here is made to serve the needs of or contribute to the enrichment of the culture; it is never allowed to dictate terms to the culture. Even when the state is used as a critique of the culture and the culture is sought to be transformed, the final justification for the criticism and the transformation is not sought in the intrinsic logic of statecraft or in the universal laws of state formation. That justification is sought in the self-perceived needs of the culture and the people and in the moral framework used by the people.

This dichotomy between the state and the culture-oriented views of society, of course, dissolves if one uses the older idea of the state as part and parcel of culture (as obtains in many traditional societies) or if one refuses to accept the modern idea of nation-state as the only genuine version of state (as is assumed by most modern political and social analysts today). In most nonmodern societies, among people who work with the older idea and not with the modern idea of the nation-state, the culture-oriented approach to state is seen as natural and the state-oriented approach as an imposition.[1] At the same time, in modern societies the nation-state-oriented approach seems natural and rational, and the culture-oriented one unnatural, irrational or primitive. The choice, therefore, boils down to one between the culture-oriented and the nation-state-oriented. Still, for the sake of simplicity, I shall use here the expression state-oriented or statist to mean the nation-state–oriented, hoping that the reader will not confuse this concept of 'statist' with that used in debates between the socialist thinkers and the liberals believing in a minimal state.

I am not considering here either the nature of the state or that of culture. These are vital issues which need to be discussed fully. For the moment I wish to avoid them because I want to do justice to the culture-oriented approach that believes that a state can destroy the civilization of which it is a part even when—forgive the anthropomorphism—the intentions of the state are 'honourable' and even when it is 'honestly' trying to improve a decaying civilization. When a state becomes ethnocidal, the culture-oriented approach believes, the remedy does not lie merely in capturing the state, since this provides no check against the captured state becoming as ethnocidal in scope as it was before being captured.

I

For the last 150 years, westernized, middle-class Indians have learnt to look at the first approach—the one that orients the needs of the culture to the needs of the state—as the very epitome of political maturity, achievement and development. Since the nation-state system acquired its present global predominance in the nineteenth century, most political analysis in the West, too, has forgotten the alternative. And since a global science of politics became fully operational after World War II, the state-oriented attitude to culture has become the only way of looking at culture the world over. Nearly all the studies of political development and political culture of the 1950s and 1960s have this cultural-engineering

[1] In traditional India, for instance, the state was clearly expected to be a part of culture and the king was expected to see himself not only a protector of *dharma* but also as a protector of multiple ways of life and a promoter of ethnic tolerance. While the *Arthashastra* may not provide a clue to this, the *puranas*, the folklore and *lokachara* do.

component built into them. From Talcott Parsons, Edward Shils and David Easton to Karl Deutsch, Samuel Huntington and Lucian Pye, it is the same story. So much so that, under their influence, modern political analysts and journalists are forced to fall back on state-oriented analytic categories, even after the categories have shown poor interpretative power, as often happens when figures like M.K. Gandhi, Ayatollah Khomeini, Maulana Bhashani and Jarnail Singh Bhindranwale (to give random examples) become politically consequential.

This is part of a larger picture. Take, for instance, studies of the cultural contexts of economic growth done during the same period. The main function of culture, according to these studies, was to facilitate economic growth. Aspects of culture that stood in the way of such growth had to be ruthlessly excised. In 'stagnant' cultures, that is, in cultures which did not nurture a thriving modern economy, the engineering challenge was to rediscover or introduce cultural elements which would trigger or sustain economic growth and the spirit of the market that went with it. This was the thrust of the psychological studies of achievement motivation done by David McClelland and company, and the studies of Protestant-ethics-like elements in nonwestern cultures by a drove of social anthropologists. Even the tough-minded economists of the period, who did not believe in the relevance of such woolly psychological or cultural anthropological work, never faltered in their belief that a society had to give primacy to the needs of the modern economy, however defined, over the needs of culture. So did the mercenaries among them vending the materialist—read economic—interpretation of history to ensure the centrality of their dismal science in the world of social knowledge. In India, at least, I have not come across a single work of any Marxist economist of the period which challenged the basic priority of economics and sought to restore, even as a distant goal, Marx's original vision of a society freed from the bondage of economism.[2]

A similar case can be made about science. Most science-and-culture studies of the 1950s and 1960s sought to make the society safe for modern science. For this purpose, all nonmodern cultures were to be

---

[2]One of the first Marxist thinkers in the Third World to explicitly recognize the primacy of culture was Amilcar Cabral (1924–74). See his *Return to the Source: Selected Speeches* (New York: Monthly Review Press, 1973). He, of course, drew upon the work of Aimé Césaire and Leopold Senghor. One suspects that the African heritage of the three had something to do with their sensitivity. The disintegrating native cultures they saw around them were more threatened than threatening, something which a Mao Zedong could not say about China. In India, unfortunately, even the Marxism of classical scholars like D.D. Kosambi and D.P. Chattopadhyay has remained in essence another version of western Orientalism and colonial anthropology.

retooled and made more rational or modern. Thus, scientific criticisms of culture were encouraged but cultural criticisms of science were dubbed obscurantist. Occasionally, shallow criticisms of the social relations of science were allowed—in the sense that the control over science exercised by imperialism or capitalism or by army generals was allowed to be exposed. But this was done as part of an attempt to protect the text and the core values of modern science which were seen as absolute and as the last word in human rationality. As if, somehow, the forces of violence and exploitation, after taking over much of the context of modern science, hesitated when they encountered the contents of modern science and refused to enter its sanctum sanctorum. Here, too, culture was always at the receiving end, while science kept the company of modern political and economic institutions.

We are however talking of politics at the moment, not of the witchcraft called economics or the mega-corporation called modern science. And I want to suggest that in India the primacy granted to the needs of the state—seen as a necessary part of a ruthless, global, nation-state system—is not a new idea coined in the late 1940s by the first generation of post-Independence managers of the Indian polity. The primacy of the state was not the discovery of Jawaharlal Nehru or Vallabhbhai Patel, two very different persons who arrived at roughly the same statist ideology through very different personal and intellectual paths. Nor did the primacy-of-the-state theory evolve in the 1950s or the 1960s when the structural–functional models of political development and positivist-Marxist models of the state endorsed, at two ends of the political spectrum, its primacy. The new model merely re-legitimized what had been brewing for more than a hundred years in India and, perhaps, for more than three hundred years in Europe.

The statist model first came to India in the nineteenth century, in the second phase of colonialism, when a more reactive, self-defensive Hinduism began to take shape in response to the consolidation of social theories that saw colonialism as a civilizing influence and as a pathway from feudalism to modern statehood.[3] It was towards the middle of

[3]For a discussion of the political consciousness which characterized this phase of colonial politics, and its persistence within the culture of Indian politics as an important strain, see Ashis Nandy, 'The Making and Unmaking of Political Cultures of India', in *At the Edge of Psychology: Essays in Politics and Culture* (New Delhi: Oxford University Press, 1980), pp. 47–69; and *The Intimate Enemy: Loss and Recovery of Self Under Colonialism* (New Delhi: Oxford University Press, 1983).

the nineteenth century that a series of dedicated Hindu religious and social reformers first mooted the idea that what Hinduism lacked was the primacy which most forms of post-medieval, western Christianity granted to the state. Even Islam, they felt, had a built-in space for such primacy. The Hindus did not. That was why, in their view, the Hindus were having it so bad. The sorrow of that generation of reformers was that the Hindu seemed an animal peculiarly hostile and insensitive to the subtleties of the nation-state system; their hope was that the hostility and insensitivity could be corrected through proper cultural and social engineering. This the religious reformers tried to do through a revision of the Hindu personality and way of life.

This effort, because it came as part of a defence of Hinduism, hid the fact that this was the first influential indigenous form of the primacy-of-the-state thesis advanced in India. The thesis, for the first time, brought modern statism within Hinduism, in the sense that the Hindu state of the future was not to be the Hindu polity of the past but a centralized, modern nation-state with a Brahminic idiom. Suresh Sharma's recent paper on V.D. Savarkar neatly sums up the spirit of this particular form of Hindu nationalism and the political form it later had to take. It is a measure of the cultural tragedy which colonialism was for India that even a person like Savarkar, after spending nearly forty years in intense, often violent, anti-colonial struggle and suffering for it, had ultimately to turn intellectually and culturally collaborationist, purportedly to save the Hindus from Islamic domination with the help of the culturally and politically more 'advanced' British.[4]

The earlier generation of reformers, in what can be called the first phase of British colonialism, had pleaded for greater political participation of Indians and also for greater state intervention in the society. But there were externally imposed limits to their enthusiasm; they did not stress

[4]Savarkar was a product of Marathi nationalism, which sought legitimacy by developing the European-style idea of a common culture, will and a fixed territory with 'natural' boundaries. Enrico Fasana, 'Deshabhakta: The Leaders of Italian Independence Movement in the Eyes of Marathi Nationalists', *Asian and African Studies*, 1994, 3(2), pp. 152–75. Also, Suresh Sharma, 'Savarkar's Quest for a Modern Hindu Consolidation: The Framework of Validation', in D.L. Sheth and Ashis Nandy (ed.), *Hindu Visions of a Desirable Society: Heritage, Challenge and Redefinitions* (forthcoming). Bankimchandra Chattopadhyay (1838–94) was probably the first well-known theoretician of the state-oriented approach in India. I say 'probably' because he stated his position indirectly, often through his literary and theological works or through commentaries on the works of others. Sudipta Kaviraj suggests that Bhudev Mukhopadhyaya (1827–94), a less known contemporary of Bankimchandra, was the first to explicitly accept and plead for a modern nation-state in India.

the absolute primacy of the state, partly because the state was not theirs and partly because even their British rulers had not yet shown any great ideological commitment to the state system they were running. The state for the first generation of British rulers was mainly a means of making money, not a means of cultural engineering. These rulers feared and respected Indian culture, which they tried not to disturb as long as it did not stand in the way of their money-making. Moreover, the Raj occupied a relatively small part of the subcontinent and certainly did not give the impression of being the paramount power in the country. Indians pressurizing their British rulers to intervene in Indian society could not internalize a highly activist or an awesomely grand image of the state.[5]

Nonetheless, the first generation of social reformers had provided the base on which the second generation of reformers built their adoration for the modern idea of the nation-state and their suspicion of all grass-roots politics. Certainly, these latter reformers did not put any premium on participatory politics, which they accepted theoretically only as a vague, populist possibility. Even when they spoke of mass politics as desirable, they saw it as something that had to come later—after the Hindu had been morally and educationally uplifted and after he or she had learnt to take on modern responsibilities.[6] This shielded them from the awareness that they were unwilling or incapable of mobilizing ordinary Indians for basic political changes, including full participation in the anti-imperial struggle.

The votaries of a Hindu nation-state, thinking that they were pleading for a Hindu polity, were also mostly unaware that the nation-state system was one of the more recent innovations in human civilization and that it had come into being only about two hundred years earlier in Europe, in the mid-seventeenth century. They chose to see it as one of the eternal verities of humankind. Naturally, they diagnosed Hindu inadequacy in state-oriented politics as the result of a major defect in the Hindu

[5]There was also probably a feeling among Indians that there should be limits to which a colonial state should be involved by its subjects in the matter of social reform. Consider, for instance, the ambivalence of Rammohun Roy (1772–1833), who worked aggressively for the abolition of the practice of sati but who doubted the wisdom of a state-imposed ban on it.

[6]Aurobindo Ghose (1872–1950) in his revolutionary years, when he was under the influence of Mazzini, was a good example of such romantic populism. The hero of Saratchandra Chattopadhyay's novel *Pather Dabi*, Sabyasachi, is a faithful idealization of this approach to political participation. The pathological possibilities of the approach have been explored in some detail in Rabindranath Tagore's novels *Gora*, *The Home and the World* and *Char Adhyay*.

personality and culture, which had to be reformed as the first step to political freedom. (The British in India, for their own reasons, endorsed this priority of the cultural over the political enthusiastically.) Many of these social reformers, inappropriately called Hindu revivalists, were later to have much sympathy for the anti-British terrorist movements. But that sympathy was not accompanied by any passion for wider political participation of the people. Indeed, they were always a little afraid of the majority of Hindus who lived in the 500,000 Indian villages. Hindu *rashtra*, yes; but not with the full participation of all the Hindu *praja*, at least not with that of the *praja* as they were, and certainly not with the participation of all Hindus in the short run. The conspiratorial style of the terrorists was handy here since it automatically restricted mass participation in politics. Even the constant invocation of the Hindu past by the revivalists—the practice which gave them their distinctive name—was a criticism of living Hindus. It was a compensatory act. It hid the revivalists' admiration for the West and for western Christianity and middle-eastern Islam, seen as martial and valorous, and it hid the desperate search for the same qualities in the Hindu past. The political consequence of this admiration for the conquerors of the Hindus was the continuous attempt by many to re-educate the 'politically immature', anarchic, living Hindus, so that the latter could rediscover their lost western and Islamic values and play their proper role in the global system of nation-states. Swami Vivekananda, when he envisioned a new race of Vedantic Hindus who would build a western society in India, was only being true to the primacy-of-the-state thesis.[7]

I am arguing that the nineteenth-century characters whom modern Indians have learnt to call revivalists were never truly anti-West or anti-Islam. They were only anti-British and anti-Muslim in the Indian context. Their ideal, in important respects, was western Christianity or West Asian Islam. And as for their concept of the state, it was perfectly modern. If anything, they were fundamentally and ferociously anti-Hindu.[8] The only good Hindu to them was the Hindu who was dead, that is, the Hindu who had lived a few thousand years ago. They wanted to enter the world scene with an engineered Hindu who, but for his ideological commitment to classical Hinduism, would be a western man, a man who would accept

[7]It was the same statist vision of India which explains Sister Nivedita's (1867–1911) discomfort with Ananda Coomaraswamy (1877–1947) whom she considered too conservative.

[8]This has been discussed in Nandy, *The Intimate Enemy*. See also 'The Twilight of Certitudes', pp. 61–82.

the rules of the game called the nation-state system and who could not be shortchanged either by the westerner or by the Muslim.

It was this heritage on which both the mainstream liberal and the official Marxist ideologies in India were to later build. Strange though it may sound to many, there *was* a cultural continuity between the early primacy accorded to the state and the strand of consciousness which was later to seek legitimacy in popular modern theories of the state in India. Both liberals and official Marxists like to trace their origins to the earlier integrationist tradition of social reform, the one beginning with Rammohun Roy (1772–1833) and more or less ending with Rabindranath Tagore (1861–1940) and Gopal Krishna Gokhale (1866–1915). This ignores the checks within the ideological frame of these pioneers. Rammohun Roy, for instance, was a modernizer, but he located the origins of the problems of Hindu personality and culture in the colonial situation and not in Hindu traditions. He believed that the pathologies of Hinduism he was fighting could be found only around the institutional structures introduced by British rule and, therefore, his own religious reforms and the new Hindu sect he established were directed only at 'exposed' Hindus, not at parts of the society untouched by colonialism. As he himself put it:

From a careful survey and observation of the people and inhabitants of various parts of the country, and in every condition of life, I am of the opinion that the peasants and villagers who reside at a distance from large towns and head stations and courts of law, are as innocent, temperate and moral in their conduct as the people of any country whatsoever; and the further I proceed towards the North and West [away from British India], the greater the honesty, simplicity and independence of character I meet with.[9]

In his own crude, unsure way Roy did try to protect the architectonics of Indian culture. He did not want Indian culture to be integrated into the modern world; he wanted modernity to be integrated into Indian culture. His modern admirers have chosen to forget the checks within him—weak though the checks were. They have built him up as the father of modern India and as a mindless admirer of everything western.

Thus, as far as the role of the nation-state in the Indian civilization is

[9]For example, Rammohun Roy, 'Additional Queries Respecting the Condition of India', in Kalidas Nag and Debajyoti Burman (ed.), *The English Works* (Calcutta: Sadharan Brahmo Samaj, 1947), Part III, pp. 63–8; see especially pp. 64–5. Cf. Gandhi's critique of the railways and lawyers in *Hind Swaraj*, in *Collected Works of Mahatma Gandhi* (Delhi: Publications Division, Government of India, 1963), Vol. 4, pp. 81–208.

concerned, Indian modernists as well as radicals have drawn upon the ideological framework first popularized by Hindu nationalism. It was in their model that the modern nation-state first became an absolute value and acquired absolute primacy over the needs of the Indian civilization.

II

Yet, there has always been in India during the last 150 years another intellectual current that has looked differently at the needs of the society. This current sees state-oriented politics as a means of criticizing Indian culture, even as a means of renegotiating traditional social relationships, but it refuses to see such politics as the *raison d'être* of Indian civilization. However, though the majority of Indians may have always lived with such a concept of politics, for modern India the concept has survived only as part of an intellectual underground since the middle of the nineteenth century.

It was only under the influence of Gandhi that this current temporarily acquired a certain self-consciousness and political dominance. Gandhi has been often called an anarchist. To the extent that he suspected and fought state power and refused to grant it the primary role in guiding or controlling political and social change, he *was* close to anarchism. Also, while leading a freedom struggle against a foreign power, he could get away with his antipathy to the state. This situation could not last beyond a point. His very success dug the grave of his ideology; his antistatist political thought quickly went into recession after Independence. The demands of statecraft in a newly-independent nation were such that national leaders not only began to look with suspicion at the Gandhian emphasis on cultural traditions, they also began to encourage political interpretations of Gandhi which fitted him into the state-oriented frame of politics, neutralizing or ignoring his culture-oriented self as irrelevant saintliness or eccentricity. On this ideological issue, they were in perfect agreement with Gandhi's assassin Nathuram Godse, an avowed statist. It was no accident that Godse, though called an ultra-conservative, felt threatened not by modernists like Jawaharlal Nehru, but by Gandhi.[10]

It is only now that this recessive strain of consciousness is again coming into its own in the works of a number of young and not-so-young

[10]Ashis Nandy, 'Final Encounter: The Politics of the Assassination of Gandhi', in *At the Edge of Psychology: Essays in Politics and Culture* (New Delhi: Oxford University Press, 1997), pp. 70–98; and 'Godse Killed Gandhi?', *Resurgence*, January–February 1983 (96), pp. 28–9.

scholars—traditionalists, counter-modernists, post-Mao Marxists, anarchists and neo-Gandhians. Evidently, an open polity has its own logic. At the peripheries of the modern Indian polity itself, the demand for fuller democratic participation by people who carry the heavy 'burden' of their nonmodern culture is becoming an important component of the political idiom.

This consciousness has been endorsed by a political reality that has two facets: (1) an increasingly oppressive state-machine that constantly imperils the survival and ways of life of those Indians it has marginalized and (2) the growing efforts of these marginalized sections to interpret their predicament in terms alien to the modern world and to the state-centred culture of scholarship.[11] There is enough evidence for us to believe that this strain of consciousness may begin to set the pace of public consciousness in India in the coming decades and the following section is written as a guide and a warning for those pragmatic spirits and hard-boiled modernists of both the right and the left who might have to close ranks to fight this new menace to the modern Indian nation-state.

The first element in this odd strain, the strain that views the needs of a civilization as primary, is the belief that a civilization must use the state as an instrument and not become an instrument of the state. This of course also means that the Indian state should be reformed before Indian civilization can be reformed. It does not argue out cultural reforms or even cultural revolutions. But the needs of the state do not determine such interventions. The idea that a civilization can be destroyed or changed beyond recognition reportedly for its own survival in the jungle of the nation-state system is given up here. At the same time, the culture-oriented approach believes that if there is need either for a cultural revolution or for modest cultural changes in this society, it should begin in decultured Anglo-India and then, if necessary, end in its externed parts (to translate into English the concept of *bahiskrit samaj* used by Sunil Sahasrabudhey).[12] Culture, in this approach, is the worldview of

---

[11]The attempt to grapple with this reality has revived Gandhian social theory in India, mostly among people who reject the orthodox Gandhism of many of the direct disciples of Gandhi. The revival has as little to do with the personal life and the personal successes or failures of Gandhi as Marx's life and his successes and failures have to do with Marx's thought today. Modern Indians naturally like to give credit for the revival either to 'Hindu woolly-headedness' or to the false consciousness generated by 'romantic propagandists' like Richard Attenborough.

[12]Sunil Sahasrabudhey, 'Towards a New Theory', *Seminar*, May 1982 (273), pp. 19–23; and 'On Alien Political Categories', *Gandhi Marg*, Feb. 1983, 4(11), pp. 896–901. Sahasrabudhey is one of the few serious Marxists in India who have self-consciously built into their models indigenous cultural categories.

the oppressed and it must have precedence over the worldview of the dominant, even when the latter claims to represent universal, cumulative rationality and sanctions the very latest theory of oppression.

Secondly, this approach believes that a cultural tradition represents the accumulated wisdom of a people—empirical and rational in its architechtonics, though not in every detail. It does not automatically become obsolete as a consequence of the growth of modern science or technology. In fact, a complex culture has its own ethnic science and technology which are sought to be destroyed by modern science and technology with the help of state power and in the name of the obsolescence of traditional knowledge-systems and lifestyles.[13] The non-statists believe that the traditions are under attack today because the people are under attack. As classical liberalism and czarist Marxism have both by now shown their bankruptcy, many liberals and socialists have increasingly fallen upon the use of concepts like cultural lag and false consciousness to explain away all resistance to the oppression that comes in the guise of modern science and development. The primacy-of-culture approach fears that more and more models of social engineering will be generated in the modern sector which would demand from the people greater and greater sacrifices in the name of the state and in the name of state-sponsored development and state-owned science and technology. The culture-oriented approach believes that when the lowest of the low in India are exhorted to shed their 'irrational', 'unscientific', anti-developmental traditions by the official rationalists, the exhortation is a hidden appeal to them to soften their resistance to the oppressive features of the modern political economy in India.[14]

[13]In the context of Indian traditions of science and technology, this point has been made indirectly but painstakingly by Dharampal, *Indian Science and Technology in the Eighteenth Century: Some Contemporary European Accounts* (New Delhi: Impex India, 1971); and directly and passionately by Claude Alvares, *Homo Faber: Technology and Culture in India, China and the West* (New Delhi: Allied, 1979). See also Shiv Visvanathan, 'The Annals of a Laboratory State'; and Vandana Shiva, 'Reductionist Science as Epistemic Violence', in Ashis Nandy (ed.), *Science, Hegemony and Violence: A Requiem for Modernity* (Tokyo: U.N. University Press; New Delhi: Oxford University Press, 1988), pp. 257–88; and Claude Alvares, *Science, Development and Violence: The Twilight of Modernity* (New Delhi: Oxford University Press, 1991).

[14]On development as it looks from outside the modern world, some of the clearest statements are in Claude Alvares, 'Deadly Development', *Development Forum*, October 1983, 9(7); and *Science, Development and Violence*; Also see the Special Issue on Survival, *Lokayan Bulletin*, 1985, 3 (4/5); Madhya Pradesh Lokayan and Lokhit Samiti, Singrauli, *Vikas ki Kimat* (Ahmedabad: Setu, 1985); Arturo Escobar, *Encountering Development: The Making and the Unmaking of the Third World* (Princeton: Princeton University Press, 1995); Vinod Raina, Aditi Chowdhury and Sumit Chowdhury (ed.), *The Dispossessed: Victims of Development*

Third, the culture-oriented approach presumes that culture is a dialectic between the classical and the folk, the past and the present, the dead and the living. Modern states, on the other hand, emphasize the classical and the frozen-in-time, so as to museumize culture and make it harmless. Here, too, the modernists endorse the revivalists who believe in time-travel to the past, the Orientalists to whom culture is either a distant object of study or a projection of their own cultural needs, and the deculturized to whom culture is what one sees on the stage or in the gallery. Such attitudes to culture go with a devaluation of the folk which is reduced to the artistic and musical self-expression of tribes and language groups. Ethnic arts and ethnic music then become, like ethnic food, new indicators of the social status of the rich and the powerful. Correspondingly, new areas of expertise open up in the modern sector such as ethnomuseology and ethnomusicology. And cultural anthropology then takes over the responsibility of making this truncated concept of culture communicable in the language of professional anthropology, to give the concept a bogus absolute legitimacy in the name of cultural relativism.

Culture in the present context covers, apart from 'high culture', indigenous knowledge, including indigenous theories of science, education and social change. The defence of culture, according to those who stress cultural survival, is also the defence of these native theories. The defence must challenge the basic hierarchy of cultures, the evolutionist theory of progress, and the historical awareness with which the modern mind works.[15] This radical departure from the Englightenment vision the modern admirers of native cultures will never accept.

Fourth, the culture-oriented approach tries to demystify the traditional reason of the state: national security. It does not deny the importance of collective security, even though the statists feel that anyone who is not a statist jeopardizes such security. However, the culture-oriented approach believes that national security can become disjunctive with people's security and may even become a threat to the latter.[16] Some of

in Asia (Hong Kong: Arena, 1997). Also see 'Culture, Voice and Development', pp. 151–70 below; Development and Violence, pp. 171–81 below.

[15]In the Indian context such a point of view was aggressively advanced by Gandhi. See the pioneering essay of A.K. Saran, 'Gandhi and the Concept of Politics', *Gandhi Marg*, 1980, 1(1), pp. 675–726. Also Thomas Pantham, 'Thinking with Mahatma Gandhi: Beyond Liberal Democracy', *Political Theory*, 1983, 2(2), pp. 165–88; and Ashis Nandy, 'From Outside the Imperium: Gandhi's Cultural Critique of the "West" ', in *Traditions, Tyranny and Utopias: Essays in the Politics of Awareness* (New Delhi: Oxford University Press, 1987), pp. 127–62.

[16]For instance, Giri Deshingkar, 'Civilization Concerns', *Seminar*, December 1980, (256), pp. 12–17; and 'People's Security Versus National Security', *Seminar*, December 1982, (280), pp. 28–30.

those who take culture seriously fear that India is fast becoming a national-security state with an ever-expanding definition of security which threatens democratic governance within the country as well as the security of India's neighbours, who are parts of Indian civilization.[17]

The culture-sensitive approach to Indian politics seeks to demystify the two newer reasons of state: conventional development and mainsteam science (including technology). It believes that new forces of oppression have been unleashed in Indian society in the name of these new reasons of state and the new legitimacies they have created. Those for the primacy of culture believe that these three reasons of state—security, development and modern science—are creating internal colonies, new hierarchies and recipient cultures among the people, so that a small élite can live off both economic and psychosocial surpluses extracted from the people as part of the process of modernization.[18] Modernization, the argument goes, has not fallen into wrong hands; built into it are certain forms of domination and violence. The concept of the expert or the revolutionary vanguard is part of the same story or, as it looks to the nonmoderns, part of the same conspiracy.[19]

[17]For instance, Bharat Wariavwallah, 'Indira's India: A National Security State?', *Round Table*, July 1983, pp. 274–85; and 'Personality, Domestic Political Institutions and Foreign Policy', in Ram Joshi (ed.), *Congress in Indian Politics: A Centenary Perspective* (Bombay: Popular Prakashan, 1975), pp. 245–69; also Deshingkar, 'People's Security Versus National Security'.

[18]For some culture-sensitive Indian intellectuals, the only valid definition of conventional development is the one given by Afsaneh Eghbal in the context of Africa in her 'L'état Contre L'ethnicité—Un Nourvelle Arme: Le Development Exclusion', *IFDA Dossier*, July–August 1983 (36), pp. 17–29:

Development is a structure in which a centralized power, in the form of a young sovereign state, formally negotiates international funds for rural populations representing ethnicity ... no external aid, in the field of development, can relate directly to ethnic groups caught in the problematique of survival. All aid is first absorbed and often plundered by state power.

The Indian critic of development will however further generalize the principle and affirm that it holds for internal resources, too. A good summary description of the process of development in Indian from this point of view is in Alvares, 'Deadly Development'. For a theoretically alert description of the political context within which such developmental pathologies emerge, see Rajni Kothari, 'The Crisis of the Moderate State and the Decline of Democracy', in Peter Lyon and James Manor (ed.) *Transfer and Transformation. Political Institutions in the New Commonwealth* (Leicester: Leicester University Press, 1983), pp. 29–47.

[19]A proper critique of the rhetoric of revolution has not yet emerged in India. Revolution could be considered, in certain contexts, a reason of a shadow state, the state which would come into being after the present one is captured by middle-class, urbane, upper-caste revolutionaries. The sacrifices that revolutionaries demand serve, in this sense,

It is a feature of the recipient culture which is to be created through the modern state system, that the superstitions of the rich and the powerful are given less emphasis than the superstitions of the poor and lowly. This is the inescapable logic of development and scientific rationality today. Only the young, the 'immature' and the powerless are left to attack the superstitions of the powerful. (For instance, the belief popularized by the two post-World War II superpowers that national security requires the capacity to kill all living beings of the world thirty times over, as if once is not good enough; the belief of our rulers that every society will one day reach the level of prosperity of the modern West, as if the earth had that kind of resources; or the faith of our science bosses that the expansion of TV or nuclear energy would strengthen development without setting up a centralized political control system.) The so-called mature scientists, the ultra-rational liberals and professional progressives are kept busy attacking superstitions such as astrology because these are the small-scale enterprises of ill-bred, native entrepreneurs, not the trillion-dollar enterprise which the arms trade, cosmetics and pet-food industries are. It is part of the same game to emphasize the unequal economic exchanges between the East and the West and under-emphasize the unequal cultural exchanges between the two, which has already made the modern western man the ideal of the official culture of India. The culture-oriented activists believe that the latter form of unequal exchange is more dangerous because it gives legitimacy to the 'proper' dissenters wanting to lead the masses to a utopia which is but an edited version of the modern West. The first step in the creation of this new set of élites for the future is the destruction of the confidence of the people in their own systems of knowledge and ways of life, so that they become recipients both materially and non-materially.[20]

Fifth, faith in the primacy of culture over the state does not mean the absence of a theory of state. It connotes another kind of a theory of the state, a theory rooted in the nonmodern understanding of modernity and in a worm's-eye-view of the imperial structures and categories that go with modernity. It can also be called an outsider's theory of statist politics. (I have said earlier that this approach does give a role to the state as a protector, an internal critic and thermostat for the culture.) How-

the class interests of the shadow rulers of a shadow state. However, a critique of statism and a nonmodern awareness of culture has just begun to take shape at the peripheries of the Marxist movement in India.

[20]Ashis Nandy, 'A Counter-Statement on Humanistic Temper', *Mainstream*, 10 October 1982, and *Deccan Herald*, 18 October 1981.

ever, it is an undying superstition of our times that only the moderns can handle the complexities or negotiate the jungle of international politics, ensure internal and external security, maintain national integration and inter-communal peace. It is a part of the superstition to believe that politics is exclusively the politics organized around the state and the prerogative of the self-declared professional politicians.[21]

The theories of the state used by outsiders—by those who take the cultural approach seriously—differ in important respects from the dominant theories of political modernization. It is the use of such alternative theories which accounts for the allegations of irrationality or false consciousness made against these outsiders. These theories look bottom up towards the modern sector of India and they are therefore not palatable to the political élite or the counter-élite dreaming of capturing the state in the future. Such nonmodern theories of the state have no commitment to the ideas of one language, one religion or one culture for India; nor do they think that such linguistic, religious or cultural unification advances the cause of the Indian people. Unlike the modernists and Hindu revivalists, those viewing Indian politics from outside the framework of the nation-state system believe it possible for a state to represent a confederation of cultures, including a multiplicity of religions and languages. To each of these cultures, other cultures are an internal opposition rather than an external enemy. Thus, for instance, true to the traditions of Hinduism, many of these outsiders believe that all Indians are definitionally Hindus, crypto-Hindus or Hinduized; it sees the modern

---

[21]I must again emphasize that the culture-oriented approach to the state stands for greater democratic participation and, thus, for more politics, not less. It wants to pursue the logic of an open polity to its end, to widen the compass of democratic politics. On other hand, state-oriented politics, in societies where there are living nonmodern traditions, have often shown the tendency to throttle democratic institutions the moment participation by the underprivileged crosses a certain threshold.

I should also emphasize that non-statist politics is not the same as non-party politics. However, the two can sometimes overlap. The new interest in non-party politics is not the same which inspired some of the earlier writers on the subject such as M.N. Roy and J.P. Narain. The new interest, however, builds upon the old. For a sample of recent writings on the non-party political processes in India, see D.L. Sheth, 'Grass-Roots Stirings and the Future of Politics', Alternatives, 1983, 9(1), pp. 1–24; and some of the papers in Harsh Sethi and Smitu Kothari (ed.), The Non-Party Political Process: Uncertain Alternatives (Delhi: UNRISD and Lokayan, 1983), pp. 18–46, mimeo. On the issue of culture and authoritarianism in India, particularly on how authoritarianism often rears its head in such societies as part of an effort to contain the nonmodern political cultures of the peripheries, see Ashis Nandy, 'Adorno in India: Revisiting the Psychology of Fascism', in At the Edge of Psychology, pp. 99–111; and 'Political Consciousness', Seminar, 1980, (248), pp. 18–21.

meaning of the exclusivist concept 'Hindu' as a foreign imposition and as anti-Hindu. The culture-oriented do have a commitment to India as a single political entity, mainly because it helps Indian civilization to resist the suffocating embrace of the global nation-state system and the homogenizing thrust of the culture of the modern West. But they are willing to withdraw this commitment if statist forces begin to dismantle the civilization to make it a proper modern nation-state and a modern culture, that is, if India is sought to be fully de-Indianized for the sake of a powerful Indian nation-state. This does not imply any innocence about the nature of the global system. It indicates a refusal to accept the games nations play and an awareness that the problem of internal colonialism in India is part of the global structure of dominance.

Sixth, as should be obvious from the foregoing, the cultural approach draws a distinction between political participation and participation in state-oriented politics—between *lokniti* and *rajniti*, as some following Jayaprakash Narain put it—and it stresses the former. This is the kind of participation that tries to bring all sections of a society within politics without bringing all aspects of the society within the scope of the state. To those stressing such participation, the politics of the nation-state is only part of the story and democratization must have priority over system legitimacy. Alas, this also means that the non-state actors refuse to accept the need for democracy as secondary to the need for a strong state. In recent years, this approach to politics has spawned a vigorous human-rights movement in India which is trying to make democratic participation more real to the lowest of the low.[22]

To the statists, this other kind of political participation is a danger signal. It looks extra-systemic and non-institutionalized—the kind of participation that the well-trained political scientist, if brought up on Samuel Huntington et al., has learnt to identify as a sure indicator of political decay—a situation where political participation outstrips system legitimacy.[23] No wonder, that many of those militantly allegiant to the Indian state would prefer to see the peripheries and the bottom of this society either remain apolitical or, if the latter are already in politics, systematically depoliticized.[24]

[22]See the *PUCL Bulletin* and *Vigilindia* for an idea of the scope and concerns of various such groups, of which the better-known examples are, of course, the People's Union of Civil Liberties, People's Union of Democratic Rights, and Citizens for Democracy.

[23]Evidently, liberal democracy in a multi-ethnic society has built-in limits on its own commitment to democracy. See Kothari, 'Crisis of the Moderate State'.

[24]Such depoliticization may come through the increasing criminalization of politics

In other words, the culture-oriented approach takes the concept of open society seriously. It knows that the glib talk of culture often hides Third-World despotism. Indeed, the approach takes the principles of democratic governance to their logical conclusion by refusing to accept the definition of civic culture vended by those in control of the state. Culture, this approach affirms, lies primarily with the people. Next door in Pakistan, the army rulers pretending to be defenders of faith, would find no consolation in the new culturist point of view which is emerging in many traditional societies and, particularly, in this subcontinent. Nor could the Ayatollah of Iran in his late-life incarnation as an Islamic Dracula. Their Islam is a state-controlled set of slogans and gimmicks; it had little to do with Islamic culture, for such a culture can be identified only through open democratic processes. Hopefully, a culture-sensitive polity in India will not stop at mechanical electoral representation of atomized individuals or secularized classes; it will extend representation also to the myriad ways of life in the hope that in the twenty-first century Indian democracy will reflect something of the uniqueness of this civilization, too, and pursue the principle of 'freedom with dignity' as a basic human need.

III

Finally, I must borrow two terms from the contemporary philosophy of science to explain the link between the worldview which swears by the primacy of the state and that which swears by the primacy of culture. The former thinks it has an explanation of the latter. The statists see the emphasis on culture as a product of the frustrations of those who have been displaced from their traditional moorings by the force of modernity. More, not less, modernity is seen as the antidote for the insane, anti-scientific worldview of the disgruntled, culture-drunk, uprooted nonmoderns. This is the tired crisis-of-change thesis. The latter worldview believes that alternative paradigms of knowledge—whether they come from updated Indian traditions or from powerful post-modern theories of the state—cannot be legitimized by categories generated by the presently dominant paradigms of political analysis. There is a fundamental and irreconcilable incommensurability between the two paradigms. This is one instance, this worldview claims, where no genuine common language or dialogue is possible. However, the nonmoderns

---

or from the apathy brought about by the failure of the political opposition to the basic social problems. Both can be found in India today.

do believe that it is possible for parts of the modern vision to survive in another incarnation, as a subset of a post-modern, and simultaneously more rooted Indian vision—somewhat in the way the Newtonian worldview survives in the Einsteinian world. With the growing cultural self-confidence of Indian intellectuals and informed activists, it is possible that the modern West will be seen by a significant number of Indians the way Gandhi used to see it; as part of a larger native frame— valuable in many ways, but also dangerous by virtue of its ability to become cancerous.

It is known that when one attempts to explain the Newtonian worldview in Einsteinian terms, elements of it such as 'mass' and 'velocity' retard rather than facilitate communication. This is because the concepts supposedly common to the two worldviews are rooted in different theories and, thus have different meanings. (This is the well-known meaning-variation argument in post-Popperian philosophy of science.) In the context of the issues we are discussing, concepts such as rationality, empirical data, mathematization and experimental verification provide no bridge between the state-oriented and the culture-oriented worldviews. Nor do concepts like history, injustice, patriotism or dissent. No sentiment-laden lecture by the national-security chap on how much he loves his culture is going to appease the activist working among tribals to protect their lifestyle. Nor will the copious tears shed by the ultra-modern, rationalist scientist for the Indian villager move the person to whom the superstitions of the rich (such as the billion-dollar con-games involving anti-diarrhoeal drugs, so-called health-food products like Horlicks and Bournevita, or mostly unnecessary surgeries such as tonsilectomy, removal of impacted molar and Caesarean section) are more dangerous than the pathetic antics of the small-time pavement palmist, being pursued by urban rationalists for conning someone out of a few rupees (somewhat in the manner in which village lunatics are pursued by stone-throwing teenagers while greater lunatics are allowed to become national leaders or war heroes.) If you speak to culture-oriented Indians about the superstitions of the witch doctors or *mantravadis*, they will shrug their shoulders and walk away. They are more concerned about the irrational search for permanent youth that helps the annual cosmetics bill of American women outstrip the combined budgets of all the African countries put together. They are more worried about the superstitious fear—of being left behind by other nations—that prompted the Indian Sixth Five-Year Plan to invest more than Rs 9000 million in only the R&D for space and nuclear programmes when the corresponding figure in the case of education was Rs 1.2 million.[25]

The two sides—the statists and the culturists—speak entirely different languages. It is the unmanageable crisis of one worldview—in this case that of the nation-state-oriented modernity which has prodded some to switch sides, in some cases willingly, in others unwillingly. Call this defection another kind of political realism or call it an act of faith. I like to call it the latter; after all, faith does move mountains.

[25]Dhirendra Sharma, *India's Nuclear Estate* (New Delhi: Lancers, 1983), p. 141.

PART TWO

An Anti-Secularist Manifesto

To be no part of this is deprivation
Never could I claim a circumcised butcher
Mangled a child out to my arms, never rave
At the milk-imbibing, grass-guzzling hypocrite
Who pulled off my mother's voluminous
Robes and sliced away at her dugs.

from 'The Ambiguous Fate of Gieve Patel,
He being Neither Muslim nor Hindu in India'

Gandhi said once in a while that he was secular. Yet he thought poorly of those who wanted to keep religion and politics separate. Those who believed in such separation, he said, understood neither religion nor politics.

This contradiction has its roots in two meanings of secularism current in contemporary India. The first meaning is known to every modern westerner; the second is an Indianism that has not yet found place in English dictionaries, though it has some unclear place in Anglo-Indian usage. According to the first, religious tolerance could come only by devaluing religion in public and by freeing politics from religion. The less politics is contaminated by religion, this argument goes, the more secular and tolerant a state will be. The sense of the word 'secular' here is the opposite of 'sacred'.

According to its second meaning, secularism is not the opposite of 'sacred' but of 'ethnocentrism', 'xenophobia' and 'fanaticism'. That is, one could be secular either by being equally disrespectful towards all religions or by being equally respectful towards them. And true secularism, the second meaning insists, must opt for respect. It is this nonmodern meaning of secularism that the anticolonial Indian élite stressed, given the need for broad-based mobilization in a deeply religious society. The leaders of the freedom movement sensed that the European meaning of secularism would make little sense to the average Indian rooted in a religious worldview and not exposed to the kinds of debate the church–state divide produced in premodern Europe.

The Indian meaning recognizes that even when a state is tolerant of religions, it need not lead to religious tolerance in a society. For tolerance by the state cannot guarantee tolerance in society. State tolerance may ensure, in the short run, the survival of a political community; in the long run the community must give it a deeper social content. This meaning of secularism recognizes covertly what many Indians are now finding out painfully, namely that the growth of vested interests in a secular public sphere is an insufficient basis for the long-term survival of a political community. Otherwise the Irish, the Scots, the Basques and the French Canadians or, for that matter, the Sikhs, Kashmiri Muslims and the Assamese would not be creating so many problems for their countries.

Previously, thanks to a number of fortunate circumstances, one could follow the logic of the second, more local meaning of secularism in Indian politics, while paying lip-service to the first. In recent years, the nature of the democratic process in India is forcing the political actors to choose between the two meanings.

First, the condition of the Indian state is such today that to advise the religious to abide by values inscribed in the culture of the Indian state is likely to fall on deaf ears. Few believe that Hinduism, Sikhism or Islam has any moral lesson to learn from the Indian state. For the same reason, the hope that the state can be an impartial arbiter among different religious communities in its present state appears a rather pallid one. The trite, once-popular slogan, 'We are Indians first, and then Hindus, Muslims or Sikhs', may have become a means of condemning certain communities, but cannot make moral sense to most Indians. It is now a pious hope rather than a state of affairs in most sections of Indian society.

Second, despite the tremendous growth in the power of the state in India, political analysts as well as activists are in no doubt as to who or what will be abolished if the Indian nation-state today takes on the task of abolishing religious and cultural identities. The secularization of the Indian state has gone far but there are limits to its capacity to secularize society. (As I am primarily writing for the modern English-speakers, I shall from now use 'secularism' in its proper English sense in the rest of this essay and forget the other connotation as an avoidable Indianism.)

Awareness of these issues has created problems for the contemporary Indian concept of the state. Since about the seventeenth century, the modern western ideology of the state has required the state to be secular by separating religion and politics. Since Indians first began to borrow this ideology in the 1830s, the ideology has also dominated modern Indian consciousness. So much so that even the ultra-Hindu formations, which have fought for Hindu nationalism, have never quite been able to give up the idea of the secular state. Many of them have tried to 'fix' the minorities by pushing the logic of a secular state to its limits and emphasizing a form of absolute secularism by pushing ideas like a universal civil code and abolishing religion-based affirmative action. That absolute secularism, they hope, would 'cut down to size' India's more assertive minorities like the Muslims and Sikhs, who seem less reconciled to the idea of secularism. This, in spite of many like Gandhi trying to be 'secular' by rejecting secularism in its pristine form and bringing the right kind of religion and the right kind of politics together.

Now we suddenly confront the embarrassing fact that not only many Indians but a significant proportion of humankind has become suspicious of the western concept of secularism and become receptive to non-secular ideas of religious and cultural tolerance. (I am aware of the inadequacies of the term 'tolerance'. What I have in mind is neither mechanical tolerance nor a tolerance based on the supposedly non-violent nature of South Asian faiths. It is closer to the concept of understanding and presumes cultural interdependency of the kind which encourages that tolerance of others because that tolerance represents the tolerance of less acceptable aspects of one's own self.)

To understand this suspicion we must first recognize that a modern nation-state, being usually wary of the presence of culture in politics and keen to carve out a domain of public life where only the values of statecraft will rule, work with the following ordering of the citizen (I also give examples from South Asian public life):

Nonbeliever in public and private	>	Nonbeliever in public; believer in private	>	Believer in public; nonbeliever in private	>	Believer in private and public
Jawaharlal Nehru M.N. Roy		Vallabhbhai Patel Indira Gandhi		V.D. Savarkar M.A. Jinnah		M.K. Gandhi Abdul Gaffar Khan, Maulana Bhashani

In other words, to those properly socialized to the ideology of the modern state, the ideal political man or woman is someone like Nehru or Roy. And they believe that, given the ineluctable laws of social progress, more and more citizens will enter the first category, to shed, as a first step, their religious beliefs in public and, then, as a second step their beliefs in private.

This hierarchy of citizens, which persists despite the official and unofficial veneration of Gandhi as the father of the Indian nation, follows naturally from the modern ideology of secularism and provides the basis of the Indian state's claim to a monopoly on religious and ethnic tolerance. At the level of the person, such tolerance is definitionally the prerogative of one who has some western education and some exposure to modernity, especially the modern idiom of politics.

A Gandhian criticism of the approach could be three-fold. First, that it ignores the finer differences within traditions, while playing up such differences within modern culture. It ignores the fact that some forms of religion do lead to intolerance, other forms do not. Thus, while the approach draws a line between vulgar and non-vulgar Marxism and one between the oppressive and the non-oppressive West, it refuses to draw a line between vulgar religion and non-vulgar religion or between tolerant and intolerant forms of culture.

Often, such secularism—I shall call it official secularism—goes farther. It compares the ideals of modernity with realities of religions and cultures. Thus, the ideals of modern politics are compared with the realities of the caste system (to show how bad the latter is), the way many zealous apologists of Hinduism compare the ideals of the caste system against the realities of hierarchical, soulless, modern bureaucracy (to show how good the former is).

Second, official secularism tries to limit the democratic process by truncating the political personality of the citizen. While the personality of those within the fully secular, modern sector is well-represented in the democratic order, those outside the modern sector have only a part of their selves represented in politics. The other part they have to carefully keep outside the public domain.

This, of course, also means pre-empting the creative role which politics might play within a religious or cultural tradition, by playing up some cultural strains against others, by re-ordering the hierarchy of these strains, or by generally maintaining the fluidity of relationships among them. Instead of a dialogue between the public and the private within a person— and between politics and culture—the two spheres are rigidly separated and the latter is frozen in time. As a result, the religious and cultural traditions are forced to become, as the moderns invariably accuse them of being, symbols of *status quo*. This does not of course keep religion out of politics; it only ensures that religion enters politics by a different route. We shall return to this point.

Third, official secularism is almost totally insensitive to the politics of cultures today. It sees the believer as a person with an inferior political consciousness and it celebrates the fact that we live more and more in a world where all faiths and cultures, except modernity, are in recession. Such secularism fails to sense that critical social consciousness, if it is to retain its radical thrust and not to become a reformist sect within modernity, must respect and build upon the faiths and the visions that have refused to adapt to the globally dominant worldview.

I have spoken of the growing marginalization of religions, cultures and visions. This may sound odd at a time when the secularists are obviously having a hard time. In Lebanon, Quebec, Scotland, Bosnia and Basque—and in Punjab, Kashmir, Assam, Sri Lanka and Sind in this subcontinent itself—ethnicity is challenging established modern nationalism; racism is on the rise in parts of the liberal First World; and the Church is ascendant in countries where the super-secular Second World had once tried to banish all religions, from not merely public life, but from life itself. Even in societies not torn by ethnic passions, a new cultural pride and exclusivism are visible in many communities. Blacks and Hispanics in the United States are examples.

Though often viewed as unique, the self-affirmation of parts of the Muslim world can also be seen as part of this larger picture. The Muslims now find themselves at the centre of the world stage precisely because for long they were treated as the et ceteras and and so-forths of the world, whereas their ethnic self-affirmation is now backed by wealth and a new capacity to be a political nuisance. Though Muslims might not be more numerous than the Buddhists, Confucians and the Hindus, they also constituted, as if to spite the modern West, a majority in a large number of states.

This is not a world where one can talk glibly about the marginalization of faith. Yet, the fact remains that the affirmation of religion in our times has gone hand-in-hand with the erosion of religions; exactly as the victory of the idea of the nation-state has co-extended with a new cultural and psychological crisis in the modern nation-state system. The two crises however become one in the Third World, and each society in our part of the world is faced with a dilemma.

On the one hand, the existing hierarchy of nations and the cultural domination of the modern West have created a new concern for, and defensiveness about, nonmodern cultures. Modernity no longer looks like something in the distant future; it is now dominant globally. The awareness of the power of modernity has been sharpened by the Orwellian awareness that one by one the main modern theories of man-made suffering and this-worldly liberation have themselves been co-opted by new forces of oppression; these theories themselves now legitimize new forms of greed, violence and obscurantism. In such a world, the older objectivist interpretations of religious intolerance are bound to look incapable of handling the need for survival, with justice and dignity, of many cultural entities.

On the other hand, the pathologies of religion have become more obvious, due to the greater visibility of many forms of religion and the empowerment of some of them. Even in the few Third World polities where democratic participation has expanded, religion has ridden piggy-back on the newly politicized to enter visible politics and move centrestage. Democratization and politicization have not eliminated religion from politics; they have given xenophobic and anti-democratic forms of religion new power and salience. On the one hand is the late Shah of Iran and the vision of modernization he represented, on the other Ayatollah Khomeini. The choice, even in this terribly crude formulation, is painful.

I

The concept of secularism in India, I have already said, is borrowed from western history and has been during the last hundred years or so, a symbol of the efforts to internalize that history and redesign contemporary Indian life according to the demands of that history. This concept has a clear normative component: religion and ethnicity should be banished from the public sphere and an area should be marked out in politics where rationality, contractual social relationships, and *realpolitik* would reign. This sanitized sphere of politics may throw up rulers who are believers, but if it does do so, these leaders should be weak, secret or apologetic believers. It also follows from the same normative frame that in open societies, some citizens may choose their leaders on religious grounds or the leaders may exploit this weakness of the citizens, but both sides—the leaders and the led—should be embarrassed about this state of affairs and know the limits of their game.

Thus, a section of the Indian citizenry too feels more at home with a temple-going prime minister such as Indira Gandhi, the same way a section of the American public applauds a church-going president and sees him as potentially more honest or straightforward. Yet, most vocal Hindu Indians would be shocked if Nepal were declared a natural ally of India because it is the world's sole Hindu kingdom.

There is a tacit theory behind this ambivalence to religion which cuts across nearly all state-centric ideologies in the Indian polity. It posits two secular trends in history: (1) the gradual erosion of faith and culture because of the growth of science, rationality and modern education; and (2) the consequent expansion of an area of monocultural, universal, contractual, impersonal, massified, public sphere where only values like self-interest, *realpolitik*, and national security rule. The theory is an indirect plea to educate, guide and 'break in' the citizenry into this secular sphere, the sphere of *rajadharma*, with the help of a modern vanguard acting as a pace-setter in matters of social change.

The vanguard sets the pace by exercising its political choices in a rational and, hence, moral fashion from the point of view of the state. It may not be the Christian, the Hindu or the Islamic concept of morality, the theory goes, but it is morality all right; it is the morality of modern statecraft. To put it differently, the vanguard sets the pace by being a collection of exemplary persons who live with their fellow humans without illusions, yet ethically, and by building their ethics not on traditions, cultural myths or on cultural definitions of empathy or compassion, but on scientific rationality, history and reasons of state.

When post-colonial India began its journey in 1947, political mobilization, despite the existence of a powerful nationalist movement since the 1920s, was still at a manageably low level. The Indian power élite was choosy about whom it admitted to the highest levels of government, and the memory of what could be done in the name of religion in public life was fresh in the minds of citizens, for the generation that had lived through the great Partition riots of 1946–78 was at the helm of affairs.

There was a wide consensus that an area of sanity had to be maintained in the polity, community-based nepotism had to be contained, confidence had to be created in the new political institutions and in the impartiality of the state's peace-keeping forces. Above all, there was a consensus that acknowledged—against the beliefs of the various forms of liberal, Fabian and Marxist ideologies which informed the ruling ideology of the Indian state—that Hindu and Islamic exclusivism and zealotry were the strongest among the urban middle classes, not in the so-called peripheries of the country, and therefore the main battle against religious and ethnic conflicts had to be fought among the middle classes which dominated Indian political consciousness. The secularization of Indian politics, so far as it involved mainly the middle classes, did hold such conflicts in check.

That consensus and that strategy have gone as far as they could have. They have now not only begun to break down but to work against many forms of ethnic tolerance. First, political participation has grown enormously, thanks to the eight general and innumerable local elections and thanks to the way politics has entered virtually every sphere of Indian life. No longer is it possible to screen those entering politics for their commitment to modern secular ethics. This is another way of saying that democratization itself has set limits on the secularization of Indian politics. The new entrants, coming from what was, until recently, part of the ethnic 'backwaters' of India, have given Indian democracy its power and resilience.

Second, partly negating the first process, the new entrants carrying their religion or ethnicity into their politics have self-consciously begun to shed their ethnic consciousness while retaining their ethnic links. These links they use in a secular fashion for electoral, especially factional ends. That is, they end up by joining the third category of political participants (exemplified by persons like Jinnah and Savarkar) rather than the first or the second (exemplified by Nehru and Indira Gandhi respectively). Instead of making religious use of politics, they make political use of religion, turning it into an instrument of political mobilization within a psephocratic model—a model in which elections and elected 'kings' dominate the system.

Thus, religion as a repository or expression of cultural values no longer remains available for checking the pure politics of public life, often seen by the newly politicized as an area where only the laws of the jungle apply. Religion is primarily seen as a legitimate instrument for the advancement of personal and collective self-interest. Consequently, there is now a peculiar double-bind in Indian politics: the ills of religion have found political expression but the strengths of it have not been available for checking corruption and violence in public life.

Third, self-doubts have arisen in many modern Indians because the older concept of secularism has been losing its shine since the late 1960s in exactly those countries which were said to be way ahead of India on the road to secularization and nation-building. The positivist, science-centred ideologies of nationality and the conservative and radical theories of progress have come under attack there as the new opiates of the masses which allow the ruling classes to hand over the state to the technocrats and controllers of mass media.

After rejecting and very nearly defeating religion as false consciousness in society after society in the First and Second Worlds, social critics and activists there have found that the secular state has begun to claim—along with its new priestly classes like the scientists, the bureaucrats and the development experts—exactly the same blind faith from its followers as the Church once did. It has begun to equip itself with the technological means to be omniscient, omnipotent and omnipresent, like God himself. In the north that process is called scientific advancement, in the south development.

All these experiences have been unkind to secular Indians. Recently, they have been subjected to further stress because, as a part of secularization itself, the private lives of politicians have become public property. Jawaharlal Nehru, it now turns out, was a votary of astrology and a sneaking Hindu in personal life; Subhas Chandra Bose was a Gita-devouring crypto-*sannyasi*; and by now it is well-known that Indira Gandhi, that open worshipper of the secular Indian nation-state, given half a chance, would not miss a *havan* or pilgrimage.

Even the implicit, third model of secularism used by the *bête noire* of Indian secularists, Mohammed Ali Jinnah, is in crisis today. Most well-known Indian secularists of recent decades, by their personal faith, would have put Jinnah to shame, who in private life was a nonbeliever. But Jinnah made a rather profitable mix of private agnosticism and public religiosity, which of course was the exact reverse of the dominant mode of linking religion to politics in Indian nationalism: private faith and public non-belief. Jinnah's goal was to create a political culture in Pakistan which ultimately, he hoped, would gradually delink Islam from the Pakistani state, confine it to private life, and then move towards a secular modern state where a highly westernized, lapsed Muslim like him would not be a misfit.

Jinnah's main fear, the fear which made him leave the Congress camp, was that the Gandhian movement would create a culture of politics in which, under the guise of Gandhian 'secularism', a Hindu culture would discomfit both the Indian secularist and the Indian Muslim. Being a westernized ethnic, Jinnah could not differentiate between a Hindu zealot and a spokesman of the peripheral Hindu. He had no clue as to why a zealot like V.D. Savarkar should be more hostile to Gandhi than to a modernist like Nehru.

However, if Jinnah had been alive, he would have been happy to see that his political style survives in other parts of the subcontinent, even though in crisis in his 'homeland', having been taken over by the zealots. In India often fully secular, even anti-religious Muslim politicians get access to power in the name of their Muslim origins which they themselves see in purely instrumental terms. In Pakistan and Bangladesh, the Zulfikar Ali Bhuttos and the Zia-ur-Rahmans, who were weak believers themselves, constantly tried politically to encash the appeal of Islam.

The experience of Islam in this respect has been the experience of every religion of the subcontinent. It is the experience of being often reduced to the status of a hand-maiden of politics, subservient to the needs of a nation-state and to the class interests of the zealot and the westernized secularist, both of whom hold the vast majority of the people of their own religion in contempt; one for their lack of zealotry; the other for their incomplete westernization.

In sum, formal, western-style secularization has shown an incapacity to keep pace with politicization in this part of the world, and it shows no sign of being able to do so in the future. As with countries long held up as models for India for their developmental performance (at different times Britain, the United States, Soviet Russia, Maoist China and even the Shah's Iran), in this subcontinent, too, ethnicity is refusing to obligingly sing its swan song. Yet, as I have already said, the survival of ethnicity has not strengthened ethnicity or religious traditions; it has only allowed the pathologies of the latter to find political expression.

We thus come to the small minority of those working for religious or ethnic tolerance in India who paradoxically use a 'method' based on the faith and the culture of the majority of Indians. The method is implied in the Indian use of the word 'secularism'; it is explicit in the Gandhian and proto-Gandhian theories of inter-religious harmony.

Those loyal to the modern idea of the nation-state accept the idiom of secularism, and try to hitch ethnicity to politics in a more or less pragmatic way. They try to create a social basis for secularism by linking it to the reward system of the state, thus creating a vested interest in at least the secular political style. Those sympathetic to the Gandhian vision—to the utter embarrassment of the modern Indian state with its new-found global power ambitions and its fear of the growing political self-affirmation of the nonmodern Indians—try to shift the emphasis from actors to texts, and from outer to inner incentives, so as to reaffirm 'true' religion and 'true' culture which they see as by definition tolerant of other religions and cultures.

Such a vision has many features. The most crucial of them is the recognition that the clash between modernity and religious traditions in much of Asia and Africa elicits from each culture four political responses to ethnicity. The responses are neither exclusive nor orthogonal to each other, though they often seem so, for they are half ideal-types, half mythic structures.

The first of the four, which does not really fit in with the other three, is the cultural constructions of the *western man*, a personality type the presence of which is viewed as the cause of the West's success and the absence of which is viewed as the ultimate cause of the non-West's failure. This western man is a shadow category or a dummy. Not merely because he is often physically absent in the Third World but also because the way the non-West construes him is not exactly how he sees himself or even the way he has existed in or lived through his history. However, the category is not unreal either; millions of human beings have lived by that image and millions have suffered because of the existence of that image. Important sections of the West also have often tried to live up to that image, with immense cost to itself and others.

Usually the western man is construed by sections of a nonwestern culture as an odd form of double—to criticize or correct the allegedly faulty personality types available in the home culture. The shadowy western man then becomes a critique of the indigenous personality as well as a projection of the ego-ideal of these sections of the indigenous population. If the sections are powerful, they may even manage to set up this sectoral ideal as *the* ideal for the entire society. It then begins to represent a new eupsychia (to use Abraham Maslow's concept of a utopian concept of personality) in opposition to the traditional eupsychias surviving in the society.

Along with the image of the western-man-as-the-ideal-political-man goes a managerial attitude to ethnic and religious divisions, often expressed in the belief that successful nation-building involves hard decisions relating to ethnic minorities, decisions not based on the chauvinism of the majority, but on inspired, hard-headed statecraft.

In other words, what is in store for the minorities in the model is not very different from what is generally in store for them in a theocratic state. Only instead of facing the prospect of being Islamized under, say, an Islamic theocracy, the minorities face the prospect of being westernized—the usual euphemism is modernized—in a western-style nation-state. However, in the second case, the situation is morally 'redeemed' by the fact that what is in store for ethnic minorities in the short run is no different from what is in store for the ethnic majority in the long run. Both become objects of social engineering and both face cultural extinction.

The second category of response is that of the *westernized native*, the ethnic who has internalized and approximated the western man (though his syncretism may include sometimes a touch of defiance, too). From a Rammohun Roy (1772–1833) who took a Brahmin cook with him to England to observe his food taboos after a life-long defiance of Hindu caste codes, to a Jawaharlal Nehru (1889–1964) who, in his weaker moments, gave in to astrologers and *tantriks* of all hues, a long and colourful list of individuals provide clues to the inner contradictions of the westernized native in India. But it also happens to be a list of the men who have fought for western secular ideals in this part of the world, and turned against their own cultural self, partly to identify with their western tormentors.

Corresponding to the personality type is a reconstructed history which locates in the past persons who purportedly represented the same ideals. Thus, modern India has rediscovered Ashoka from the third century BC and Akbar from the sixteenth century AD as proper 'secular' rulers and it has reinterpreted traditional texts (such as the one dealing with the different *dharma*s of the king and the Brahman, or the ones dealing with the morality of statecraft) to legitimize western ideals of secular statecraft.

The westernized native may differ politically from the western man, he may even be the western man's political antagonist, but his ultimate aim is to westernize—he prefers to say 'modernize' or 'universalize'—his own culture. He takes the ideal of one world seriously and he believes in a theory of progress in which progress stands for uniformity according to the nineteenth-century European vision of a desirable society. He believes that the western nations—or, if the westernized native happens to be orthodox socialist or positivist Marxist, the socialist West—are more advanced culturally; that the peripheries of the world will slowly and painfully have to traverse the same path of progress.

The two main obstacles to this for the westernized native are the backward, religious masses, unexposed to modern scientific rationality, and their unscrupulous leadership, ever willing to take advantage of irrational, superstitious faiths. To fight the two obstacles he invokes the image of the eupsychia he has set up and constantly compares it with the realities of the nonwestern cultures.

Thirdly, there is the *zealot*—the aggressive Hindu, Muslim or Sikh who, reacting to and yet internalizing the humiliation inflicted on all faiths by a triumphant anti-faith called western modernity, has accepted the western Englightenment's attitude to all faiths, including his own. He is the one the westernized native fears the most as the fanatic who might mobilize the otherwise unmobilizable masses suffering from an acute case of false consciousness (even though such zealots mostly operate from urban bases and appeal to the semi-modern). If such a zealot is a Muslim or a Sikh we call him a fundamentalist; if he is a Hindu we call him a revivalist or a Hindu nationalist.

Strangely enough, the zealot only *uses* the traditional religious or ethnic boundaries as units of mobilization, means of coalition building and settling scores (as a means of giving vent to the free-floating violence that an urban-industrial life often sires). To him the faith of the ordinary Hindu, Muslim or Sikh is an embarrassment. The latter does not seem to show the right kind of respect to the purity of his or her own religion; has neither any sense of unity nor of *realpolitik* and lacks the martial spirit shown by the zealot himself. This is no accident; the one universal trait of an ideology is always a certain contempt for the targeted beneficiaries of the ideology.

In this respect, the Hindu revivalist or Muslim fundamentalist is often only a variation on the secular political man of post-Enlightenment Europe and his ethnicity is skin-deep and reactive. He, too, has identified with the aggressors; he, too, has turned against his cultural self. Ultimately, the zealot's is more a political than a civilizational self-affirmation. To the zealot the idea of his own religion or culture is appealing, not the actuality of it. That explains his strong commitment to the classical version of his religion and culture.

He is one who has internalized the 'defeat' of his religion or culture at the hands of the modern world and he is one who believes that that defeat can be avenged only when the peripheral faiths or ethnicities have internalized the western technology of victory and decided to fight under the flag of their own faiths. The zealot hates the westernized ethnic as one who has sold himself to the western man but his hatred is deeper for the ordinary ethnic who wants to live unburdened by *historical* memories and being put on a heavy diet of cultural and political self-consciousness. For the zealot shares with the westernized ethnic the reference point called the western man.

Finally, there are the numerically preponderant, ordinary *peripheral believers* eking out their lives in the backwaters of South Asia in the ways in which such people eke out their lives throughout the South. They are peripheral only because both the zealots and the secularists have declared them so. These believers are the ones who have learnt to fight with, as also to survive the zealots of the others faiths as well as their own. The modern secularist and the crypto-modern zealot know of the battles for survival against the zealots of other faiths, not of the other battle against the zealots of one's own. Neither the secularist nor the zealot has the sensitivity to stand witness to this other battle for survival. Neither has the time to remember the experience of neighbourliness and co-survival, which characterizes the relationship among the peripheral believers of different faiths.

The nonmodern, peripheral ethnic—I have deliberately retained the term of contempt 'peripheral', for it accurately reflects the political status of the sector—has a longer and deeper memory. It is to that memory and the consciousness that went with it that Gandhi turned to give a political basis to his concept of religious and ethnic tolerance. A number of scholars, such as T.K. Mahadevan and Agehananda Bharati in recent decades, have written about Gandhi's poor knowledge of textual Hinduism. An impartial scholar of classical Hinduism cannot but agree with them. Surely Gandhi had little patience with the greater Sanskritic culture. He sometimes paid lip service to it but there could be little doubt that his primary allegiance was to the folk theologies and ways of life of Hinduism and Islam.

His family belonged to the Pranami sect, a sect deeply influenced by Islam and he belonged to a region where Muslim communities were in turn deeply influenced by Hindu folk theology. He had reason to be confident that religions not merely divided but also united human aggregates.

Once the ethnic personality in politics has been thus classified (see page 48), it becomes obvious that in any situation involving two religious communities, the overt affinity is between the modern believers of the two communities. The westernized Hindu and the westernized Muslim, for instance, can spend days discussing their commonness, especially how the two of them are different from the common run of Hindus and Muslims who are willing to kill each other for the sake of their faiths, and how in the distant future, they, the barbarians, might be persuaded to shed their faith, modernize and then live happily ever after. In the interim period they hope that faiths can be contained by containing the zealots who, given the depth of awareness the westernized secular élite have, look the natural leaders of a people caught in an earlier stage of history. To that extent, there is a less overt affinity between the decultured westernized ethnic and the partly decultured zealot.

The covert affinity is between the peripheral Hindus and peripheral Muslims, much less accessible to the modern Indian and to modern scholarship. This may not be the place for a detailed analysis of that affinity, but two features of peripherality in South Asia need to be emphasized. First, unlike in the Brahminic traditions, faith is more lived out than articulated; and tolerance or forgiveness is given expression in the actualities of living, not in ideological or even theological propositions, positions or briefings. In fact, ideological or even theological intolerance often serve formal textual purposes (such as the maintenance of internal consistency) and are not allowed to enter life, except under mammoth

1. *Nonbeliever in private and public*
Examples:
Persons: Jawaharlal Nehru, M.N. Roy

Groups: The various positivist-Marxist parties, having mainly urban, educated, westernized social base; or movements having a high proportion of leaders with these traits and a small proportion of nonmodern followers.

Typical Pathology: Denial of politics and fear of participatory democracy. Compare M.N. Roy's early analysis of Gandhi where he assesses Gandhi mainly ideologically with Roy's latter works in which he recognizes the political, particularly the mobilizational, role of Gandhi.

2. *Nonbeliever in public, believer in private*
Examples:
Persons: Indira Gandhi, Vallabhbhai Patel

Groups: The Indian National Congress in the 1940s–1960s; the second tier of leadership in the Communist Party of India (Marxist) in recent years. Frequently parties which originate in the modern sector and at some point quickly acquire a large base among the rural or less westernized populations.

Typical Pathology: Can end in secular use of religion (as in 3). Many forms of revivalism, though popularly perceived as belonging to 4, belong to this category. See Nathuram V. Godse's last testament in court in which he suggests that Gandhi had flouted the principles of secular politics.

3. *Believer in Public, nonbeliever in private*
Examples:
Persons: Mohammad Ali Jinnah, V.D. Savarkar

Groups: None, because this is a self-contradictory category. Leaders belonging to the category mostly have followers who belong to 1 or 4 e.g., some of the Maoist activists in rural India who, while they themselves think or work with secular categories, accept the non-secular cosmologies of oppressed sections (poor peasantry, tribals, etc.) Also, the instrumental support given by the CPI to the Pakistan movement in the 1940s.

Typical Pathology: Instrumental uses of religion and ethnicity.

4. *Believer in private and public*
Examples:
Persons: Vinoba Bhave, Jarnail Singh Bhindranwale

Groups: Can take the shape of the nationalist movement in India in the 1920s and 1930s, the Black movement in the US led by Martin Luther King, or some of the Latin American revolutionary movements led by sections of the Christian church. Ali Shariati represents another trend within the category.

Typical Pathology: Exclusivism and nihilism, often accompanied by a search for martyrdom.

or catastrophic social stress. Second, each faith acknowledges the cultural and theological necessity for formalized, textual intolerance (theories of how the ruler should treat the *kafir* or the *mlechcha*, for instance) and handles them as over-statements that are culturally balanced by mutual recognition of deep and darker forces in each community or culture that need to be contained, but also provide a check against powerful tendencies or possibilities in one's own culture that one is constantly contending with. Inter-faith 'dialogue' here is maintained not on the basis of syncretism but on the basis of dynamic balance or stability. Thus, for instance, the aggressively monotheistic, anti-idolatrous and even iconoclastic passions of Islam, may be moderated by the demands of life in what is contemptuously called folk Islam. (Aggressive nationalism, on the other hand, may weaken this moderation by emphasizing high culture.)

Broad worldview	Personality type	Referent	Primary concerns
Modern secular-rationalism	Westernized Hindu/westernized Muslim	'western' man (dummy variable)	History, mega-science, nation-state, nationalism, national security, progress, cultural development
Semi-modern zealotry	Hindu revivalist/ Muslim fundamentalist		
Nonmodern or traditional ethno-religious identity	Peripheral or everyday Hindu or Muslim	Self	Survival, including cultural survival; plural, non-absolute, moral, but often empirically or experimentally non-sustainable constructions of the past; piety and knowledge

The overt hostility is that between Hindu and Muslim zealots who seem to hate each other but understand each other's motivations perfectly and inhabit the same psychological world. The less overt one is the hostility of the westernized ethnic towards the peripherals of his own as well as other faiths whom the westernized ethnic sees as passive or prospective zealots. The covert hostility is that of the zealot whose hatred for the everyday practitioner of his own faith is nearly total.

I have more or less completed my analysis. All that remains to be done is to mention some features of the peripheral majority, their folk religions and folk theologies, and the politics of tolerance implicit in them. This tolerance—better described as a principle of co-survival—bypasses the three enmities mentioned above and has the capacity to withstand and possibly even enrich the process of democratic participation, unlike the 'official' tolerance of the modernized sector which proves fragile in a situation of expanding participation.

First, peripheral believers in a traditional society face a worldview which seeks to preempt and deny the validity, even the existence, of their traditions of tolerance. Thus, modern India talks of Ashoka and Akbar without admitting that they did not build their tolerance the way the Indian state or a Jawaharlal Nehru would have wanted them to; they built their tolerance on tenets derived from Buddhist and Islamic worldviews. By projecting into history the conceptual grid of the European Enlightenment and dishonestly claiming them as part of the secular worldview, Indian secularists have participated in an ethnocidal project the direct results of which are the impoverished versions of faiths that have come to dominate Indian public life.

Likewise, the chieftains of Hindu zealotry like to refer to the profound truth that India is tolerant because it is Hindu. But their claim has a hollow ring about it, for they violently disagree if one claims that Akbar was tolerant because he was Muslim or Ashoka so because he was a Buddhist first and a king second. It is impossible to convince the zealot that to deny Akbar's Islamic base or to incorporate Ashoka into contemporary secularism's statist projects is nothing less than an assault on the organizing principles of the Indic civilization.

All Gandhi did as a *sanatani* or traditional Hindu was to take both these positions seriously—the one which says that India is tolerant because it is Hindu and the one which says that Akbar was tolerant because he was a Muslim—and to openly admit the religious basis of ethnic tolerance in India. He did the same thing with Christianity and tried to do so haphazardly with Sikhism and Judaism, too.

Instead of committing himself to the hopeless task of banishing religion while expanding democratic participation in politics he dared seek a politics which would be infused with the right kind of religion and be tolerant. That is why a Hindu zealot found him a serious opposition and killed him. As I have already said, Hindu zealotry has never found the secular Indian a serious enemy; it has found in him only an effete, self-hating Hindu.

Secondly, Gandhi recognized that India's most effective preachers of inter-communal harmony in the past have mostly been pre-modern, nonmodern or anti-modern. Persons like Nehru, he felt, were only a partial or apparent exception to this rule. Sensing the critique of modernity implied in this recognition, embarrassed moderns have tried to integrate Gandhi into their framework by conceptualizing Hinduism and Islam as two cultures which could be freed from their religious moorings and fitted into a composite whole called 'the Indian culture' to which all right-thinking Indians should be allegiant.

Unfortunately, politicians and scholars make bad cultural machinists. The best of Hinduism and the best of Islam may make excellent titles for two popular books in the same series, but hardly invoke two living religious traditions trying to cope with each other or with real-life issues.

Those outside the modern sector in India sense this. They are conscious of the existence of two religions called Hinduism and Islam, as well as of the diverse Hindu construction of Islam and the diverse Muslim construction of Hinduism. It is on the basis of such constructions—and these are something more than stereotypes—that they operate in everyday life. At this plane the 'languages' of Hinduism and Islam—and for that matter of all major faiths or cultural traditions in South Asia—now have interlocking and/or common grammars. These grammars survive, in spite of the efforts of learned scholars to read them as folk theologies—as inferior, disposable versions of Hinduism and Islam. They survive as a mode of mutuality and a major source of Indian creativity.

Creativity, after all, presumes a certain marginality and, in the matter of culture, a certain dialectic between the classical and the folk. It has to transcend the classicist—and élite—formulation that classicism is the centre of the culture, to protect the classicism itself from becoming a two-dimensional frozen instance of a culture museumized or shelved.

Let us consider for a moment what many consider to be the finest expression of Indian creativity today, north Indian classical music. Is it Hindu? Is it Muslim? Is it secular? One need not do a very imaginative empirical work on Indian creative musicians to find that while Muslim musicians think north Indian classical music to be mainly Muslim, the Hindu musicians think it to be mainly Hindu.

This could be read as a source of possible conflict; it could be read as the possible source of the cultural power of such music. One of the major symbols of the north Indian classical tradition in this century, Allauddin Khan, when he wanted to honour his wife Madina Begum by composing a new raga in her name, could not apparently find anything less Vaisnava than *madanmanjari*.

Modern secularism fails to see the religious sources of such creativity and acceptance, in fact celebration, of other faiths. It sees the public refusal of Bade Ghulam Ali to sing paeans to Pakistan or to its founder during his brief stay in that country as an expression of his secularism. Traditional theories of ethnic tolerance see it as an expression of *his* Islam or of a true Islam. They recognize that song texts in north Indian classical music have a tradition behind them and they bear a direct relationship with an artist's or a *gharana*'s mode of creativity. The tradition has a direct religious meaning—simultaneously Hindu and Islamic. It cannot be artificially given a religious meaning exclusively identified with one faith. Nor can it ever be fully secularized.

Similarly with architecture: P.N. Oak has worked for years on a 'Hindu' history of the Taj Mahal. Now carbon dating seems to be lending partial support to this theory; some carvings used in the mausoleum, it is said, might be older. Trying pathetically to be a proper modern historian, Oak never owns up the psychological insight he is tacitly articulating: the Taj Mahal does seem sanctified to a religious Hindu, and deeply Islamic to the believing Muslim. There lies the meaning of its grandeur as well as appeal. Disconnect the Taj from either of the two traditions, and it becomes a monument mainly for the non-Indian tourist, cultural nationalist and art historian. Oak's history is not only irrelevant to the majority of Hindus, it is anti-Hindu.

What is true of the zealot's approach to culture is also true of the modern secular Indian's attempt to preserve the Taj as a purely artistic statement and a monument for tourists with an oil refinery next to it. Their modernity is also linked to the Taj through the market and through the sulphuric acid that industrializing India is producing to corrode it. The traditional concept of ethnic tolerance, cornered, powerless and at bay, can only pray at the mosque hoping that the modern world will pass it by.

Both examples provide clues to an alternative awareness of the culture of India. This awareness admits that at one plane Hinduism has become a part of Indian Islam and Islam a part of Hinduism, that the ordinary Indian Muslim knows—even if being part of a minority he or she finds it more difficult to admit—that South Asian Islam, one of the most creative in the world, owes its creativity to its encounter with the other faiths of India, exactly the way the Hindu knows that the creativity of Hinduism has been sharpened over the centuries by its encounters with other faiths, mainly Islam, Buddhism, Christianity and Sikhism.

It is true that the uprooted or marginalized Muslim, increasingly ghettoized in urban India, often looks to the West Asia and desert Islam for salvation. And so does sometimes the Mullah, trying desperately to protect his status among followers whose peripheral Islam does not often grant him the centrality he seeks. But can one not make a strong case that such defensiveness follows not so much from faith as from the frustrations and insecurities in one's immediate political environs?

The Gandhian response to this question is clear. If the rules governing the treatment of *mlechchas* and *vidharmis* in Manu, Yajnavalka and Kautilya do not handicap the Hindu in a democratic order, because he has other *shastras* and traditions to fall back upon, the concept of *dar'ul Islam* also should not make the Muslim a congenital misfit in a plural society. There are alternative traditions in Islam, too.

In the *Indian Express* of 19 January 1983, there was a brief biographical note written by a journalist which, abbreviated and slightly edited, I reproduce for the seasoned secularist as my last word on the inner capacities of faiths in the matter of ethnic tolerance.

On 9 January, the house of a young Telugu poet in the old city of Hyderabad was raided by a band of communalists. They stabbed him, his wife and his child. The woman died immediately, the poet on the way to the hospital. The orphaned boy is in hospital, dangling between life and death. Communal frenzy does not know what it claims. They did not know that they were destroying a promising Telugu poet, who was writing the 17th version of ... Ramayana.

The poet was born on 2 January 1946 at Kalwakurty, a big tehsil village in Mahboobnagar district of the Telengana region. His mother was a teacher in the village school. He too followed in her footsteps. 'Teaching is the noblest profession', he used to say. But he was not content being a matric-passed trained basic teacher. His ambition was to become a *vidvan* of Sanskrit. But Kashi Vidyapeeth rejected him. ... Then he met a scholar, Pandit Gunday Rao Harkarey, who taught him the secret of learning a language by the self-taught method. ... Thus, studying privately, be obtained Master's degrees in three ... languages—Sanskrit, Telugu and Hindi.

He had started composing small poems in Telugu when he was just 12 years old. After his marriage, he produced four volumes of *kavyas* and three volumes of *khanda kavya*. After the publication of 'Vijaya Bheri', 'Asru Dharu' and 'Bharati', he was hailed as the most significant poet since Umar Ali Shah. Presenting him at a Telugu mushaira, Viswanatha Satyanarayana ... said, 'This is a gathering of poets in their 70s. This young poet being only 25 should not have been here. But if he is here, it is because he already was 50 when he was born.' Such a rich tribute ... is all the more significant because the poet was from Telengana and the literary élite of the Godawari district dismisses Telengana's 'ulligaddi, bandnikai' Telugu with disdain ... the unspoilt villager in the poet had survived despite the many degrees he obtained. ...

The young poet now began studying all the versions of Ramayana—Valmiki, Ranganatha, Bhaskara, Kambha, Molla, Viswanatha, Kalpa Vruksha and Tulsi. 'I have discovered rational and logical flaws in Valmiki in his description of places and situations', he said, 'I want to write my version of Ramayana. ... I want to name it *Yaseen ramayana*. It will be my gift to posterity'. That is what Ghulam Yaseen, the teacher and the poet, was busy doing when fanaticism struck its deathly blow. ... And the Ramayana which Ghulam Yaseen wanted to leave behind him ... remains unfinished.

What was Ghulam Yaseen? A secular Muslim who did not know his real vocation? A good man with a Muslim name who could be *used* by dedicated social reformers or by the Indian state to establish bridges between faiths? A crypto-Hindu killed by the Hindus by mistake? Or a true Muslim who could express his religious sensitivities through other people's faiths? Or an Indian whose assassination has simultaneously impoverished Hinduism, Islam and Indianness?

Gandhi's response to these questions, I am sure, would have been unambiguous. What about ours?

II

Only one thing remains to be discussed now. And the case of poet Ghulam Yaseen brings us back to it with a vengeance: riots.

From the growing volume of data on religious violence in India it is now fairly obvious that riots have only indirect links with traditions or faiths. Though the modern Indian loves to see all riots as products of insufficient modernization, a very large majority of all riots takes place in urban and semi-urban India where only one-fourth of Indians live. Within urban India in turn, riots co-vary significantly with industrialization, uprooting, breakdown of traditional social ties and habitats.

Likewise, the frequency of riots go down as we go back into recorded history. Even if one accepts the favourite argument of Indian modernists that all positive interpretations of the Indian past are products of inadequate data and imperfect history, it is difficult to believe that earlier centuries could match the going rate of more than one violent communal incident a day in India. Nor can the modernists adequately explain the five-fold increase in the number of riots in the last three decades when the collection of data have not seen any qualitative or quantitative change.

One is forced to admit that communal riots in India have a modern connection. This connection is not surprising. While religious violence was certainly not unknown in pre-modern or nonmodern India, the kind of 'rational', 'managerial', inter-communal violence we often witness nowadays can only be a by-product of secularization and modernization. Only a secular, scientific concept of another human aggregate or individual—only total objectification—can sanction the cold-bloodedness and organization which have recently come to characterize many riots.

True, there has always been an element of organization in riots. Religious violence in our times is rarely, if ever, a spontaneous expression of faith or of the desire for martyrdom. True, during this century, this element of organization has often been provided by zealots and by political formations controlled by zealots. This is but 'natural'. Only partly modern zealots, trying to organize their fellow believers as a political community—as an instrument of heroic, death-denying cause—can have the motivation and ideology to provide the organizational base for riots.

For that very reason, however, there is a built-in check in the situation. In an open system, zealots rarely have anything more than a temporary control over the fate of a community. Take for instance the self-conscious Hindu zealot who, embarrassed by his own un-Hindu zealotry, always defensively asserts that Hinduism is more tolerant than other faiths, while admiring, deeper down, the 'intolerance' of the other faiths. He also recognizes that this tolerant spirit of Hinduism is based on the unorganized, polycentric nature of the faith. The Hindu who is tolerant is not a zealot; he does not even talk of his tolerance. The zealot who talks of Hindu tolerance is actually the one embarrassed by it. That is why the 'natural' support base of Hindu revivalist groups in the Indian electoral system has rarely exceeded ten per cent. More or less the same argument can be given for the Islamic fundamentalists in Pakistan and Bangladesh.

This poses a dilemma for the zealot. On the one hand he hates run-of-the-mill Hindus for what they are; on the other, the more he demonstrates his zealotry, the more isolated he gets from them. (Modernists searching the sources of zealotry in the everyday Hinduism forget the limited electoral support it has enjoyed outside modernizing, urban India). In other words, the zealot's success is self-limiting, even though it can be fearsome in the short run.

No such limit works when the westernized Hindu uses religion in politics. The zealot as a semi-westernized, marginal Hindu can only look wistfully at the fully westernized, modern Hindu and his command of modern statecraft, organizations and mass media. The zealot has to look even more wistfully at the support the peripheral Hindu has given till now to many westernized, secular leaders and denied the zealot, even though the zealot claims to fight for the Hindu cause and the westernized Hindu does not. As if the ordinary peripheral Hindu knew that the westernized Hindu was engaged in the hopeless task of abolishing Hinduism, whereas the zealot was engaged in the more attainable and therefore dangerous task of radically altering the content of Hinduism.

It is the westernized Hindu's command over modern statecraft, combined with his efforts to protect his earlier hegemony in competitive mass politics, and his hard-boiled secularism which has created a volatile situation in India today. The modern, secular Hindu, like his counterparts among the Sinhala Buddhists in Sri Lanka and Punjabi Muslims in Pakistan, is now constantly pushed towards the political use of religion. He is so pushed because he has two natural assets: (1) better access to the mass media, compared to that of the zealot and the peripheral Hindu, and (2) greater ability to use dispassionately the passions of faith of the zealot and the peripheral Hindu. Both assets give him unique advantages which the zealot envies and has now begun to match.

In other words, when secular modernists get involved in the game of organized religious or ethnic violence to fight off political defeat, they play the game not as fanatics trying to advance the cause of their own community or faith but as politicians who must take advantage of human passions to mobilize the political, especially electoral, support of the numerically preponderant 'passive' believers. And as the roles of modern communication and modern organizations expand in politics, the temptation as well as capacity of the secular, modern politicians to organize religious or ethnic violence in a fully secular and scientific manner increases. In that *dispassionate use of passions* lies the roots of authoritarianism, not in the presence of religion in politics.

It is the unfolding of this process which we are witnessing in India today. In earlier riots, organization by the zealot and political cost-calculation by everyone used to play an important but small role. A larger role was played by religious fanaticism, stereotypes and prejudices. Over the years the role of organization and rational cost-calculations have expanded enormously. During the 1980s, Bhiwandi, Delhi and Ahmedabad have seen fully planned and expertly executed pogroms run by hired rioters who not only start and sustain mob violence but do so without necessarily believing in much of the fanaticism, stereotyping and prejudice they spread, promote or sustain.

Though the new breed of riots depends more on rationality, objectivity and self-interest—on hard materialism, secular cost-benefit analysis, and greed—than on religious fanaticism or stereotypes, fanaticism and stereotyping provide the morally troubled middle-classes with post facto rationalization of what the local toughs and the political machines do. In other words, rationality is now used to generate violence while the passions are used to sustain the idea of a moral world where instances of mob violence become not arbitrary acts of God but deserved punishments for the victims' community. In this sense, we are now witnesses to primarily secular riots, justified later on in non-secular terms for the benefit of the victims and the instruments of violence.

No other violence of recent times illustrates this point better than the carnage of Sikhs in Delhi in November 1984. The Sikhs had been traditionally seen by the Hindus and the Sikhs themselves not as an alien community but as part of a larger Hindu social order. After all, the principle of endogamy was never strictly observed in the case of Hindu–Sikh relations and the traditional social ties which bound the two communities were deep. That is, by conventional criteria, the Sikhs were not a political minority nor did they see themselves as such. It took a long period of political skullduggery and the experience of the 1984 riots to turn them into a distinct minority.

Because of this background it had not been possible, till 1980s, to arouse in Hindu–Sikh conflicts the fanaticism associated with the Hindu-Muslim conflicts in this century. It was not easy, during the days of violence in November 1984, to induce Hindu neighbours to take part in the pogrom against the Sikhs. At best they could be turned into passive observers who later on, if guilty about their passivity, could be given ready-made packaged 'reasons' as to why the Sikhs needed to learn a lesson. Thus, except in a few localities, Hindu neighbours tried to help Sikh families to escape the killers, sometimes at great risk to their own security. Communities with a shared past did even better. For instance, many erstwhile refugee colonies, set up in the 1940s by victims of the Partition riots, formed joint Hindu–Sikh defence committees and protected their Sikh members successfully. The exceptions were localities where there were no neighbourly ties, either because they were new settlements or because they were dominated by uprooted, economically deprived isolates and criminals.

Second, organizations like the Rashtriya Swayamsevak Sangh (RSS), which generally take a lead in organizing violence against minorities, also got into the act this time. However, according to the Sikhs themselves, these zealots acted as small-time activists, not as kingpins of the pogrom. In the majority of cases, the attackers came from outside the community, in organized groups and in busloads. Often they came from the nearby state of Haryana. As if they were being unleashed especially against the poorer, less defended Sikh communities, beyond the psychological boundaries of middle-class city life, so as to not disturb the conscience of the average middle-class citizens. As if the organizers knew that many middle-class Hindus would find it easier to justify the pogrom if the major killings did not take place before their own eyes or before the eyes of their families, and if the killings did not indicate a total breakdown of the moral order. Attacks against those living at the geographical and psychological peripheries of Delhi's civic life ensured such a 'numbing' of the citizens' moral self.

The attackers on their part were motivated not so much by anger or sorrow at the assassination of Indira Gandhi, usually given as the reason for the carnage, but mainly by the prospect of loot. In many cases, they joked and laughed when participating in the arson and the killings. From the available accounts of the victims, even the police, docile bureaucrats and the Congress-I activists who took part in the pogrom did so not as a spontaneous revenge for Mrs Gandhi's assassination but as part of a well-oiled machine. This is best evidenced by the way in which the police got rid of all evidence of the carnage in an organized, calculated fashion. The other clue is the way rumours were deliberately spread in the city (such as the one about the city's drinking water being poisoned by Sikhs) to provoke the citizenry, to further numb its moral sense, and to buy its passivity.

Third, before, during and after the pogrom, a propaganda barrage against the Sikhs was kept up by the government controlled media, represented by the radio, the television and sections of the press. This propaganda dubbed as seditious even things which had previously been looked upon as innocuous or minor, such as the alleged anti-national demands of the Anandpur Sahib Resolution.

This resolution had been passed twelve years earlier in the presence of Congress-I stalwarts; it was later on blessed by persons like Jayaprakash Naraian, and considered harmless enough by Indira Gandhi for her to have supported and financed Jarnail Singh Bhindranwale even after he had become a strong votary of the resolution. Evidently, aware that the minorities were gradually abandoning the Congress-I, the ruling party was keen to win over a sizeable chunk of the Hindu vote, even at the cost of unleashing a Hindu backlash and making a target of the Sikhs.

At this plane, Sikhs were replaceable victims, as were Muslims in Hyderabad a few months earlier in September 1984, and Muslims and Dalits in Ahmedabad were to be a few months later, in April–May 1985. Only the organizers of such pogroms are not fully substitutable; they have to belong to the sector from which India's political élite come; they have to take advantage of the print and audio-visual media and the state's law-and-order machinery.

It is not easy to organize a pogrom against a community not commonly seen as a minority. Despite efforts by Sikh zealots and despite the Sikhs being a crushing majority in the Punjab countryside, it was not possible to organize a single riot against the Hindus there during 1982–4. The Sikh zealots had to depend on a small band of assassins and they too ended up killing more Sikhs than Hindus. Similarly, it was not easy to induce the ordinary Hindu to attack the Sikhs in Delhi; in most cases one had to use imported gangs or the criminal underworld of

Delhi, provide them with transport and weapons, and motivate them with the promise of loot, rape and protection. I like to believe that at one time, perhaps fifty or a hundred years ago, it must have been as difficult to organize a Hindu–Muslim riot. It is not easy to make a fanatic out of the ordinary believer, be he Hindu, Muslim or Sikh.

Finally, while in all riots it is the poor and the powerless who suffer the most, in 'secular riots' their lot becomes worse. Fanaticism cuts across social classes. A riot which is precipitated by a quarrel about playing music before a mosque, smoking before a gurudwara, or cow slaughter, touches a wider range of classes than does a riot which is fully organized. In the latter case, the demand for secrecy, the fear of public protest, the need to protect the rioting cadres from the hands of the law, and the need to destroy evidence of party or state involvement in the riots, force the organizers to choose dispensable victims who are less visible and have less access to law courts and the media.

In the Delhi carnage, available data suggest that less than two per cent of the Sikhs killed were well-to-do. The rest were poor or very poor. Electorally, these poor Sikhs were mostly supporters of the Congress-I, the party that led the riots against the Sikhs, and in most cases they did not even speak Punjabi. A majority of them were Rajasthani Sikhs and they were hostile to the political demands of the Punjabi Sikhs. All this did not save them. Their poverty and their marginality doomed them. Secular communal violence, one suspects, is always more decisively anti-poor than the non-secular one. Roughly similar was the case of the Ayodhya Muslims who more than fulfilled every criteria of cultural integration set by the ultra-nationalists, including those who organized the riots at Ayodhya on 7 December 1992. But when the need for finding easy scapegoats arises, it supersedes the need for ideological consistency.

To sum up, the Delhi carnage suggests that religious violence is becoming increasingly a product of hard political cost-calculations, level-headed organization, and dispassionate arousal of communal feelings. It is now primarily a product of faulty rationality, not of faulty passions. The idea of secularism may be able to cope with religious riots which grow out of faulty passions, but it is unable to cope with the riots which grow out of rationally-managed violence. Instead of resisting such violence, secularism endorses the worldview from within which such violence flows.

Recognizing this new role of secularism is also to recognize that the major threats to religious tolerance now come from modernizing India. Hence the secularists have no answer when the minorities are attacked— or a base is laid for an attack on them—with reference to modern, secular criteria, when for example the Sikhs as a community are attacked for their links with external powers or for anti-national ideology, the Muslims for multiplying like bedbugs and for not accepting a uniform civil code, or the South Indians for not speaking Hindi or being in touch with Sri Lankan Tamil zealots.

Likewise, the Delhi carnage has made it clear that little help can be expected from secularists when the state or a party with a 'correct' ideology gets involved in organizing communal violence. A few naive, well-meaning secularists may break ranks, but the remainder, led by the state and the media, goose-step and redefine all uncomfortable cultural distinctiveness as antithetical to the interests of the state and the political community, thus, as culpable.

Probably the thrust of the last part of the argument is that we can no longer define any sector, class or ideology as intrinsically incapable of producing communal violence. Each grouping or subculture has its own potential pathology which becomes patent once the group or the subculture establishes its hegemony in the society. It follows that neither a mechanical reiteration of the principle of secularism nor its mechanical exclusion from public life or public documents (such as the Constitution) will ensure religious tolerance.

A humane society can only be built or sustained on the basis of open polities. And both in South Asia demand the defiance of the ruling categories of our times. These categories have allowed the concept of secularism (which is but one of many ways of moving towards a more tolerant society—a not very successful one at that) to hegemonize the idea of tolerance, so that anyone who is not secular becomes *definitionally* intolerant, particularly in the wog empire variously known as modern India or Indian middle classes. The defiance must involve attempts to recover the first-hand experience of religious and ethnic conflicts and co-operation from the ready-made interpretations of them given by the secularists.

The Twilight of Certitudes: Secularism, Hindu Nationalism and Other Masks of Deculturation

What follows is basically a series of propositions. It is not meant for academics grappling with the issue of ethnic and religious violence as a cognitive puzzle, but for concerned intellectuals and grass-roots activists trying, in the language of Gustavo Esteva, to 'regenerate people's space'.[1] Its aim is three-fold: (1) to systematize some of the available insights into the problem of ethnic and communal violence in South Asia, particularly India, from the point of view of those who do not see communalism and secularism as sworn enemies but as the disowned doubles of each other; (2) to acknowledge, as part of the same exercise, that Hindu nationalism, like other such ethno-nationalisms, is not an 'extreme' form of Hinduism but a modern creed which seeks, on behalf of the global nation-state system, to retool Hinduism into a national ideology and the Hindus into a 'proper' nationality; and (3) to hint at an approach to religious tolerance in a democratic polity that is not dismissive towards the ways of life, idioms and modes of informal social and political analyses of the citizens even when they happen to be unacquainted with—or inhospitable to—the ideology of secularism.

I must make one qualification at the beginning. This is the third in a series of papers on secularism, in which one of my main concerns has been to examine the political and cultural–psychological viability of the ideology of secularism and to argue that its fragile status in South Asian politics is culturally 'natural' but not an unmitigated disaster. For there are other, probably more potent and resilient ideas within the repertory of cultures and religions of the region that could ensure religious

[1] Gustavo Esteva, 'Regenerating People's Space', *Alternatives*, 1987, 12(1), pp. 125–52.

and ethnic co-survival, if not creative inter-faith encounters. Few among the scores of academic responses to the papers—some of them hysterically hostile—have cared to argue or examine that part of the story, which I once foolishly thought would be of interest even to dedicated secularists. They were more disturbed by my attempts to identify the spatial and temporal location or limits of the ideology of secularism. Evidently, for some academics, the ideology of secularism is prior to the goals it is supposed to serve. Much less provoked were those who had some direct exposure to religious or ethnic strife as human rights activists, first-hand observers or victims, for whom the papers were written in the first place. For even when uncomfortable with M.K. Gandhi's belief that 'politics divorced from religion becomes debasing',[2] they seemed to intuitively gauge the power of Raimundo Panikkar's pithy formulation: 'the separation between religion and politics is lethal and their identification suicidal'.[3]

The Paradox of Secularism

Secularism as an ideology can thrive only in a society that is predominantly non-secular. Once a society begins to get secularized—or once the people begin to feel that their society is getting cleansed of religion and ideas of transcendence—the political status of secularism changes.[4] In such a society, people become anxiously aware of living in an increasingly desacralized world, and start searching for faiths to give meaning to their life and to retain the illusion of being part of a traditional community. If faiths are in decline, they begin to search for ideologies linked to faiths, in an effort to return to forms of a traditional moral community that would negate or defy the world in which they live. If and when they find such ideologies, they cling to them defensively—'with the desperate ardour of a lover trying to converse life back into a finished love', in the language of Sara Suleri. What sometimes happens to com-

[2] M.K. Gandhi, in Raghavan Iyer (ed.), *The Moral and Political Writings of Mahatma Gandhi* (Oxford: Clarendon Press, 1986), p. 374.

[3] Raimundo Panikkar, 'The Challenge of Modernity', *India International Centre Quarterly*, Spring–Summer 1993, 20(1/2), pp. 183–92; see p. 189.

[4] The decline of faith I am speaking of has its rough counterpart in the erosion of beliefs surveyed in a somewhat different context by Mattei Dogan, 'Decline of Religious Beliefs in Western Europe', *International Social Science Journal*, 1995, 47(3), pp. 405–17; and Ronald Inglehart, 'Changing Values, Economic Development and Political Change', ibid., pp. 379–403. See also Ronald Inglehart, *Culture Shift in Advanced Societies* (Princeton: Princeton University Press, 1991).

munities can also happen to sections of a community or to individuals. Thus, in recent years, many expatriate South Asians in the West have become more aggressively traditional, culturally exclusive and chauvinistic. As their cherished world becomes more difficult to sustain, as their children and they themselves begin to show symptoms of getting integrated in their adopted land, they become more protective about what they think are their faiths and cultures.

The enthusiasm of some states to aggressively impose secularism on the people sharpens these fears of deracination. Already sensitive about the erosion of faith, many citizens are particularly provoked by a secularizing agenda imposed from the top, for that agenda invariably carries with it in this era a touch of contempt for believers. Such secularism is:

essentially a religious ideology, not based on any scientifically demonstrable propositions. ... It is the religion of a divinized human rationality of a particular kind, making critical rationality the final arbiter. This religious ideology is then imposed on our children in schools—from which all other religions are proscribed. ... This religion spread in the UK and the USA for two generations. Sunday schools were established. Catechisms of the new religion were published. With the rise of Nazism and the Second World War it fizzled out, and merged with modern liberalism, which is also the religion of the new civilization now sweeping Europe. ... Secularism creates communal conflict because it brutally attacks religious identity, while pretending to be tolerant of all religions.[5]

When Indian public life was overwhelmingly nonmodern, secularism as an ideology had a chance. For the area of the sacred looked intact and safe, and secularism looked like a balancing principle and a form of legitimate dissent. Even many believing citizens described themselves as secular, to keep up with the times and because secularism sounded like something vaguely good. Now that the secularization of Indian polity has gone far, the scope of secularism as a creed has declined. Signs of secularization are now everywhere; one does not have to make a case for it. Instead, there has grown the fear that secularization has gone too far, that the decline in public morality in the country is due to the all-round decline in religious sensibilities. Many distorted or perverted

---

[5]Paulos Mar Gregorios, 'Speaking of Tolerance and Intolerance', *Indian International Centre Quarterly*, Spring 1995, 22(1), pp. 22–34; see pp. 24–5, 27. On the contempt for believers that lies at the heart of secularism and the capacity this contempt has to legitimize western dominance over all traditional societies, see Ziauddin Sardar and Merryl Wyn Davies, *Distorted Imagination: Lessons from the Rushdie Affair* (London: Grey Seal, and Kuala Lumpur: Berita, 1990).

versions of religion circulating in modern or semi-modern India owe their origins to this perception of the triumph of secularization rather than to the persistence of traditions.

As part of the same process, many 'non-secular' ideologies and movements have become more secular in style and content. They do try to look religious, for the sake of their constituency, but they can pursue political power in a secularized polity only through secular politics, secular organization and secular planning. They increasingly resemble the jet-setting gurus and *sadhus* who, while criticizing the 'crass materialism of the West', have to use at every step western technology, western media and western disciples to stay in business. A popular way of recognizing this in India is to affirm that politicians misuse religion. But that affirmation usually fails to acknowledge that only a person or a group at least partly repudiating the sanctity of religion can 'misuse' religion or 'use' it only instrumentally.[6] In this sense, the Bharatiya Janata Party and the Shiv Sena, though called fundamentalist, are two of the most secular parties in India, for they represent most faithfully the loss of piety and cultural self-doubts that have come to characterize a section of urban, modernizing India. While other parties observe, even if by default, some limits to their instrumental use of religion, there seems to be no such restraint in the BJP or the Shiv Sena. The people these parties mobilize may sometimes be driven by piety—in the Shiv Sena's case even that is doubtful—but their leaders value that piety only as a part of their political weaponry.

Even religious riots or pogroms are secularized in South Asia. They are organized the way a rally or strike is organized in a competitive, democratic polity and, usually, for the same reasons—to bring down a regime or discredit a chief minister here or to help an election campaign or a faction there. Some political parties in India today have 'professionals' who specialize in such violence and, like true professionals, do an expert job of it. Often these professionals, though belonging to antagonistic

[6]The great European witch-hunt, it has frequently been pointed out, peaked not during the period when European Christendom and the Church were secure, but when modernity had weakened their bases. Speaking of the belief in witches in the sixteenth and seventeenth centuries, H.R. Trevor-Roper says, 'It was not, as the prophets of progress might suppose, a lingering ancient superstition, only waiting to dissolve. It was a new explosive force, constantly and fearfully expanding with the passage of time.' H.R. Tevor-Roper, 'The European Witch-Craze in the Sixteenth and Seventeenth Centuries', in *The European Witch-Hunt in the Sixteenth and Seventeenth Centuries and Other Essays* (New York: Harper, 1967), pp. 90–192. See also Norman Cohn, *Europe's Inner Demons* (New York: Basic, 1975).

religious or ethnic communities, maintain excellent personal, social and political relationships with each other. Fanaticism, they appear to believe, is for the hoi polloi, not for serious politicians playing the game of ethnic politics.[7] It is not difficult today to find out the rate at which riots of various kinds can be bought, how political protection can be obtained for the rioters and how, after a riot, political advantage can be taken of it.

There is even a vague consensus among important sections of politicians, the bureaucracy and the law-and-order machinery on how such specialists should be treated. Despite hundreds of witnesses and detailed information, hardly anyone has ever been prosecuted for complicity or participation in riots in India or, for that matter, in the whole of South Asia. The anti-Sikh riot in Delhi in 1984 provides dramatic evidence of such a consensus. Though over 3,000 Sikhs were killed in the three-day pogrom in India's capital, for over fifteen years its instigators and active participants have not only escaped prosecution but have risen high in the political hierarchy. At least two have been in the Union cabinet and another three have been Congress party MPs from the capital. It does not need much political acumen to predict that more or less the same fate awaits the self-declared instigators and perpetrators of the anti-Muslim violence in Bombay in January 1993 and in Gujarat in March 2002.

On the other hand, though by now human-rights activists and students of communal violence have supplied enough data to show that riots are organized, they have rarely pushed this point to its logical conclusion. Riots *have* to be organized because ordinary citizens—the 'illiterate', 'superstitious' South Asians, uncritically allegiant to their primordial identities—are not easy to arouse to participate in riots. To achieve that

[7]In the context of the films of Woody Allen, Barbara Schapiro speaks of the 'clever, manipulative technique by which Allen attempts to control his critics by demonstrating an awareness of his own potential weaknesses. ... The character displays awareness of his problem while in the very act of demonstrating the problem, and that self awareness, of course, creates the humour.' Barbara Schapiro, 'Woody Allen's Search for Self', *Journal of Popular Culture*, Spring 1986, 18, pp. 47–62. I am speaking here of an analogous process which produces, instead of humour, tragedy for millions.

However, there is some scope for irony, if not humour, within such tragedies. Recently, when Brijbhushan Sharan Singh, an MP of the Bharatiya Janata Party (BJP), the most powerful political front of the Hindu nationalist formations, was accused of harbouring criminals with terrorist connections and protecting them from the law, the criminals turned out to be associates of the notorious don of Bombay's underworld, Dawood Ibrahim. Likewise, when the former BJP President Lal Krishna Advani was accused of being involved in criminal money-laundering, the main source of payments to him was said to be one Ameerbhai. The party has established its secular credentials the hard way!

end, one needs detailed planning and hard work. It is not easy to convert ordinary citizens into fire-spitting fanatics or killers; they may not be epitomes of virtue, but they are not given to blood-curdling Satanism either—not even when lofty modern values like history, state and nationalism are invoked.[8] South Asian loves and hates, being often community-based, are small-scale. In the case of communal violence, the most one can accuse them of is a certain uncritical openness to the rumours floated before riots, which help them make peace with their conscience and their inability to resist the violence.

Yet, they do resist. Each riot produces instances of bravery shown by persons who protect their neighbours at immense risk to their own lives and that of their families.[9] Often entire families and communities participate in the decision to resist. There is no empirical basis whatever to explain away this courage as a function of individual personality while, at the same time, seeing the violence it opposes as a cultural product. In South Asia as much as in Nazi Germany, those who resist such violence at the ground level derive their framework from their religious faith.[10] I have been hearing since my childhood literally hundreds of caustic accounts of the victims of the great Partition riots—about their suffering in 1946–7. In most cases, the experiences have made them bitterly anti-Muslim, anti-Sikh or anti-Hindu. Despite the bitterness, however, most accounts include a story of someone from the other community who helped the family. The loves and hates of everyday life, within which usually are fitted ethnic and religious prejudices and stereotypes, may be small-scale but they are not always petty.

The resistance is stronger where communities have not splintered into atomized individuals. Not only do riots take place more frequently in the cities, but also they are harder to organize in villages. The village community is breaking down all over the world, but it has not broken down entirely in South Asia. Even the smaller towns in South Asia have often

---

[8]Probably the rational–legal values of an individualized, mass society have not yet made inroads into the interstices of the South Asian personality and the values and faiths most South Asians live with cannot be mobilized too easily for collective action cutting across sects or denominations. Urbanization and massification is changing this profile, but the changes so far affect only a minority.

[9]For instance, Tariq Hasan, 'How Does it Matter Who is the Victim?', *The Times of India*, 3 April 1995. See also, Ashis Nandy, Shikha Trivedy, Shail Mayaram and Achyut Yagnik, *Creating a Nationality: The Ramjanmabhumi Movement and Fear of the Self* (New Delhi: Oxford University Press, 1995).

[10]Cf. Eva Fogelman, 'Victims, Perpetrators, Bystanders, and Rescuers in the Face of Genocide and its Aftermath, in Charles B. Strozier and Michael Flynn (ed.), *Genocide, War and Human Survival* (New York: Rowman and Littlefield, 1996), pp. 87–98; see pp. 91–2.

escaped massification. It is no accident that, despite the claim of some Hindu nationalists that more than 350,000 Hindus had already died fighting for the liberation of the birthplace of Rama, Ramjanmabhumi, during the previous 400 years, the residents of Ayodhya themselves lived in reasonable amity till the late 1980s. The Sangh Parivar sensed this; till the mid-1980s, the case for demolishing the Babri mosque at Ayodhya was not taken up by any of the noted Hindu nationalists, from V.D. Savarkar, Balkrishna Munje and Keshav Hedgewar to Bal Thackeray, Lal Krishna Advani and Murli Manohar Joshi. The Babri mosque was turned into a political issue only after India's urban middle class attained a certain size and India's modernization reached a certain stage.[11]

The first serious riot in the sacred city of Ayodhya took place on 6–7 December 1992. For seven years, despite all efforts to mobilize the locals for a riot, no riot had taken place.[12] This time, it was organized by outsiders and executed in many cases by non-Hindi-speaking rioters with whom the local Hindus could not communicate. These outsiders were not traditional villagers, but urbanized, semi-educated, partly westernized men and, less frequently, women. They broke more than a hundred places of worship of the Muslims in the city to celebrate the 'fall' of the unprotected Babri mosque.[13]

In the final reckoning, the demolition of the Babri mosque in 1992 was proof that the secularization of India has gone along predictable lines.

The Politics of Secularism

Over the last fifty years or so, the concept of secularism has had a good run. It has served, within the small but expanding modern sector in India, as an important public value and as an indicator of one's commitment to the protection of minorities. Now the concept has begun to deliver less and less. By most imaginable criteria, institutionalized secularism has failed. Communal riots have grown more than ten-fold and have now begun to spread outside the perimeters of modern and semi-modern India.[14] In the meanwhile, the ruling culture of India, predominantly modern and secular, has lost much of its faith in—and access to—the

[11]Nandy et al., *Creating a Nationality*.

[12]In the case of both Kashmir and the Punjab, despite the bitterness produced by the militants and the agencies of the state and despite some determined efforts to precipitate riots, there has been no communal riot till now.

[13]Nandy et al., *Creating a Nationality*.

[14]Ibid., ch. 1.

traditional social and psychological checks against communal violence.

In this respect, one is tempted to compare the political status of secularism with that of modern medicine in India. Traditionally Indians used a number of indigenous healing systems, and did so with a certain confidence and scepticism. These systems were seen as mixed bags; they sometimes worked, sometimes not. But they were not total systems; they did not demand full allegiance and they left one with enough autonomy to experiment with other systems, including the modern ones. Slowly well-meaning reformers broke the confidence of their ignorant compatriots in such native superstitions. In the second half of the nineteenth century, modern medicine was introduced into India with great fanfare. It was introduced usually with the backing of the state and sometimes with the backing of the coercive apparatus of the state, not merely as a superior science but also as a cure for the irrational faith of the natives in traditional systems of healing.[15] People were constantly bombarded with the message that the older systems were bogus or, at best, inefficient; that they should, therefore, shift to the modern, 'truly universal' system of medicine.

Once the confidence of a sizeable section of Indians in the older, more easily accessible healing systems were destroyed, the inevitable happened. Most of those who converted to modern medicine found it prohibitively costly, more exclusive, often inhuman and alienating. They also found out that their proselytizers had other priorities than to give them easy access to modern medicine. In the meanwhile, the converts had lost some of their faith in the traditional systems of healing. Many of the practitioners of the traditional systems, too, had lost confidence in their vocation and had begun to pass themselves off as deviant practitioners of modern medicine; they had begun to copy allopaths in style and, more stealthily, in practice.

Similarly, the concept of secularism was introduced into South Asian public life by a clutch of social reformers, intellectuals and public figures— seduced or brainwashed by the ethnocidal, colonial theories of social evolution and history—to subvert and discredit the traditional ideas of inter-religious understanding and tolerance. These traditions had allowed the thousands—yes, literally thousands—of communities living in the subcontinent to co-survive in reasonable neighbourliness for centuries. The co-survival was not perfect; it was certainly not painless. Often there

---

[15]See for instance Frédérique Apffel-Marglin, 'Smallpox in Two Systems of Knowledge', in Frédérique Apffel-Marglin and Stephen A. Marglin (ed.), *Dominating Knowledge: Development, Culture and Resistance* (Oxford: Clarendon Press, 1990), pp. 145–84.

were violent clashes among communities, as is likely in any 'mixed neighbourhood'. But the violence never involved such large aggregates or generic categories as Hindus, Muslims, Sikhs, Tamils or Sinhalas. Conflicts were localized and sectored, and were almost invariably seen as cutting across religious boundaries, for such boundaries were mostly fuzzy.[16] More important, both conflict and resolution were explained and negotiated in languages that were reasonably transparent to a majority of the people living in the region.[17] To the reformers, thinkers and politicians—brought up on the colonial state's classification of Indians into broad European-style religious categories—this 'living past' was an anachronism, an embarrassment and a sure prescription for ethnic and religious strife. To them, some of the clashes between sects, denominations or ethnic groups in earlier centuries began to look in retrospect like clashes between entire religious communities. Simultaneously, the categories that sustained such interreligious adaptations or tolerance—or, to put it modestly, the categories that contained communal animosities within tolerable limits—were systematically devalued, attacked and ridiculed as parts of an enormous structure of irrationality and self deceit, and as sure markers of an atavistic, retrogressive way of life.

In place of these categories, the concept of secularism was pushed as *the* remedy for all religious conflicts and fanaticism, something that would do away with the constant religious violence and bloodletting that had reportedly characterized the region from time immemorial. 'Reportedly' because no one produced an iota of empirical evidence to show that such conflicts had existed on a large scale and involved religious

[16]See Kumar Suresh Singh, *People of India: An Introduction* (New Delhi: The Anthropological Survey of India, 1992), Vol. 1, part of a voluminous and authoritative survey which almost incidentally shows that even in the 1990s, nearly 50 years after the Hindu–Muslim divide has become the most dangerous cleavage in the subcontinent, of the 2800 old communities identified as Hindu and Muslim, about 400 cannot be identified as exclusively Hindu or Muslim. There are probably something like 600 such communities which live, not with multiculturalism without, but with multiculturalism within in South Asia. In a personal communication Singh estimates that the proportion of such fuzzy-bordered communities had been much higher in earlier times. For a fascinating case study, see Frédérique Apffel Marglin, 'On Pirs and Pandits', *Manushi: A Journal about Women and Society*, 1995, (91), pp. 17–26. Also, Shail Mayaram, 'Representing the Hindu–Muslim Civilizational Encounter: The Mahabharata of Community of Muslims', Jaipur: Institute of Development Studies, 1996; and 'Ethnic Co-Existence in Ajmer', Project on Culture and Identity, Colombo, Centre for Ethnic Studies and Delhi, Committee for Cultural Choices, 1995.

[17]Ashis Nandy, 'Time Travel to Another Self: Searching for the Alternative Cosmopolitanism of Cochin', *Japanese Journal of Political Science*, 2000, 1(2), pp. 295–327.

communities as they are presently defined.[18] That did not cramp the style of well-educated South Asian liberals and progressives. They seemed convinced that the data did not exist because their societies were ahistorical; had a proper scientific, objective history existed, it would have shown that pre-modern South Asia had been a snake pit of religious bigotry and blood lust.

That innocent social–evolutionist reading today lies in tatters. Yet, the dominance of the ideology of secularism in the public discourse on religious amity and ethnic plurality in India continues. Why? Why do even the Hindu nationalists uphold not religion but genuine secularism (as opposed to what they call the pseudo-secularism of their political enemies)? Above all, who gets what from secularism and why? Any attempt to even raise this question triggers deep anxieties; it seems to touch something terribly raw in the Indian bourgeoisie. As if secularism was a sacred trans-historical concept, free from all restraints of space and time, and any exploration of its spatial and temporal limits was a reminder of one's own mortality. As if those disturbed by the questions knew the answers, but did not wish to be reminded of them. I shall risk political incorrectness here and obstinately turn to these very questions.

First, once institutionalized as an official ideology, the concept of secularism helps identify and set up modernized Indians as a principle of rationality in an otherwise irrational society and gives them, seemingly deservedly, a disproportionate access to state power. After all, they are the ones who have reportedly freed themselves from ethnic and religious prejudices and stereotypes; they are the ones who can even be generous and decide who among the majority of Indians who do not use the idiom of secularism are nevertheless 'objectively' secular. Secularism for them is often a principle of exclusion. It marks out a class that speaks the language of the state, either in conformity or in dissent. At this plane, secularism is emblematic of a person or group willing to accept two corollaries of the ideology of the Indian state: the assumption that those who do not speak the language of secularism are unfit for full citizenship, and the belief that those who speak it have the sole right to determine what true democratic principles, governance and religious tolerance are.[19]

[18]For a concise, if non-committal coverage of this part of the story, see C.A. Bailey, 'The Pre-History of "Communalism"? Religious Conflict in India, 1700–1860', *Modern Asian Studies*, 1985, 19(2), pp. 177–203.

[19]An apparently harmless but chilling example of this attitude is Sumanta Bannerji, 'Sangh Parivar and Democratic Rights', *Economic and Political Weekly*, 1993, 28(34), pp. 1715–18.

The main function of the ideology of secularism here is to shift the locus of initiative from the citizens to a specialist group that uses a special language.

To be more generous to this sector and those mentoring them in the mainstream global culture of scholarship, secularism has become mainly modern India's way of 'understanding' the religious tolerance that survives outside modern India. It has become a concept that names the inexplicable and, to that extent, makes it more explicable. Its necessity depends on modern India's loss of touch with Indian traditions and loss of confidence in the traditional codes of religious tolerance that constitute an alternative vantage ground for political intervention in a democratic polity. Hence the modern Indian's fear of the void that the collapse of the concept of secularism might produce.

Many secularists are secular on ideological or moral grounds. They consider their ideology to be compatible with radical or leftist political doctrines and seem oblivious of its colonial connections and class bias. Evidently, class analysis for them, unlike charity, does not begin at home. Some of them have personally fought for religious and ethnic minorities, but now face the fact that, with the spread of participatory mass politics, they are being reduced to a small minority among the very section within which they expected to have maximum support—the westernizing, media-exposed, urban middle classes. They can neither give up their faith in secularism, because that would mean disowning an important part of their self-definition, nor can they shake off the awareness that it is doomed, at least in ground-level politics.[20] Such politics is already getting too secularized to be able to sustain secularism as a popular ideology.

Second, the ideology of secularism not merely fits the culture of the Indian state, it invites the state to use its coercive might to actualize the model of social engineering the ideology projects. Secularism and statism in India have gone hand in hand—perhaps the main reason why Hindu nationalism, statist to its core, has not given up the language of secularism.[21] The goal of both is to retool the ordinary citizen so that he

[20]For a profile of westernizing, media-exposed urban India as the site of rivalry between secularists and Hindu nationalists, see Nandy et al., *Creating a Nationality*.

[21]Theologian Jyoti Sahi claims that both the modern state and secularism owe their origins to the Judaeo-Christian worldview and secularism particularly has no theological status outside Christianity. 'Monotheism has created its own understanding of the state and its relation to the nation. ... The concept of a nation-state based on a religious identity derives from a Judaeo-Christian background, but now has been adopted by other faith systems, giving rise to a very new idea like a Hindu nation-state. ... The concept of a secular state has also come from a Christian debate on the relation of church to State. ... Hinduism and Buddhism have never discussed or defined this kind of distinction; in fact the sacred

or she, though given democratic rights, would not exercise the rights except within the political limits set by South Asia's westernizing élite, constituting the steel-frame of the region's Wog empires. Secularism too, has its class affiliations; it too, has much to do with who gets what and when in a polity. Tariq Banuri compares the dominant position of the ego in Freudian psychology with the dominant position of the nation-state in contemporary ideas of political development.[22] To complete his evocative metaphor, one must view secularism as a crucial defence of the ego.

Banuri's metaphor also supplied a clue to the fanaticism of many secularists in India, eager to fight the cause of secularism to the last Muslim, Christian, or Sikh. It is their version of a passionate commitment to interests or, if you like, irrational commitment to rationality (a typical nineteenth- and twentieth-century psychopathology in which allegiance to an ideology outweighs the welfare of the targeted beneficiaries of the ideology). Such romantic realism is the underside of what Banuri calls 'the overly enthusiastic pursuit of national integration'.[23] Though carrying the white man's burden after the demise of empires in the subcontinent, these secularists seem particularly unhappy at the South Asian failure to internalize the psychological traits and social skills congruent with the ideology of secularism. Underlying the unhappiness, however, is a certain glee at the persistence of religious belligerency. It is proof that the average South Asian's internship to qualify for full citizenship is not yet complete and it justifies further postponement of the day when the plebeians would be allowed to 'legitimately' claim their full democratic rights and exercise the power of numbers.

The third reason for the survival of secularism as an important ideological strain in Indian public life is for some reason even less accessible to political analysts, journalists and thinkers. Though the culturally rootless constitute a small, if audible, section of the population, to many of them, secularism is not just a way of communicating with the modern world but also with compatriots trying to enter that world. These neophytes do not have much to do with the European associations and

---

and the profane are interwoven. ... even in Islam there is no clear distinction drawn between the sacred and profane, or religious and secular.' Jyoti Sahi, 'Response to Asghar Ali Engineer's "Imaging and Imagining Religious Symbolism in Mass Media"', Paper presented at the conference on Globalization of Mass Media: Consequences for Indian Cultural Values, United Theological College, Bangalore, 29 June–1 July 1998.

[22]Tariq Banuri, 'Official Nationalism, Ethnic Conflict and Collective Violence', (Islamabad: Sustainable Development Policy Institute, 1993), p. 8.

[23]Ibid.

cultural baggage of the term 'secularism'. But they have stretched the meaning of the term for their own purposes and adapted it in such a fashion that it manages to communicate something to others who have to cope, however unwillingly, with Indian realities.[24] They seem satisfied that such secularism allows one to break the social barriers set up by castes, sects and communities, and helps one to converse not only with the political and social élite, but also with the metropolitan intellectuals and professionals. Secularism for them is a marker of cosmopolitanism. Many Indian politicians—when they pay lip service to the standard, universal concept of secularism—have one eye on the response of the national media, the other on their clever competitors who have profited from the secular idiom.

Finally, there are the self-avowed 'genuine secularists'—political actors and ideologues who have an instrumental concept of secularism. They see secularism partly as a means of mounting an attack on the traditional secularists and partly as a justification for majoritarian politics. (The appeal that this majoritarianism has to an urban, deracinated minority can be a frustrating experience and this frustration probably contributes significantly to organized violence against constructed 'others' in South Asia.) These are the people who often use, participate in, or provoke communal frenzy, not on grounds of faith but on grounds of secular political cost calculations. Occasionally, in place of political expediency, they are motivated by political ideology and that ideology may *appear* to be based on faith. But on closer scrutiny it turns out to be only a secularized version of faith or arbitrarily chosen elements of faith packaged as a political ideology.[25] I accept the self-definition of the genuine

---

[24]I am afraid that much of the recent academic defence of secularism, however elegantly formulated, is totally irrelevant to South Asian political life from this point of view. See, for instance, Akeel Bilgrami, *Secularism, Nationalism and Modernity* (New Delhi: Rajiv Gandhi Institute for Contemporary Studies, 1995), paper no. 29, pp. 1–29; and Amartya Sen, 'Secularism and its Discontents', in Kaushik Basu and Sanjay Subramanyam (ed.), *Unravelling the Nation: Sectarian Conflict and India's Secular Identity* (New Delhi: Penguin, 1996), pp. 11–43. It is a pity that the academic viability of many ideas in the mainstream global culture of universities does not ensure their political survival in the tropics.

[25]There has been some discomfort about the distinction between faith and ideology I have drawn in this and other papers on the subject. As should have been obvious from the context, my use of the concept of ideology is not Marxian or Mannheimian but conventional social–psychological and cultural–anthropological. However, I now find that at least one respected scholar-activist and a historian of religion has arrived at the same dichotomy, starting from altogether different concerns. Abdolkarim Soroush claims that 'Islam, or any other religion, will become totalitarian if it is made into an ideology, because that is the nature of ideologies.' Quoted in *Communalism Combat*, October 1997,

secularists simply because their world *is* entirely secular. They use religion rationally, dispassionately and instrumentally, ·intouched by any theory of transcendence. They genuinely cannot or do not grant any intrinsic sanctity to the faith of even their own followers.

At one time, secularism did have something to contribute to Indian public life. That context presumed a low level of politicization, a personalized, impassioned quality in collective violence, its expression and execution.[26] As ethnic and religious violence has become more impersonal, organized, rational and calculative,[27] it has come to represent, to rework my own cliché, more a pathology of rationality than that of irrationality. As part of the same process, the ideology of secularism too has become ethnocidal and dependent on the mercies of those controlling or hoping to control the state. It has become chronically susceptible to being co-opted or

---

(37), p. 24. A similar distinction informs Julius J. Lipner, *Brahmabandhab Upadhyay: The Life and Thought of a Revolutionary* (Delhi: Oxford University Press, 1999). The relevance of the distinction to contemporary India is reflected in, for instance, Pratap Bhanu Mehta, 'Hollow Hinduism: The VHP's Self-Defeating Vision', *The Times of India*, 18 February 1999, and Sukla Sen et al., 'Savarkar Memorial' (letter to the editor) *Economic and Political Weekly*, 26 December 1998, pp. 3286.

I should clarify here that, following the conventions of contemporary social psychology, I make no assumption regarding the truth or falsity of the consciousness that underlies faith or ideology: I am merely underscoring the psychological organizational principles of two distinct forms of consciousness, one of which includes a theory of transcendence, while the other does not or is not supposed to. The distinction echoes the differences in emotive tone of most collective violence in our times and the more hate-filled religious violence that marked earlier centuries. Ethnic cleansing carries the psychological stamp of the modern farmer's attitude towards pest control rather than that of a crusade or *jihad* (see below). This is a difference to which others also, notably Hannah Arendt and Robert J. Lifton, have drawn our attention. See also 'Introduction: Science as a Reason of State', in Ashis Nandy (ed.), *Science, Hegemony and Violence: A Requiem for Modernity* (Tokyo: UN University Press and New Delhi: Oxford University Press, 1990), pp. 1–16.

[26]See Ashis Nandy, 'The Politics of Secularism and the Recovery of Religious Tolerance', *Alternatives*, 1998, 13(3), pp. 177–94. See especially the table on p. 189.

[27]According to Zygmunt Bauman, 'The most shattering of lessons deriving from the analysis of the twisted road to Auschwitz' is that—in the last resort—*the choice of physical extermination as the right means to the task of* Entferung *was a product of routine bureaucratic procedures:* means–ends, calculus, budget balancing, universal rule application. ... The 'Final Solution' did not clash at any stage with the rational pursuit of efficient, optimal goal-implementation. On the contrary, *it arose out of a genuinely rational concern, and it was generated by bureaucracy true to its form and purpose.*' Quoted in Akbar S. Ahmed, 'Ethnic Cleansing: A Metaphor for Our Time', *Ethnic and Racial Studies*, 1995, 18(1), pp. 1–25; see p. 4.

hijacked by the politically ambitious. Simultaneously, religion as the cultural foundation for the existence of South Asian communities has increasingly become a marker of the weak, the poor, and the rustic.

As a result, modern India, which sets the tone of the culture of the Indian state, now fears religion. That fear of religion, part of a more pervasive fear of the people and of democracy (which empowers the majority of Indian who are believers), has thrown up the various ready-made, packaged forms of faith for alienated South Asians—Banuri calls them Paki-Saxons—who populate urban, modernized South Asia.[28] For that feared, invisible majority, on the other hand, the religious way of life continues to have an intrinsic legitimacy. That majority seems to believe, with Hans-Georg Gadamer, that 'the real force of morals ... is based on tradition. They are freely taken over but by no means created by a free insight grounded on reasons'.[29] If that religious way of life cannot find normal play in public life, it finds distorted expression in fundamentalism, revivalism and xenophobia. That which is only a matter of Machiavellian politics at the top does sometimes acquire at the ground level the characteristics of a *satyagraha*, a *dharma yuddha* or a *jihad*.

I do not mean to identify secularism as a witches' brew in South Asia. Perhaps in parts of the region where political participation has not outstripped the legitimacy of the nation-state, secularism still has a political role, exactly as it had a creative role to play in India in the early years of Independence. But its major implications are now ethnocidal and statist, and it cedes—in fact, lovingly hands over—the entire domain of religion, in societies organized around religion, to the genuine

[28]These packaged forms go with various circus-tamed versions of religion, meant for easy consumption. In India, these versions are bookish, high-cultural, pan-Indian, and go well with modern cults, political skullduggery, and fashionable, jet-setting gurus—both within India and among the decultured, uprooted, expatriate Indians and Indophiles in the West. Those given to this modern version of religion find all other spiritual experiences low-brow, corrupted and, thus, meaningless, uncontrollable and fearsome. That fear of religion of the uncontrollable kind (to which the majority of Indians of all faiths give their allegiance) is part of the fear of the vernacular, the democratic, and the plural. It is the fear that the majority of Indians are religious in a way that is not centrally controllable and does not constitute a 'proper' religion in contemporary times.

[29]Hans-Georg Gadamer, quoted in Arindam Chakrabarti, 'Rationality in Indian Philosophy', Lecture given at the Devahuti-Damodar Library, 13 July 1996, mimeo, p. 15. Of course, neither Gadamer nor Chakrabarti seems aware that this is also a typical Gandhian formulation.

secularitsts—the ones who deal in, vend or use as a political technology secularized, packaged versions of faith. Secularism today is threatening to become a successful conspiracy against the minorities.

Is secularism doomed to political impotency in the southern world where historicization of consciousness and individuation are not complete? What is the fate of secularists who are dedicated crusaders for communal peace and minority rights? There is no reliable answer to the questions but some secularists, I suspect, *will* survive the vicissitudes of South Asian politics. They are the ones in whom there is no easy, cheerful assumption that one day they would abolish categories, such as Hindus, Muslims, Buddhists and Sikhs, including their myriad subdivisions, and have the luxury of working with newly-synthesized categories such as Indians, Sri Lankans or Pakistanis. They do what they do—by way of defending the human and cultural rights of the minorities—not so much as a well-considered, ideological and cognitive choice, but as a moral reaction set off by a vague sense of rebellion against the injustice and cruelty inflicted on fellow citizens. The social evolutionary project sits lightly on such secularists. They do not really expect the world to be fully secularized over time. Nor do they expect the 'rationality' of modern science to gradually supplant the 'irrationality' of religion. (Somewhat like Sigmund Freud who, propelled simultaneously by the optimism of the Enlightenment and a tragic vision of life, hoped that the human ego would gradually win over more and more territory from the id, without fully giving up the belief that the dialectic between the two was an eternal one. I am sure Banuri will accept this qualification of his metaphor.)

It is not much of an inheritance. However, I like to believe that that inheritance is not trivial either, for it has something to do both with the very core of our humanness and the key civilizational categories that distinguish this part of the world. It cannot be written off as ethically pointless or politically futile.

I have said that the huge majority of South Asians knows neither the literal meaning of the word 'secularism' nor its connotative meaning derived from the separation of the state from the church in post-medieval Europe; and, sadly, in an open polity, the choices of this majority matters. I have also pointed out that most properly educated Indians love to believe that life in pre-colonial India was nasty, brutish and short; that communal violence was a daily affair till the imperial state forcibly imposed some order on the warring savages. Strangely, many secular South Asians are not comfortable with that 'history' either. They feel compelled to remind us, often in maudlin detail, how gloriously syncretic India was before religious fanaticism and scheming politicians spoilt it all.[30] Only they do not stop to ask if that syncretism was based on secularism or on some version of 'primitive proto-secularism' and if those who did so well without the ideology need it now.

These secularists seem oblivious that mass politics in an open polity demands an accessible political idiom, even when that idiom seems crude and unbecoming of the dignity of a modern state or looks like a hidden plea to return to the country's brutal, shabby past. That is why, at times of communal and ethnic violence, when the state machinery and the newspaper-reading middle classes keep on harping on the codes of secularism, at the ground level, where survival is stake, the traditional codes of tolerance are the ones that matter, however moth-eaten they may otherwise look.[31]

Finally, I should like to venture two formulations. First, religion as the foundation of social life is true for mainly the weak, the poor and the rural. Modern India, which sets the tone of the culture of the Indian state, fears that kind of religion. Second, the opposite of religious and ethnic intolerance is not secularism but religious and ethnic tolerance. Secularism is merely one way of ensuring that tolerance. However, in societies where most citizens have been uprooted from traditional life-styles, secularism *can* become the counterpoint of religious chauvinism, because both begin to contest for the allegiance of the decultured, the atomized and the massified. In other societies, religious fanaticism mainly contests the tolerance that is part of religious traditions themselves.

That is why in South Asia secularism can mostly be the faith of— and be of use to—the culturally dispossessed and the politically rootless. In favourable circumstances, it can make sense even to the massified in the growing metropolitan slums, but never to the majority living its life with rather tenuous links with the culture of the nation-state. True, when such a concept of secularism is made profitable by the state and the élite— that is, if lip-service to the concept pays rich enough dividends—many begin to use it, not in its pristine sense but as an easy, non-controversial synonym for religious tolerance. If such a reward system functions long enough in a society, political institutions may even begin to protect the view that religion is essentially a drag on civil society. The primary function

[30]For a random example, see the superbly executed television series made by Saeed Naqvi and shown on Doordarshan between 1992 and 1994.

[31]Nandy et al., *Creating a Nationality*.

of secularism then becomes management of the fear of religion and the religious.

To function thus, the ideology of secularism must presume the existence of an individual who clearly defines his or her religious allegiance according to available census classifications and does not confuse religion with sect, caste, family traditions, *dharma*, culture, rituals and *deshachara* or local customs. That is, the ideology presumes a relatively clear, well-bounded self-definition compatible with the post–seventeenth-century ideal of the individual, comfortable in an impersonal, contractual-relations-dominated society. There is nothing terribly wrong with such a presumption and many people might in fact wish to live in such an individualistic society, seeing in it the scope for true freedom. Only, they have to take into account two political developments, working at cross purposes.

On the one hand, the majority, impervious to the charms of the official ideology of secularism, has now *some* access to political power. And with quickening politicization in this part of the world and large-scale efforts to empower newer sections of people by parties and movements of various kinds, this access is likely to increase. So, the contradiction between the ideology of secularism and the democratic process is likely to sharpen further in the future. To be implemented, the secularist project may then have to depend even more on the coercive power of the state. Not merely to keep in check the enemies of secularism, but also to thought-police history (through the production of official histories, history textbooks, time capsules, and other such sundry tricks of the trade to which both India's intellectual left and the liberals are privy).[32] This should not be much of a shock to the Indian secularist. Secularism has always had a statist connection, even in the West, and most South Asian, especially Indian, secularists are confirmed statists. As the legitimacy of the state as a moral presence in society declines, this state connection may produce new stresses within the ideology of secularism.

On the other hand, there is now a powerful force that may find meaning in the secularist worldview. Modern India—by which I mean the westernized, media-exposed India, enslaved by the urban–industrial vision—is no longer a small, insignificant oasis in a large, predominantly rural, tradition-bound society. One-fourth of India is a lot of India. In absolute terms, modern India is itself a society nearly four times the size

[32]That is partly the reason why even the Bharatiya Janata Party, being ideologically committed to unqualified statism, is unable to shed the idiom. It has to define its position as loyalty to 'true' secularism, in opposition to what it calls the 'pseudo-secularism' of other parties dependent on minority vote banks.

of its erstwhile colonial master, Britain. It is—to spite Thomas Macaulay, that intrepid, romantic ideologue of the Raj—no longer a buffer between the rulers and the ruled. Modern India is the world's fourth largest country in itself.

This India does have sufficient exposure to the ideology of the state to be able to internalize the concept of secularism and sections of it are willing to go to any length to ensure that the concept is not questioned. But that by itself is not particularly surprising. There are plenty of Indians now who are willing to sacrifice the unmanageable, chaotic, real-life Indians for the sake of the idea of India. They are miserable that while Indian democracy allows them to choose a new set of political leaders every five years, it does not allow them to choose, once in a while, the right kind of people to populate the country. Instead, they have to do with the same impossible mass of a billion Indians—uneducable, disorganized, squabbling and, above all, multiplying like bedbugs. For in the Indianness of Indians who are getting empowered lies, according to many learned scholars, the root cause of all the major problems of the country.

Hindu Nationalism and the Future of Hinduism

When a secularizing society throws up its own versions of religion, extremist or otherwise, to cater to the changing psychological and cultural needs of the citizenry, what is the link between these versions and the faith that serves as their inspiration? The relationship between Hindutva, the encompassing ideology that inspires all Hindu nationalist movements in India, and Hinduism provides the semblance of an answer.

Speaking pessimistically, Hindutva will be the end of Hinduism. Hinduism is what most Indians still live by. Hindutva is a response of the mainly Brahminic, middle-class, urban, westernizing Indians to their uprooting, cultural and geographical. According to V.D. Savarkar, the openly agnostic, westernized nationalist who coined the term, Hindutva is not only the means of Hinduizing the polity but also of militarizing the effeminate, disorganized Hindu. It is a critique of—and an answer to the critique—of Hinduism, as most Indians know the faith and an attempt to protect, within Hinduism, the flanks of a minority consciousness—including the fears and anxieties—that the democratic process threatens to marginalize.[33]

[33]This critique of Hinduism, often masquerading as a personological critique of the Hindus, is central to Hindutva. For a useful discussion of this part of the story, see Chaturvedi Badrinath, *Dharma, India and the World Order: Twenty Essays* (New Delhi: Centre for Policy

Though I have stressed earlier the pathology of rationality that characterizes this minority consciousness, there is also in it an element of incontinent rage. It is the rage of Indians who have decultured themselves, seduced by the promises of modernity, and who now feel abandoned. With the demise of imperialism, Indian modernism—especially that sub-category of it that goes by the name of development—has failed to keep these promises. Hence the paradoxical stature of Hindutva; it is simultaneously an expression of status anxiety and a claim to legitimacy. At one plane, it is a *savarna purana* that the lower-middle class ventures while trying to break into the upper echelons of modern India; at another, it is an expression of the fear that they may be pushed into the ranks of the urban proletariat by the upper classes, not on grounds of substance, but 'style'. The 'pseudo-secularists' represent for them the ambition; the Muslims (in India, consisting mostly of communities of artisans getting proletarianized) the fear. Hence, the hatred for both.

It is as part of the same story that Hindutva represents in popular, mass-cultural form some of the basic tenets of the worldview associated with secularism and the secular construction of the Muslim. Built on the principles of religious reform movements in the colonial period, Hindutva cannot but see Hinduism as inferior to the Semitic creeds— monolithic, well-organized, and capable of being a sustaining ideology for an imperious state. And, being a mass-cultural ideology, it *can* do to Hinduism what the secularists have always wanted to do to it. Hindutva at this plane is a creed which, if it succeeds, might end up making Nepal the world's largest Hindu country. Hinduism will then survive not as a faith of the majority of Indians, but in pockets, cut off from the majority

---

Research, 1991). A flavour of the intellectual and cultural climate that produced Hindutva can be had from Dhananjay Keer, *Veer Savarkar* (Bombay: Popular Prakashan, 1966). For a succinct comment on the Rashtriya Swayamsevak Sangh as a lower-middle-class, political expression of the ideology of Hindutva and its relationship with Hinduism, see Parsa Venkateshwar Rao Jr, 'The Real RSS: Not Hindu, Cultural or Nationalist', *The Times of India*, 8 July 1998.

The line drawn between Hinduism and Hindutva is visible at the ground level, when communal violence spreads to or breaks out in rural India, where communities have not yet fully broken down and where the ideology of Hindutva faces resistance from every day Hinduism. Some have academic objections to such a separation, but I doubt if those who offer such resistance would worry about that. They will draw sustenance either from the 'lowbrow' Hinduism of everyday life (see for instance, Marglin, 'On Pirs and Pandits'; and Mayaram, 'Representing the Hindu–Muslim Civilizational Encounter') or from even some of the pillars of Brahminic/classical orthodoxy, such as Shankaracharya Chandrasekharendra Saraswati Swami, *Hindu Dharma: The Universal Way of Life* (Bombay: Bharatiya Vidya Bhavan, 1996).

who will claim to live by it—perhaps directly in Bali, indirectly in Thai, Sri Lankan and Tibetan Buddhism and, to the chagrin of many Hindu nationalists, in South Asian and Southeast Asian Islam. The votaries of Hindutva will celebrate that death of Hinduism. For they have all along felt embarrassed and humiliated by Hinduism as it is. Hence, the pathetic, counterphobic emphasis in Hindutva on the pride that Hindus must feel in being Hindus. Hindutva *is* meant for those whose Hinduism has worn off. It *is* a ware meant for the supermarket of global mass culture where all religions are available in their consumable forms, neatly packaged for buyers. Predictably, its most devoted consumers can be found among the expatriate Hindus of the world.

I go back once again to the important question that many years ago H.R. Trevor-Roper raised in the context of the great European witch-hunt: did the inquisitors discover a new 'heresy' beneath the faith of the heretics or did they invent it?[34] He reached the conclusion that, on the whole, the witch-craze did not grow out of the social and religious processes operating in medieval Europe; it 'grew by its own momentum' from within modernizing Europe.[35] The growth of Hindutva has depended heavily upon invented heresies that are organized around themes that have no place in Hindu theology: the modern state, nationalism and national identity. It has borrowed almost nothing from existing Hindu theology in its construction of the non-Hindus; it has followed its own trajectory in the matter. This is another crucial difference between Hindutva and Hinduism. It is a pity that, to some extent, the same can be said about some of the more fanatical opponents of Hindutva in the modern sector, too. That fanaticism comes from a tacit recognition that, beneath the skin, they are each other's doubles. Only, while the ideologues of Hindutva have already found Indian analogues of *The Protocols of the Elders of Zion*, some opponents of Hindutva are still desperately looking for them.[36]

Speaking optimistically, Hindu nationalism has its territorial limits. It cannot spread easily beyond the boundaries of urban, westernizing India. Nor can it easily penetrate those parts of India where Hinduism is more resilient and Hindus are less prone to project on to Muslim the feared, unacceptable parts of their self. Hindutva cannot survive where

[34]Trevor-Roper, *The European Witch-Craze*, pp. 115–27.

[35]Ibid., p. 119.

[36]For a while, they found it in M.S. Golwalkar's book, *We or Our Nationhood Defined* (Nagpur: Bharat Publications, 1939). Things became a little convoluted when his disciples disowned it and claimed that Golwalkar, too, had disowned it. That was not what self-respecting fascists were expected to do and it was considered almost a betrayal by important sections of the Indian Left.

the citizens have not been massified and come to speak only the language of the state.

To those who live in Hinduism, Hindutva is one of those pathologies that periodically afflict a faith. Hinduism has, over the centuries, handled many such pathologies; it still retains the capacity, they feel, perhaps over-optimistically, to handle one more. It will, they hope, consume Hindutva once a sizeable section of the modernized Hindus finds an alternative psychological defence against the encroaching forces of the market, the state, and the urban–industrial vision.

Whether one is a pessimist or optimist, the choices are clear. They do not lie either in a glib secularism talking the language of the state or in pre-war versions of nationalism seeking to corner the various forms of increasingly popular ethnic nationalism breaking out all over South Asia. It lies in alliance with forces that have risen in rebellion against the social forces and the ideology of dominance that have spawned Hindutva in the first place. As the world built by nineteenth-century imperialism collapses around us, Hindutva, too, may die a natural death. But, then, many things that die in colder climes in the course of a single winter survive in the tropics for years. Stalinism has survived better in India than even in the Soviet Union and so probably will imperialism's lost child, Hindutva. Maybe its death will not be as natural as that of some other ideologies. Maybe post-Gandhian Hinduism—combined with a moderate, modest and, what Ali Mazrui calls, ecumenical state—will have to take advantage of the democratic process to help Hindutva die a slightly unnatural death. Perhaps that euthanasia will be called politics.

History's Forgotten Doubles

However odd this might sound to contemporary historians, millions of people still live outside 'history'. They *do* have theories of the past; they *do* believe that the past is important and shapes the present and the future, but they also recognize, confront and live with a past different from the one constructed by historians and historical consciousness. They even have a different way of arriving at the past.

Some historians and societies have a term and a theory for such people. To them, those who live outside history are 'ahistorical', and though the theory has contradictory components, it does have a powerful stochastic thrust. One might even say that the historians' history of the ahistorical—when grounded in a 'proper' historical consciousness, as defined by the European Enlightenment—is usually a history of the pre-historical, the primitive, and the pre-scientific. By way of transformative politics or cultural intervention, that history basically keeps open only one option—that of bringing the ahistoricals into history.

There is a weak alternative—some would say response—to this position. According to their modern historians, the idea of history is not entirely unknown to some older civilizations like China and India. It is claimed that these civilizations have occasionally produced quasi- or proto-historical works during their long tenure on earth, evidently to defy being labelled as wholly ahistorical and to protect the self-respect of their modern historians. These days the historian's construction of ahistoric societies often includes the plea to rediscover this repressed historical self.[1]

---

[1] A creative variation on the same response is found in works like Gananath Obeyesekere's *The Apotheosis of Captain Cook: European Mythmaking in the Pacific* (Princeton: Princeton

The élites of the defeated societies are usually all too eager to heed this plea. They sense that the dominant ideology of the state and their own privileged access to the state apparatus are both sanctioned by the idea of history. Many of their subjects too, though disenfranchised and oppressed by history, believe that their plight—especially their inability to organize effective resistance—should be blamed on their inadequate knowledge of history. In some countries of the South today, these subjects have been left with nothing to sell to the ubiquitous global market except their pasts and, to be saleable, these pasts have to be, they now suspect, packaged as history. They have, therefore, accepted history as a handy language for negotiating the modern world. They talk history with tourists, visiting dignitaries, ethnographers, museologists, and even with human-rights activists fighting their cause. When such subjects are not embarrassed about their ahistorical constructions of the past, they accept the tacit modern consensus that these constructions are meant for private or secret use or for use as forms of fantasy useful in the creative arts.

On this plane, historical consciousness is very nearly a totalizing one, for both the moderns and those aspiring to their exalted status; once you own history, it also begins to own you. You can, if you are an artist or a mystic, occasionally break the shackles of history in your creative or meditative moments. (However, even then you might be all too aware of the history of your own art, if you happen to be that kind of an artist, or the history of mysticism, if you happen to be that kind of practitioner of mysticism.) The best you can hope to do, by way of exercising your autonomy, is to live outside history for short spans of time. For instance, when you opt for certain forms of artistic or spiritual exercises, perhaps even when you are deliriously happy or shattered by a personal tragedy. But these are *moments* of 'freedom' from history, involving transient phases or small areas of life.

University Press, 1992). Obeysekere argues that history can be part-mythic and myths part-historic, that is, there is no clear discontinuity between the two. His narrative, however, seems to suggest that he dislikes the mythic-in-history and likes the historical-in-myths.

Shail Mayaram pushes Obeysekere's argument to its logical conclusion in her 'Oral and Written Discourses: An Enquiry Into the Meo Mythic Tradition', report to the Indian Council of Social Science Research, Delhi 1994, p. 6: 'No civilization is really ahistorical. In a sense, every individual is historical and uses his/her memory to organize the past. ... The dichotomy between history and myth is an artificial one. History and myth are not exclusive modes of representation.'

Here I reject formulations that impose the category of history on all constructions of the past or sanction the reduction of all myths to history. I am also uncomfortable with formulations that do not acknowledge the special political status of myths as the preferred language of a significant proportion of threatened or victimized cultures.

At one time not long ago, historical consciousness had to co-exist with other modes of experiencing and constructing the past even within the modern world. The conquest of the past through history was still incomplete in the late nineteenth century, as was the conquest of space through the railways. The historically-minded then lived with the conviction that they were an enlightened but threatened minority, that they were dissenters to whom the future belonged. So at least it seems to me, looking back upon the intellectual culture of nineteenth-century Europe from outside the West. Dissent probably survives better when its targets are optimally powerful, when they are neither too monolithic or steam-rolling nor too weak to be convincing as a malevolent authority. As long as the non-historical modes thrived, history remained viable as a baseline for radical social criticism. That is perhaps why the great dissenters of the nineteenth century were the most aggressively historical.

Everyone knows, for instance, that Karl Marx thought Asiatic and African societies were ahistorical. Few know that he considered Latin Europe, and under its influence the whole of Some America, to be ahistorical, too. Johan Galtung once told me that he had found, from the correspondence of Marx and Engels, that they considered all Slavic cultures to be ahistorical and the Scandinavians to be no better. If I remember Galtung correctly, one of them also added, somewhat gratuitously, that the Scandinavians could be nothing but ahistorical, given that they bathed infrequently and drank too much. After banishing so many races and cultures from the realm of history, the great revolutionary was left with only a few who lived in history—Germany, where he was born, Britain, where he spent much of his later life, and the Low Countries through which, one presumes, he travelled from Germany to England.

Times have changed. Historical consciousness now owns the globe. Even in societies known as historical, timeless or eternal—India for example—the politically powerful now live in and with history. Ahistoricity survives at the peripheries and interstices of such societies. Though millions of people continue to stay outside history, millions have, since the days of Marx, dutifully migrated to the empire of history to become its loyal subjects. The historical worldview is now triumphant globally; the ahistoricals have become the dissenting minority.

Does this triumph impose new responsibilities on the victorious? Now that the irrational savages, living in timelessness or in cyclical or other forms of disreputable non-linear times, have been finally subjugated, should our public and intellectual awareness include a new sensitivity to the cultural priorities, psychological skills, and perhaps even the ethical concerns represented by the societies or communities that in different ways are still cussed enough to choose to live outside history? Are they protecting or holding in trust parts of our disowned selves that we have dismissed as worthless or dangerous? Is ahistoricity also a form of wilderness that needs to be protected in these environmentally conscious times, lest, once destroyed, it is lost forever as a 'cultural gene pool' in case the historical vision exhausts itself while fighting our profligate ways and we are forced to retrace our steps? Before we make up our minds and answer the question, let me draw attention to what seem to be two of the defining features of ahistorical societies.

This is not an easy task. It is my suspicion that, broadly speaking, cultures tend to be historical in only one way, whereas each ahistorical culture is so in its own unique style. It is not easy to identify the common threads of ahistoricity: I choose two that look like being relatively more common to illustrate my point. The task is made even more difficult for me because I want to argue the case of ahistoricity not on the grounds of pragmatism or instrumentality, of the kind that would require me to give a long list of useful things that ahistoricity could do for us. I wish to argue the case on the grounds of diversity being a moral value in itself, especially when its locus lies in the worldview of the victims.

The major difference between those living in history and those living outside it, especially in societies where myths are the predominant mode of organizing experiences of the past, is what I have elsewhere called the principle of principled forgetfulness. All myths are morality tales. Mythologization is also moralization; it involves a refusal to separate the remembered past from its ethical meaning in the present. For this refusal, it is often important *not* to remember the past, objectively, clearly, or in its entirety. Mythic societies sense the power of myths and the nature of human frailties; they are more fearful than the modern ones—forgive the anthropomorphism—of the perils of mythic use of amoral certitudes about the past.

Historical consciousness cannot take seriously the principle of forgetfulness. It rejects the principle as irrational, retrogressive, unnatural, and fundamentally incompatible with historical sensitivities. Remembering, history assumes, is definitionally superior to forgetting. Unwitting forgetfulness, which helps a person to reconcile with and live in this world, is seen as natural and, to that extent, acceptable. Adaptive forgetfulness is also seen as human; human beings just cannot afford to remember everything and non-essential memories have to be discarded both by individuals and societies.

The moderns are willing to go further. Since the days of Sigmund Freud and Marx, they recognize that forgetfulness is not random, that there are elaborate internal screening devices, the defences of the ego or the principles of ideology, which shape our forgetfulness along particular lines. As understandable is unprincipled forgetfulness, the kind Freud saw as part of a person's normal adaptive repertoire, even though he chose to classify it under the *psychopathologies* of everyday life, presumably because of the non-creative use of psychic energy it involved.

But principled forgetfulness? That seems directed against the heart of the enterprise called history. For historians, the aim ultimately is nothing less than to bare the past completely, on the basis of a neatly articulated frame of reference that implicitly involves a degree of demystification or demythologization. The frame of reference is important: history must order its data in terms of something like a theme of return (invoking the idea of cultural continuity or recovery), progress (invoking the principle of massive, sometimes justifiably coercive, irreversible intervention in society) or stages (invoking the sense of certitude and mastery over the self, as expressed in an evolutionary sequencing of it). The aim is to unravel the secular processes and the order that underlie the manifest realities of past times, available in readymade or raw forms as historical data-textual and graphic records, public or private memories that are often the stuff of oral history, and a wide variety of artefacts.[2]

[2]Speaking of the Partition of British India and the birth of India and Pakistan, Gyanendra Pandey ('Partition, History and the Making of Nations', presented at the conference on State and Nationalism in India, Pakistan and Germany, Colombo, 26–8 February 1994) asks: 'Why have historians of India (and Pakistan and Bangladesh) failed to produce richly layered, challenging histories of Partition of a kind that would compare with their sophisticated histories of peasant insurrection; working class consciousness; the onset of capitalist relations in agriculture; the construction of new notions of caste, community, and religion, ... and, indeed, the writing of women's autobiographies ...? Or, to ask the question in another way, why is there such a chasm between the historian's history of Partition and the popular reconstruction of the event, which is to such a large extent built around the fact of violence?'

He continues, 'The answer lies, it seems to me, in our fear of facing ... this history as our own: the fear of reopening old wounds. ... It lies also in the difficulty that all social science has faced in writing the history of violence and pain. But, in addition, it inheres ... in the very character of historian's history as "national" history and a history of "progress"'.

Could Pandey have added that, when faced with a trauma of this magnitude, when the survival of communities and fundamental human values are at stake, popular memories of Partition have to organize themselves differently, employing principles that are ahistorical but not amoral? Do the historians of South Asia have a tacit awareness that they are in no position to supplant memories which seek to protect the dignity of the one million or so who died in the violence and the approximately sixteen million who were uprooted? Are popular memories obligated to protect normal life and basic human values?

Because as the authentic progeny of seventeenth-century Europe, history fears ambiguity.[3] The ultimate metaphor for history is not the *double entendre*; it is synecdoche: the historical past stands for all past because it is presumed to be the only past. Hence the tenuous legitimacy of psychological history as a subdiscipline of history. Psychoanalysis at its best is a game of *double entendre* loaded in favour of the victims of personal history—the pun is intended—but it has to be sold to the historically minded as a technology of analysis that removes the ambiguities human subjectivity introduces into history.

The enterprise is not essentially different from that of Giambattista Vico's idea of science as a form of practice. There is nothing surprising about this, for the modern historical enterprise is modelled on the modern scientific enterprise, whether the historian admits it or not. This is not the scientization that leads to the use of experimental methods or mathematization—though even that has happened in a few cases—but to an attempt to make history conform to the spirit of modern science (as captured more accurately, I am told, by the German word *wissenschaftlich*). I know that the idea of scientific history has acquired a certain ambivalent load ever since the great liberator of our times, Joseph Stalin, sent twenty million of his compatriots marching to their death in its name, with a significant proportion of the historically-minded intelligentsia applauding it all the way as a necessary sacrifice for the onward march of history. But it is also true that to the savages, not enamoured of the emancipatory vision of the Enlightenment, the orthodox Marxist vision of history was never very distinct from that of its liberal opponents, at least as far as the molar philosophical assumptions of its methodology went. These assumptions owed much to the ideas of certitude, reliable and valid knowledge, and the disenchantment of nature to which Francis Bacon gave respectability. (It is the same concept of knowledge that made history in the nineteenth century a theory of the future masquerading as a theory of the past. More about that later.)

In recent decades, there has been much talk about history being primarily a hermeneutic exercise. It is now fairly commonplace to say that there can be no true or objective past; that there are only competing

---

[3] On the fear of ambiguity as a gift of the Enlightenment, see Donald N. Levine, *The Flight from Ambiguity: Essays in Social and Cultural Theory* (Chicago: University of Chicago, 1985). On the psychological and cultural correlates of ambiguity, once a popular subject of research in psychology, see for instance, Anthony Davids, 'Pychodynamic and Sociocultural Factors Related to Intolerance of Ambiguity', in Robert W. White (ed.), *The Study of Lives: Essays in Honour of Henry A. Murray* (New York: Atherton Press, 1963), pp. 160–78.

constructions of the past, with various levels and kinds of empirical support. The works of a number of philosophers of science, notably that of Paul Feyerabend, have in recent years contributed to the growing self-confidence of those opposing or fighting objectivism and scientism in history.[4] Contributions to the same process have also been made by some of the structuralists and post-modernists, Louis Althusser being the one who perhaps tried the hardest to bypass history. The anti-historical stance of post-modernism, not being associated with the ahistoricity of the older civilizations, has even acquired certain respectability.[5]

There have also been attempts to popularize other modes of time perception built on some of the new developments in science, especially in quantum mechanics and biological theory. Attempts have also been made to base such modes on the rediscovery of some of the older modes of knowledge acquisition, such as Zen and Yoga, and on theories of transcendence celebrated in deep ecology and ecofeminism. As important has been the growing awareness in many working at the frontiers of the knowledge industry—though it is yet to contaminate the historians— that the historical concept of time is only one kind of time with which contemporary knowledge operates, that most sciences and now even a few of the social sciences work with more plural constructions of time.

Many will see all this as an exercise in self-correction, as an attempt to correct the excesses of what could be called a history modelled on the Baconian concept of science. Some will identify this as an effort to incorporate into the historical consciousness crucial components of the moral universe of the ahistorical. (Both are implied in the work of a number of psychologists venturing new psychological utopias— eupsychias, Abraham Maslow used to call them—in the wake of the breakdown of some of the post-war certitudes in the late 1960s.) A few cynical ones though will continue to say that the effort is nothing less than an effort to capture, for preservation, what according to the moderns are the necessary or valuable components of the worldview of those living outside the post-seventeenth-century concept of history. So that the people

---

[4]For instance Paul Feyerabend, *Against Method: Outline of an Anarchistic Theory of Knowledge* (London: Verso, 1978); and *Science in a Free Society* (London: NLB, 1978).

[5]For a pithy critique of post-modernism's anti-history from the point of view of the non-West, see the series of essays by Ziauddin Sardar: 'Surviving the Terminator: The Post-Modern Mental Condition', *Futures*, March 1990, 22(2), pp. 203–10; 'Total Recall: Aliens, "Others" and Amnesia in Post-Modernist Thought', *Futures*, March 1991, 23(2), pp. 189–203; 'Terminator 2: Modernity, Post-Modernism and the "Other"', *Futures*, June 1992, 24(6), pp. 493–506; and 'Do Not Adjust Your mind: Post-Modernism, Reality and the Other', *Futures*, October 1993, 25(10), pp. 877–94.

who have kept alive the art of living outside history all these centuries can be safely dumped into the dustbins of history, as obsolete or as superfluous.

The second major difference between the historically minded and their ahistorical others is the scepticism and the fuzzy boundaries the latter usually work with when constructing the past. There is one thing the historical consciousness cannot do, without dismantling the historian's self-definition and threatening the entire philosophical edifice of modern history: it cannot admit that the historical consciousness itself can be demystified or unmasked and that an element of self-destructiveness could be introduced into that consciousness to make it more humane and less impersonal.[6] In other words, while the historical consciousness can grant, as the sciences do, that historical truths are only contingent, it also assumes that the idea of history itself cannot be relativized or contextualized beyond a point. History can recognize gaps in historical data; it can admit that history includes mythic elements and that theory terms and data terms are never clearly separable in practice, that large areas of human experience and reality remain untouched by existing historical knowledge. It can even admit the idea of reversals in history. But it cannot accept that history can be dealt with from outside history; the entire Enlightenment worldview militates against such a proposition. As a result, when historians historicize history, which itself is rare, they do so according to the strict rules of historiography. It reminds me of one of the fantasies Freud considered universal, that of one's immortality. The human mind, Freud believed, was unable to fantasize itself as dead; all such fantasies ended up by postulating an observer/self that witnessed the self as dead. All critiques of history from within the modern worldview have also been ultimately historical.

Part of the hostility of the historically minded towards the ahistorical can be traced to the way the myths, legends, and epics of the latter are intertwined with what look like transcendental theories of the past. Historians have cultivated over the last two hundred and fifty years a fear of theories of transcendence. And in recent centuries, what was once avoidance of the sacred and apotheosization of the secular has increasingly become an open fear of those who reject or undervalue the secular or who choose to use the idiom of the sacred. This fear is particularly

---

[6]Actually, history has thrived on such impersonality—according to some a core value of modernity. On the role of impersonality in modern knowledge systems, see Tariq Banuri, 'Modernization and Its Discontents: A Cultural Perspective on Theories of Development', in Frédérique Apffel Marglin and Stephen Marglin (ed.), *Dominating knowledge: Development, Culture and Resistance* (Oxford: Clarendon Press, 1990, pp. 73–101.

pronounced in societies where the idiom of the sacred is conspicuously present in the public sphere. As some of the major political ideologies have re-entered the political arena in the guise of faiths, posing a threat to the modern nation-state system globally, the nervousness about anything that smacks of faith has taken the form of an epidemic in territories where history reigns supreme. Confronted with the use, or misuse, of theories of transcendence in the public sphere, historical consciousness has either tried to fit in the experience within a psychiatric framework, within which all transcendence, even the use of the language of transcendence, acquires perfect 'clarity' as a language of insanity; or it has reread what look like transcendent theories of the past as a hidden language of *realpolitik* in which all transcendence is merely a complex, only apparently ahistorical, political ploy.

Why have historians till now not seriously tried to critique the idea of history itself? After all, such self-reflexibility is not unknown in contemporary social knowledge. Sociology has produced Alvin Gouldner and Stanislav Andreski; psychology Rollo May, Abraham Maslow, Ronald Laing and Thomas Szasz.[7] Even economists, usually defensively self-certain, include in their ranks N. Georgescu-Roegen and Joseph Schumacher; and amongst philosophers, there are enthusiasts of philosophical silence and the end of philosophy.[8] Some of the self-explorations have turned out to be decisive to the disciplines concerned, others less so; some are exciting, others tame; some are explicit, others implicit. But they are there.[9]

[7]Alvin W. Gouldner, *The Coming Crisis of Western Sociology* (London: Heinemann, 1971); Stanislav Andreski, *Social Sciences as Sorcery* (London: André Deutsch, 1972); Rollo May, *Psychology and the Human Dilemma* (Princeton, N.J.: Van Nostrand, 1962); Abraham Maslow, *Toward a Psychology of Being* (Princeton: Van Nostrand, 1968); Roland Laing, *The Divided Self: A Study of Sanity and Madness* (Harmondswoth, U.K.: Penguin, 1970); Thomas S. Szasz, *The Manufacture of Madness* (London: Routledge and Kegan Paul, 1971); and *The Myth of Mental Illness* (London: Paladin, 1972).

[8]N. Georgescu-Roegen, *Energy and Economic Myths* (New York: Pergamon, 1976); J. Schumacher, *Small is Beautiful: The Study of Economics as if People Mattered* (New Delhi: Radha Krishna, 1977); and *Roots of Economic Growth* (Varanasi: Gandhian Institute of Studies, 1962); Ludwig Wittgenstein, *Tractus Logico-Philosophicus*, tr. C.K. Ogden and F.P. Ramsay (London: Routledge, and Kegan Paul, 1922); and Richard Rorty, 'The Priority of Democracy to Philosophy', in *Objectivity, Relativity and Truth: Philosophical Papers* (Cambridge: Cambridge University Press, 1991), Vol. 1, pp. 175–96; and 'Philosophy as Science, as Metaphor, and as Politics', in *Essays on Heidegger and Others* (Cambridge: Cambridge University Press, 1991), Vol. 2, pp. 9–26.

[9]So much so that in anthropology, I am told, graduate students in some universities are more keen to do cultural critiques of anthropology than empirical studies of other cultures.

Historians have sired no such species. Occasionally, some have tried to stretch the meaning of the term 'history' beyond its conventional definition. One example is William Thompson's *At the Edge of History*, which at least mentions the possibility of using myths as a means of 'thinking wild' about the future by reversing the relationship between myth and history.[10] Usually, however, when historians talk of the end of history, from Karl Marx to Francis Fukuyama, they have in mind the triumph of Hegelian history.

There have also been critics of ideas of history, direct or indirect, from outside history. Ananda Coomaraswamy, philosopher and art historian, is an obvious early example, and Seyyed Hossein Nasr (the philosopher of science, who has built on the traditions of Coomaraswamy, Frithjof Schuon and René Guénon) is a more recent one.[11] And the present-day structuralists and post-structuralists also can be thought of as critics of the idea of history itself.[12] But there has emerged no radical criticism of history from within the ranks of historians. The histories of scepticism, à la Richard Popkins, have not been accompanied by any scepticism towards history as a mode of world construction. Or at least I do not know of such efforts. Recently, in an elegant introductory text on history, Keith Jenkins sharply distinguishes between history and the past, but refuses to take the next logical step—to acknowledge the possibility that

[10]William Irwin Thompson, *At the Edge of History: Speculations on the Transformation of Culture* (New York: Harper and Row, 1972), pp. 179–80.

[11]Roger Lipsey (ed.), Ananda K. Coomaraswamy, *Selected Papers* (Princeton, N.J.: Princeton University Press, 1977), Vols. 1 and 2; Frithjof Schuon, *Language of the Self* (Bloomington, Indiana: World Wisdom Books, 1999); and *Logic and Transcendence*, tr. Peter Townsend (London: Perennial Books, 1984); René Guenon, *The Reign of Quantity and the Signs of the Times*, tr. Lord Northbourne (Baltimore, Md.: Penguin, 1972); Seyyed Hossein Nasr, *Introduction to Islamic Cosmological Doctrines* (London: Thames and Hudson, 1978); and *Islamic Life and Thought* (London: Allen and Unwin, 1981).

I hope the rest of this essay will not be now read as a convoluted plea for perennial philosopohy, though I have obviously benefitted from the critique of history ventured by such philosophy. Mine is primarily a political-psychological argument that tries to be sensitive to the politics of cultures and knowledge.

[12]For instance, Anthony Giddens, 'Structuralism, Post-Structuralism and the Production of Culture', in Anthony Giddens and Jonathan Turner (ed.), *Social Theory Today* (Cambridge: Polity Press, 1987), pp. 194–223 and pp. 212: 'The methodological repression of time in Saussure's conception of *language* is translated by Levi-Strauss into substantive repression of time involved in the codes organized through myths. ... Foucault's style of writing history does not flow along with chronological time. Nor does it depend upon the narrative description of a sequence of events. ... There is more than an echo of Levi-Strauss in Foucault's view that history is one form of knowledge among others—and of course, like other forms of knowledge, a mode of mobilizing power.'

history might be only one way of constructing the past and that other cultures might have explored other ways.[13] It is even doubtful if Jenkins himself considers his essay anything more than an intra-mural debate, for *all* his thirty-five odd references come from mainstream European and North American thought.

There are also papers written by two sensitive young Indian historians who come close to admitting the need for basic critiques of history: Gyan Prakash and Dipesh Chakrabarty. The latter even names his paper 'History as Critique and Critique of History'.[14] On closer scrutiny, however, both turn out to be hesitant steps towards such a critique; at the moment they are powerful pleas for alternative histories, not for alternatives *to* history. Vinay Lal's two unpublished papers, which explore the entry of modern history into Indian society in the nineteenth century, both as a discipline and as a form of social consciousness, and one of Chakrabarty's more recent papers go further.[15] Lal's paper, 'The Discourse of History and the Crisis at Ayodhya', comes close to being an outsider's account of history in India. And Chakrabarty acknowledges that 'insofar as the academic discipline of history—that is "history" as a discourse produced at the institutional site of the university is concerned, "Europe" remains the sovereign, theoretical subject of all histories, including the ones we call "Indian", "Chinese", "Kenyan", and so on.' He continues:

So long as one operates within the discourse of 'history' at the institutional site of the university it is not possible simply to walk out of the deep collusion between

[13]Keith Jenkins, *Rethinking History* (London: Routledge, 1991). See esp. pp. 5–20.

[14]Gyan Prakash, 'Writing Post-Orientalist Histories of the Third World: Indian Historiography is Good to Think', in Nicholas B. Dirks (ed.), *Colonialism and Culture* (Ann Arbor: The University of Michigan Press, 1992), pp. 353–88; and Dipesh Chakravarty, 'History as Critique and Critique of History', *Economic and Political Weekly*, 14 September 1991, pp. 2262–8; and D.C., 'Post-coloniality and the Artifice of History: Who Speaks for the "Indian" Pasts', *Representations*, Winter 1992, (37), pp. 1–26.

[15]Vinay Lal, 'On the Perils of History and Historiography: The Case, Puzzling as usual, of India', *Journal of Commonwealth and Postcolonial Studies*, Fall 1995, 3(1), 79–112; see also his 'The Discourse of History and the Crisis at Ayodhya: Reflections on the Production of Knowledge, Freedom, and the Future of India', *Emergences* (5/6), 1994, pp. 4–44. The latter goes further in its critique of history as a cultural project and its relationship with violence in the context of the Ramjanmabhumi movement in India, something to which I turn towards the end of this essay briefly and from a slightly different point of view.

Is it merely an accident that so many of the critics of history I have mentioned in this essay are South Asians or have a South Asian connection? Is it only a function of my own cultural origins? Or is it possible that, pushed around by powerful traditions both of modern history and the surviving epic cultures in their part of the world, many South Asians are forced to take, sometimes grudgingly, a more sceptical stance towards history?

'history' and the modernizing narratives of citizenship, bourgeois public and private, and the nation-state. 'History' as a knowledge system is firmly embedded in institutional practices that invoke the nation-state at every step.[16]

All three historians are exceptions and even they are basically pleading for what Sara Suleri calls 'contraband history'. All three leave one with the hope that some day their kind will reactivate their own cultural memories and bring in an element of radical self-criticism in their own discipline. Radicalism may not lose by beginning at home.

But the question still remains: Why this poor self-reflexivity among historians as a species? I suspect that this denial of the historicity of history is built on two pillars of modern-knowledge systems. First, Enlightenment sensitivities, whether in the West or outside, presume a perfect equivalence between history and the construction of the past; they presume that there is no past independent of history. If there is such a past, it is waiting to be remade into history. To misuse David Lowenthal's imagery, the past is another country only when it cannot be properly historicized and thus conquered.[17] And the regnant concepts of human brotherhood and equality insist that all human settlements must look familiar from the metropolitan centres of knowledge and, ideally, no human past must look more foreign than one's own. On and off I have used the expression 'imperialism of categories' to describe the ability of some conceptual categories to establish such complete hegemony over the domains they cover that alternative concepts related to the domains are literally banished from human consciousness. History has established such a hegemony in our known universe. In that universe, the discipline is no longer merely the best available entry into the past; it now exhausts the idea of the past. In what psychoanalysis might some day call a perfect instance of concretization, it is now *the* past.

Everyone has a right to one's own clichés, C.P. Snow says. So let me give my favourite example of such a hegemony from my own discipline. When intelligence tests were first devised there was much discussion in the psychological literature on the scope and limits of these tests. Scholars acknowledged that the tests were an imperfect measure of human intelligence, that they were sensitive to, and influenced by, personal and social factors; that their reliability and validity were not closed issues. Over the decades, doubts about the reliability and especially the validity

[16]Ibid., p. 19.

[17]David Lowenthal, *The Past Is a Foreign Country* (Cambridge: Cambridge University Press, 1985).

of intelligence tests have declined to nearly zero, though a debate on them raged for a while in the late 1970s.[18] Today, virtually every introductory textbook of psychology defines human intelligence as that which intelligence tests measure. IQ, once a less than perfect measure of intelligence, now defines intelligence. Other such examples are the hegemony of development and modern science over the domains of social change and science respectively. It is almost impossible to criticise development today without being accused of social conservatism of the kind that snatches milk from the mouths of hungry Third-World babies. It is even more difficult to criticize modern science without being seen as a religious fundamentalist or a closet astrologer.

History not only exhausts our idea of the past, it also defines our relationship with our past selves.[19] Those who own the past own the present, George Orwell says. Perhaps those who own the rights to shape the pasts of our selves can also claim part-ownership of our present selves. Historians have now come to crucially shape the selves of the subjects of history, those who live only with history. In the process, they have abridged the right and perhaps even the capacity of citizens to self-define, exactly as the mega-system of modern medicine has taken over our bodies, and the psychiatrists our minds for retooling or renovation. We are now as willing to hand over central components of our self to the historians for engineering purposes as to hand over our bodies to surgeons.

Second, the absence of radical self-reflexivity in history is in part a product of the gradual emergence and spread of the culture of diaspora and the psychology of the exile as a dominant cultural motif of our times.[20] The modern world has a plurality of people who have been uprooted—from their pasts, from their cultures, and from less impersonal communities that often ensure the continuity—of traditions. Modern cosmopolitanism is grounded in this uprooting. Not only have state- and nation-formation, empire-building, colonialism, slavery,

---

[18]Paradoxically, that debate, centring around Cyril Burt's ethical lapses, only consolidated the status of the tests as *the* measure and operational definer of intelligence.

[19]The moderns like to build their selfhood on the past that looks empirical and falsifiable. But it can be argued that the unsatiated search for a touch of transcendence in life is, as a result, only pushed into weird psychopathological channels and finds expression in using or living out history with the passions formerly elicited by myths, without the open-endedness and the touch of self-destructiveness associated with myths. Later on in this paper I shall give an example of this from the backwater of Asia, but the reader can easily think up similar examples from his or her surroundings.

[20]Nikos Papastergiadis, *Exile as Modernity* (Manchester: Manchester University Press, 1993).

pogroms, the two world wars and ethnic violence, taken their toll, perhaps more than anything else, development combined with large-scale industrialization and urbanization have contributed handsomely to such uprooting. These are the 'historical dislocations' that mark out, according to Robert Lifton, the 'restless context' which 'includes a sense of all the unsettled debts of history that may come "back into play" '.[21]

While direct violence produces identifiable victims and refugees, social processes such as development produce invisible victims and invisible refugees. To give random examples from this century, the United States began as a nation of uprooted immigrants. Just when it began to settle down as a new cultural entity, its farming population came down from more than 60 per cent to something like 5 per cent in about seventy-five years. Likewise, Brazil has acquired a plurality of the uprooted within two decades by going through a massive transfer of population from rural to urban settlements, probably involving as much as 60 per cent of the population of the country. Independent India, which saw colossal communal violence and forced movements of population during its early years, and China, which has seen in this century millions of refugees created by a world war and a series of famines, are going through similar changes at the moment. They are producing invisible refugees of development by the million. The dams, especially the fifteen hundred large dams built in India in the last forty-five years, presumably along with associated major development projects, have by themselves produced nearly twenty-two million refugees.[22] As in the case of the environment, the sheer scale of human intervention in social affairs has destroyed cultural elasticities and the capacity of cultures to return to something like their original state after going through a calamity.[23]

This massive uprooting has produced a cultural psychology of exile that in turn has led to an unending search for roots, on the one hand, and angry, sometimes self-destructive, assertions of nationality and

[21]Robert Jay Lifton, *The Protean Self: Human Resistance in an Age of Fragmentation* (New York: Basic Books, 1993), p. 131.

[22]Gayatri Singh, 'Displacement and Limits to Legislation', in Raajen Singh (ed.), *Dams and Other Major Projects: Impact on and Response of Indigenous People* (Goa: CCA-URM, 1988), pp. 91–7; see p. 91.

[23]Cf. Robert Sinsheimer's certainty principle, which he proposes as the inverse of Heisenberg's uncertainty principle, is particularly relevant to this argument. The uncertainty principle has to do with the effect of observation on the observed; the certainty principle with the effect of observation on the observer. Robert Sinsheimer, 'The Presumptions of Science', *Daedalus*, 1978, 107, pp. 23–5.

ethnicity on the other. As the connection with the past has weakened, desperate attempts to re-establish this connection have also grown. Paradoxically, this awareness of losing touch with the past and with primordial collectivities is mainly individual, even though it uses the *language* of collectivity. It has to use the language of collectivity because the community has in the meanwhile perished for many who are a party to the search. I have in mind something like what Hannah Arendt used to call the search for pseudo-solidarities in European fascism in the 1930s.[24]

The attempt to give a central place in our personality repertoire to formal history—in its conventional or dissenting sense—has its counterpart in organized efforts to institutionalize history as the only acceptable construction of the past. History manages and tames the past on behalf of the exile, so that the remembered past becomes a submissive presence in the exile's world. The objectivity and empirical stature of history is supposed to give a certitude that alternative constructions of the past—legends, myths and epics—can no longer give. The latter used to give moral certitude, not objective or empirical certitude; history gives moral certitude and guides moral action by paradoxically denying a moral framework and giving an objectivist framework based on supposedly empirical realities. This is what Heinrich Himmler had in mind when he used to exhort the SS to transcend their personal preferences and values, and do the dirty work of history on behalf of European civilization. He had excellent precedents in Europe's history outside Europe. His innovation was the Teutonic thoroughness and self-consistency with which the same historical principles were applied within the confines of Europe.

It is this that makes history a theory of the future for many, a hidden guide to ethics that need not have anything to do with the morality of individuals and communities. History allows one to identify with its secular trends and give a moral stature to the 'inevitable' in the future. The new justifications for violence have come from this presumed inevitability. In these circumstances, psychology enters the picture not in the sense in which the first generation of psychohistorians believed it would do—as a new dimension of history that would deepen or enrich the historical consciousness, but as a source of defiance of the imperialism of history. A practising historian, Richard Pipes, has come close to acknowledging this possibility, if not in a professional journal, at least in a respectable periodical. Pipes may be a distinguished retired cold-

---

[24]Hannah Arendt, Interview with Roger Errera, *New York Review of Books*, 26 October 1978, p. 18.

warrior and a pillar of the establishment, but in this instance at least he has chosen to identify with those uncomfortable with history, both at the centre and in the backwaters of the known world:

> History may be meaningless. The proposition merits consideration. Perhaps the time has come, after two world wars, Hitler, Lenin, Stalin, Mao and Pol Pot, to abandon the whole notion of history, writ large, as a metaphysical process that leads to a goal of which people are only dimly aware. This concept, invented by German idealist philosophers in the early nineteenth century, has often been described as a surrogate secularized religion in which the will of history replaces the hand of God, and revolution serves as the final judgement. As practitioner of history writ small, I, for one, see only countless ordinary individuals who materialize in contemporary documents desiring nothing more than to live ordinary lives, being dragged against their will to serve as building material for fantastic structures designed by men who know no peace.[25]

There is just a hint in Pipes' essay that part of the answer to this passion for 'grand history' lies in psychology, perhaps in psychopathology.[26]

I

In a well-known paper on the crisis of personal identity, psychoanalyst Erik H. Erikson, whose name is associated with serious efforts in the once-trendy disciplinary domain called psychohistory, mentions a news report on a 'smart-alecky' youth, fined twenty-five dollars for reckless driving. While in the court, the boy interrupted the judge to say, 'I just want you to know that I'm not a thief.' Provoked by this 'talking back', the judge immediately increased the sentence to six months on a road gang.[27] Erikson suggests that the judge here ignored what may have been a 'desperate historical denial', an attempt to claim that an anti-social identity had not been formed. The judge was just not sensitive enough to the reaffirmation of a moral self that transcended in this instance the history of a moral lapse.

Can this story be re-read as a fable that redefines the role of psychology in relation to history? Can we read it as an invitation to ponder if the reaffirmation of a moral self in the present by the young man should or should not have priority over the historical 'truth' of his rash driving?

---

[25]Richard Pipes, 'Seventy-Five Years On: The Great October Revolution as a Clandestine Coup d'Etat', *The Times Literary Supplement*, 6 November 1992, pp. 3–4; see p. 4.

[26]Ibid., p. 3.

[27]Erik H. Erikson, 'Youth: Fidelity and Diversity', *Daedalus*, Winter 1962, 91(1), pp. 5–27; see p. 22.

Can his historical denial be read as a defiance of history itself? Does his cognitive defiance have at least as much empirical and objective 'truth' value as the proven history of his bad driving? Is all history only contemporary history, as Benedetto Croce suggested, or is all history psychological history—diverse, essentially conflict-ridden, internally inconsistent constructions of the past that tell more about the present and about the persons and collectivities 'doing' history? Is Erikson even *empirically* flawed because he cannot, or would not, exercise his hermeneutic or exegetic rights beyond a point? Is the unwillingness to exercise these rights fully or the refusal to share them with other civilizations determined by the same forces that we are usually so keen to invoke when we embark on historical analysis? I shall address these odd questions in a very roundabout way, not necessarily to answer them, but to tell the outlines of a story about history in what was once an unabashedly ahistorical society.

Most Indian epics begin with a prehistory and end, not with a climactic victory or defeat, but with an ambivalent awareness of the end of an era. The conclusion conveys a sense of exhaustion, of the futility of it all. The Mahabharata, for instance, does not end with the decisive battle of Kurukshetra; it ends with the painful awareness that an age is about to pass. The victorious are all too aware—in the words of Yudhisthira, who with his brothers has ensured the defeat of the 'ungodly'—that the fratricide that brought them their victory in a just war, has actually been a glorified defeat. Even Lord Krishna, the lord of lords, dies a humble death, his entire clan decimated, his kingdom destroyed.

The first nonwestern psychoanalyst, Girindrasekhar Bose (1886–1953), who happened to be an Indian and a Bengali, wrote among other things a huge commentary on the ancient Indian epics, the *puranas*, which is now entirely forgotten even in his native Bengal.[28] On the face of it, the commentary has so little to do with psychoanalysis that even sensitive commentators on Bose, such as Christians Hartnack and Sudhir Kakar, have mostly ignored it.[29] The book perhaps looks to them like an attempt to construct a genealogy, which is also what it seemed to me when I first read it.

Reared in the culture of nineteenth-century science, particularly its

---

[28]Girindrasekhar Bose, *Purana Pravesha* (Calcutta: M.C. Sarkar, 1934).

[29]Christiane Hartnack, Psychoanalysis and Colonialism in British India, Ph.D. dissertation, Freie Universität, Berline 1988; Sudhir Kakar, 'Stories From Indian Psychoanalysis: Context and Text', in James W. Stigler, Richard A. Shweder and Gilbert Herdt (ed.), *Cultural Psychology* (New York: Cambridge University Press 1990), pp. 427–45.

easily exportable positivist version, Bose was in many ways an unabashed empiricist and experimentalist. That culture of science had entered India in the middle of the nineteenth century along with the European concept of history. A new space for this concept of history was created in the Indian consciousness by the manifest power of the colonial regime, its self-justification in the language of science and history, and by the Enlightenment values seeping into the more exposed sectors of the Indian élite, either as tools of survival under the colonial political economy or as symbols of dissent against the traditional authority system. On one side were those like James Mill who mentions in his *History of British India* the 'consensus' that 'no historical composition existed in the literature of Hindus' and that the Hindus were 'perfectly destitute of historical records'; on the other, there were Indian modernists like Krishna Mohun Banerjea who internalized Mill's estimate and Gibbon's more general belief that 'the art and genius of history [was] ... unknown to the Asiatics' and that the mythological legends of India showed that Indians had a sense of poetry, but that such legends could not be confused with 'historical compositions'.[30] At first, it seemed that the Muslims were better of in this respect. After all, Alberuni *did* say, even if politely, 'Unfortunately the Hindus do not pay much attention to the historical order of things, ... and when they are pressed for information and are at a loss, not knowing what to say, they invariably take to tale-telling.' But soon it became obvious to the moderns, through the likes of H.M. Elliot who wrote a voluminous history of India, that Muhammadan histories were no better than annals.[31]

[30] Lal, 'On the Perils of History', pp. 1–3.

[31] Ibid., p. 2. Could it be that things looked different in the Islamic cultures to some historians of India because for a long time the ruling dynasties of India had been Muslim? Was the earlier reading of South Asian Islam as historically-minded based on the assumption that dominance and successful statecraft required a 'proper' sense of history? I am not the right person to answer this question but it is pretty clear that the new sense of history spread unevenly in India. It became a deeper passion among the Brahminic castes—after all, history did require written texts at a time when oral histories were not fashionable—and castes aspiring to a Brahminic status (such as the Bhadraloks of Bengal, traditionally considered peripheral to the mainstream Brahminic culture, but now closer to power in the pan-Indian scene due to their colonial connection). History also became a passion with those Brahminic communities that had opted for the Kshatriya vocations of statecraft and bureaucracy, which previously contributed to one's power but not to ritual-status. These vocations now contributed to one's status because of the revaluation, under the colonial regime, of the Kshatriyas as martial and masculine and, therefore, as true indigenous rulers of people in India. Two examples of communities gaining from their non-traditional vocations and opting for history with a vengeance in colonial times are the Chitpavan Brahmins of Maharashtra and the Nagar Brahmins of Gujarat.

By the time Girindrasekhar Bose wrote his commentary on the Indian epics, the favourite lament of many Bengali thinkers was: *Bangali atmavismrita jati*—'the Bengalis are a people who have forgotten their self.' By this was meant that the Bengalis did not have a self based on history, that the traditional depositories of Bengal's awareness of its selfhood and past—its myths, folkways, shared and transmitted memories—were no longer legitimate to important sections of the Bengali élite. It was this westernized élite, not the whole of Bengal, that felt it was *atmavismrita*, truly orphaned, without a proper history. It was now looking for a different kind of construction of the past, the kind that would not humiliate them before their historically-minded rulers.[32]

Yet it became obvious to Bose, after working on the subject for a while, that no modern western historian could do justice to the *puranic* texts, for the modern West had lost access to certain forms of consciousness that were necessary for a more open, creative reading of the texts. If traditional India did not have access to the Enlightenment's idea of modern history, neither did Europe have access to Indian traditions of constructing the past.[33]

Now, Bose was no ordinary nationalist trying to re-value the Indian classics; he had accepted psychoanalysis as *the* mode of understanding his society as well as the cultural products of his society, including texts such as the *puranas*. In fact, to the best of my knowledge, he was the first nonwestern psychiatrist and psychologist to do so; he began adapting the main principles of the young discipline to his culture in the first decade of this century, when hardly anything of Freud was available in English. In fact, he emerged so early in the career of psychoanalysis that he was accepted, apart from August Aichorn and of course Freud himself, as a training analyst on the basis of his self-analysis. I suspect that Bose

[32]Surendranath Banerjea, the nationalist leader, handled the situation the way many modern Indian historians would like to handle it. After asking whether it was imaginable that a great civilization did not have proper histories, he concluded that histories did indeed exist in India but could not survive the social upheavals in the country, the carelessness of the Brahmins, and the tropical climate. Ibid., p. 6.

[33]It was certainly not an accident that the new enthusiasm for history in India was accompanied by a fear of a return to India's past. While the new acquaintance with history created an awareness of and a tendency to celebrate some aspects of European past—in particular, the legitimation of modern science in India, as in Europe, proceeded on the basis of a systematic invocation of the beauties of Europe's Hellenic traditions—any similar attempt to invoke the Indian past immediately triggered and continue to trigger accusations of retrogression or atavism. Gradually, the idea that some pasts were more equal than other pasts came to be successfully institutionalized in India's westernized élite's new-found historical consciousness.

became aware of the implicit politics of knowledge within which his work was getting located only after beginning his work on the epics of India.[34] It was as a psychoanalyst dealing with case *histories* that he deciphered some of the distinctive rules or techniques that the epics-as-*histories* followed.[35] He was a 'student of pastness itself', as Ivan Illich describes the vocation.[36] Bose came to the conclusion that the *puranas* were themselves a form of history.[37] That formulation could not have been easy to arrive at when the Indian élite were desperately trying to create within Indian civilization a place for history as the moderns understood it.

If Bose were living today, would he talk of the *puranas* as alternative history or as alternatives *to* history? Do we have to interpret the *puranas* into history? Or should we, those who have lived through the blood-drenched history of this century, learn to cherish the few who would rather interpret history into *puranas* to get out of the clutches of history? Should Bose have been sensitive to the closeness of psychoanalysis to the language of myths and its ability to be a critique of history, including case history, at the end of the twentieth century? Let me attempt some part-answers to these questions, too, by telling a story.

The 'religious' violence triggered by the Ramjanmabhumi movement in India reached its climax on 6 December 1992. As we know, on that fateful day a controversial mosque at the sacred city of Ayodhya, which many claimed was built by destroying a temple that stood at the birthplace of Lord Rama, was demolished by screaming, angry volunteers eager to avenge a historical wrong.[38]

[34]Bose, *Purana Pravesha*, pp. 212–3.

[35]For instance, among the interpretive principles Bose deciphered was *atiyukti vichara*, analysis of *atiranjana* or the stylized exaggerations of the Indian epics, which put up the back of James Mill, as part of the narrative style of the *puranas*.

[36]Ivan Illich, 'Mnemosyne: The Mold of Memory', in *In the Mirror of the Past: Lectures and Addresses 1978–1990* (New York: Marion Boyars, 1992), passim.

For the historian, the script is a vehicle which allows him to recover the events or perceptions that the document was meant to record. For the student of pastness itself, the script has a more specific function. For him, the script is a privileged object which allows him to explore two things: the mode of recall used in a given epoch, and also the image held by that epoch about the nature of memory and therefore of the past.

[37]Bose, *Purana Pravesha*, p. 179.

[38]Rama himself, though a venerated deity in much of South and South-East Asia, has been open to diverse forms of veneration and recognition within Hinduism itself. The two main sects of Hindus, Vaishnavas and Shaivas, see him differently, with the only the former granting him full divinity. There are versions of Ramayana, the epic that tells the

What was the nature of the history around which so much bloodshed has already taken place, and what is the status of that concept of history which has so frequently been invoked by Indian historians to clinch the argument on Ramjanmabhumi one way or the other? Why did the same history not move millions of Indians for hundreds of years, not even the first generation of Hindu nationalists in the nineteenth century, not even, for that matter, the founders and ideologues of the same parties that are today at the forefront of the temple movement? Though they always claimed to be ardent devotees of the idea of history, none of them ever demanded the return of the Babri mosque to the Hindus on historical grounds: neither Balkrishna Munje, nor Keshav Hegdewar, nor Vinayak Damodar Savarkar, not even Lal Krishna Advani and Murali Manohar Joshi, the present leaders of the movement.[39]

The two questions I have raised, as you will have noticed, do not lay any emphasis on the ongoing debate in India on the 'truth' about the Ramjanmabhumi. They are concerned neither with the archaeological and historical evidence on the controversial mosque nor with the ongoing legal battle on the judicial status of the territoriality of the birthplace of one believed to be an incarnation of Lord Vishnu but treated by some of his new-found political disciples as a venerable, now-dead national leader. Admittedly, the debate on the subject, particularly its style, reveals much about the psychological and cultural realities that frame the problem *today*, even if not in the sense that the protagonists believe. Was there a temple that was destroyed by the builders of the Babri mosque? Is this Ayodhya really the Ayodhya of Rama? The questions are important but only for the secularized Indians, not for the millions who have trudged to the sacred city for pilgrimage over the centuries. Can we provide at least some vague clues to the point of view of the majority to whom the idea of history itself was once an encroachment on the traditional constructions of the past, some of whom have now opted to enter the dominion of history? I shall give my response as unambiguously as I can.

---

story of Rama, where he is the villain and there are even temples dedicated to the demons Rama fought against.

[39]Almost all the main leaders of the movement have come from modern sects that explicitly attack Hindu idolatry. Till the movement succeeded in bringing to power a party committed to their cause in the state where Ayodhya is located and the new cabinet made a symbolic appearance at the Ayodhya temple, almost none of the major leaders had found time in seven years to visit the temple. For details of the Ayodhya case I have depended on Ashis Nandy, Shikha Trivedy, Shail mayaram and Achyut Yagnik, *Creating a Nationality: The Ramjanmabhumi Movement and the Fear of the Self* (New Delhi: Oxford University Press, 1995).

History is not the anthropology of past times, though it can come close to it. The growing popularity of anthropological history gives a false sense of continuity between the two disciplines, for they are separated by a deep political chasm. Victims of anthropology talk back in some cases and in many other cases retain the potential for doing so; the subjects of history almost never rebel, for they are mostly dead. In the first instance, the worst affliction is colonial anthropology, in the second the civilizational *hubris* that claims that not merely the present but even the past and the future of some cultures have to be reworked. The main tools in that redefinition till now have been devaluation, marginalization and liquidation of memories that cannot be historicized and, in the case of cultures that locate their utopias in the past, narrowing the range of alternatives 'envisionable' within the cultures. In cultures where plural visions of the future derive from plural visions of the past, unqualified historicization has opened up new possibilities of violence to eliminate plurality, directed both outwards and inwards.

In the controversy on Ramjanmabhumi, volumes have been written by scholars, journalists, and partisan pamphleteers to prove either that there was a temple where the Babri Masjid stood since the sixteenth century or that there was no such temple. Shorn of verbiage, Hindu nationalists have claimed that the Muslims are temple-breakers; the Muslims have denied that they are so. Two minor parties involved in the dispute are the secular and Hindu nationalist historians; they care for neither temples nor mosques, except for archaeological, aesthetic or political reasons. Some of India's respected historians such as Romila Thapar, S. Gopal, Bipan Chandra and Harbans Mukhia have said it all on behalf of their tribe, the secular historians, when they wrote that there was no historical proof that Rama was ever born, certainly none that he was born in the present city of Ayodhya. And one of their main opponents, the historian S.P. Gupta, whose ambition once was to do his doctoral work in history under Thapar, has said it all on behalf of the Hindu nationalists when he claimed that he took part in the archaeological expedition to Ayodhya led by B.B. Lal (which he did not). Both Thapar and Gupta share the belief that the conflict in Ayodhya is about historical truths and the rectification of historical wrongs that can only be solved by objective, scientific history.

On the whole, it will not be an oversimplification to say that secular historians either claim that Hindus are also temple-breakers—they allegedly broke Shaivite and Vaishnava temples in sectional clashes as well as Buddhist and Jain temples—or that the Muslims are not temple-breakers, at least in this instance.[40] Recently the secularists, fighting their gut reaction to Hinduism as a warehouse of superstitions and atavism, have added for political reasons a third angle to their viewpoint. They argue that the Hindu nationalists are not true Hindus, 'true Hinduism' being what the secularists find out from the traditional texts and from the writings of Hindu religious leaders through modern or post-modern textual analysis. The Hindu nationalist historians—who claim, fittingly, that they are 'positive' or genuine secularists, unlike the 'pseudo-secularists' who disagree with them—demand that Indian Muslims own up their heritage of temple-breaking and iconoclasm and atone for it by admitting. that the disputed mosque should have been handed over to the Hindus for demolition or relocation in the first place, and that the destruction of the mosque in December 1992 was a nationalist act.[41]

The Muslim responses to these demands have ranged from massive protests to violent and nonviolent resistance to even early local offers to hand over the mosque to their neighbours.[42] But one possible position has not been taken: no Muslim in India has claimed till now that the Muslims broke temples *and* are proud of that past as a measure of their piety. Nor has any Muslim affirmed the right to break temples or even retain mosques built on demolished temples. No Muslim has sought protection for the Babri mosque without insisting that the mosque had *not* been built on a razed temple or without insisting that what Muslim marauders did in India was what marauders always do and such vandalism had nothing to do with Islam and that, in any case, the past was now truly past. This has been associated with a spirited denial of the accusation that they are temple-breakers. Strangely, both the *dharmashastras*, especially the epic vision of the *smarta* texts—the vision

[40]See for instance, S. Gopal, et al., The Political Abuse of History (New Delhi: n.d.), pamphlet. Also see Romila Thapar, Harbans Mukhia and Bipan Chandra, *Communalism and the Writing of Indian History* (New Delhi: People's Publishing House, 1969), pamphlet.

[41]See for instance, Arun Shourie, Harish Narain, Jay Dubashi Ram Swarup and Sita Ram Goel, *Hindu Temples, What Happened to Them (A Preliminary Survey)* (New Delhi: Voice of India, 1990); Koenraad Elst, *Ramjanmabhumi Versus Babri Masjid: A Case Study in Hindu–Muslim Conflict* (New Delhi: Voice of India, 1990); and *Negationism in India: Concealing the Record of Islam* (New Delhi: Voice of India, 1993), 2nd ed.

[42]I found out from a local leader of the Vishwa Hindu Parishad during a field trip to Ayodhya that the local Shia leaders had offered, at least twice, to relocate the mosque and the local Hindus were willing to accept the offer. But the all-India leadership of both the Hindu nationalists and important sections of the Muslim political leadership refused to countenance such a compromise. The local Hindus and Muslims had no right to decide an issue that involved all the Hindus and Muslims of India, some of the latter said.

in which the heritage of the Ramayana is located—and the living traditions
of everyday Hinduism, exemplified above all by the majority of Hindu
residents of Ayodhya, have customarily considered that denial an important
moral statement. To them, that reaffirmation of a moral universe by
Muslims may be more acceptable than the high-pitched evangelism of
Hindu nationalists.

Traditional India not only lacks the Enlightenment's concept of
history; it is doubtful that it finds objective, hard history a reliable, ethical
or reasonable way of constructing the past. The construction of time in
South Asia may or may not be always cyclical, but it is rarely linear or
unidirectional. As in some other cultures and some of the natural sciences,
the Indian attitude to time—including the sequencing of the past, the
present and the future—is not given or pre-formatted. Time in much of
South Asia is an open-ended enterprise. The power of myths, legends,
itihasas (which at one time used to be mechanically translated as primitive
precursors of history) and *puranas* may have diminished but is not yet
entirely lost.

Elsewhere I have classified nonhistorical reconstructions of the past
under the rubric of mythography, but this may not be an appropriate
term, though politically it does seem to protect the dignity of reconstructions that are the farthest from the contemporary idea of history.[43] But
whatever name or names we give to such projects, they remain part of
a moral venture. What a contemporary mythographer in the West like
Erik Erikson has to establish in the guise of a clinical interpretation
or Joseph Campbell and others in the guise of an environmentally-sound
remembered practice, many of the not-entirely-recessive traditions of
constructing the past in India take for granted as a part of everyday life.
They take seriously the affirmation of Indian Muslims that they are not
temple-breakers, that there exist textual injunctions in Islam against
even worshipping in a mosque built on forcibly-occupied land. The marauders who broke temples are already in their minds marauders who
'coincidentally' happened to be Muslims, and I suspect that most of their
Hindu neighbours outside the reach of history have accepted that
formulation. (After all, an altogether different concept of the past moved
even the fiery nineteenth-century religious and social reformer,
Vivekananda, from whom the majority of Hindu nationalists claim to
trace their ideological lineage. As philosopher Ramchandra Gandhi tells
the story, which I cannot help repeating again, towards the end of his

---

[43]Ashis Nandy, *The Intimate Enemy: Loss and Recovery of Self Under Colonialism* (New
Delhi: Oxford University Press, 1983).

life, seeing evidences of the desecration of Hindu temples by successive invaders in Kashmir, Vivekananda asked in anguish in a temple of the Goddess Kali, 'How could you let this happen, Mother, why did you permit this desecration?' Vivekananda himself records the answer Kali whispered in his heart: 'What is it to you, Vivekananda, if the invader breaks my images? Do you protect me, or do I protect you?'[44]

The conventional truth value of, or empirical certitude, about the past is not particularly relevant from this point of view. Because once the principle of non-destruction of the places of worship of other faiths is accepted in present times, the past is 'constructed adequately', the moral point has been made, and the 'timeless truths' reaffirmed.

Collingwood or no Collingwood, for some ahistorical cultures at least, all times exist only in present times and can be decoded only in terms of the contemporaneous. There is no past independent of us; there is no future that is not present here and now. And therefore the model of decoding is subject to the morality of everyday life, not to the various derivatives of the Baconian worldview. This is the humbler 'secular' counterpart of Coomaraswamy's proposition, made on behalf of Islam and, for that matter, the major religious worldviews, that 'time ... is an imitation of eternity.'[45]

In modern India, to the extent it has got involved in the controversy over the mosque at Ayodhya, history, not Ayodhya, is the terrain for which the 'secularists' and the Hindu nationalists fight. Both want to capture and correct it. The former want to correct the intolerance that, they feel, characterizes all faiths; the latter want to correct the intolerant faiths and teach their followers a lesson.

Secular historians assume that the past of India has been bloody and fanatic, that Hindus and Muslims have been fighting for centuries, and that the secular state has now brought to the country a modicum of peace. They believe that the secular faiths—organized around the ideas of the nation-state, scientific rationality and development—are more tolerant and should correct that history (despite the nearly 210 million killed in man-made violence in this century, the killing in most cases justified by secular faiths, including Baconian science—Darwinism in the case of colonialism, biology and eugenics in the case of Nazism, and science and history in the case of communism). Hindu nationalists

[44]Ramchandra Gandhi, *Sita's Kitchen: A Testimony of Faith and Inquiry* (New Delhi: Penguin, 1992), p. 10.

[45]Ananda K. Coomaraswamy, *Time and Eternity* (Bangalore: Select Books, 1989), p. 71.

believe that, except for Hinduism, most faiths, including the secular
ones, are intolerant. But they do not celebrate that exception. They resent
it; it embarrasses them. They, therefore, seek to masculinise Hinduism
to combat and, at the same time, make it resemble what according to
them has been the style of the dominant faiths, which Hindu nationalists
see as more in tune with modern science and technology and, above all,
scientized history.[46] At the same time, they insist that the history produced
by their opponents, the Indian secularists, is not adequately scientific.
They believe, as their historically-minded opponents do, that there is
an implicit science of violence that shapes history, which itself gives us
guidance about how to tame and use that violence for the higher purposes
of history through the instrumentalities of the modern nation-state.
Like their opponents again, the Hindu nationalists are committed to
liberating India from its nasty past, by acquiring access to the state in the
name of undoing the past with the help of the same kind of history. The
secular historians have done it in the past; the Hindu nationalists are
hoping to do so in the future.

In this 'historical' battle, the two sides understand each other perfectly.
One side has attacked only pseudo-secularism, not secularism; the other
has attacked the stereotyping of minorities, never the 'universal' concepts
of the state, nationalism, and cultural integration that underpin the colonial
construction of Hinduism that passes as Hindutva. It is a Mahabharatic
battle between two sets of illegitimate children, fathered by nineteenth-
century Europe and the colonial empires, who have escaped from the
orphanage of history.

When modern history first entered the Indian intellectual scene in the
middle of the nineteenth century, many accepted it as a powerful adjunct
to the kit-bag of Indian civilization. Like Krishna Mohun Banerjea, famous
social reformer, they felt that Europe had transcended its wretched past
by acquiring a historical consciousness and India, which showed a
'lamentable want of authentic records in ... literature', could do so too.[47]
The domination of that consciousness has now become, as the
confrontation at Ayodhya shows, a cultural and political liability. In a

[46]See for instance Gyanendra Pandey, 'Modes of History Writing: A New Hindu History
of Ayodhya', *Economic and Political Weekly*, 18 June 1994, 29(25), pp. 1523–8.

[47]Krishna Mohun Banerjea, 'Discourse on the Nature and Importance of Historical
Studies', in *Selection of Discourses Delivered at the Meetings of the Society for the Acquisition
of General Knowledge* (Calcutta, 1840), Vol. 1, quoted in Lal, 'On the Perils of History and
Historiography', p. 1.

civilization where there are many pasts, encompassing many bitter memories and animosities, to absolutize them with the help of the European concept of history is to attack the organizing principles of the civilization. Particularly so, given that South Asian historians, though otherwise a garrulous lot, have produced no radical critique of history, perhaps not even an authentic history of history. They have sought to historicize everything, but never the idea of history itself. For historicizing the idea of history is to historicize the historians themselves. As I have said, such self-confrontation has not been the strong suit of historians; there are very poor checks in history against the violence and cruelty that may follow from uncritical acceptance of the idea of history.

Bertolt Brecht, I am told, strongly believed that the past had to be bared to settle all accounts, so that one could move towards the future. The traditional Indian attitude to the past, as in many other such societies, is a spirited negation of that belief. That negation resists the justificatory principles on which modern, organized violence heavily depends. Provincial European intellectuals like Brecht had no clue that the construction of the past can sometimes be, as in some of the little cultures of India, guided not by memories alone, but by tacit theories of principled forgetfulness and silences. Such constructions are primarily responsible to the present and to the future; they are meant neither for the archivist nor for the archaeologist. They try to expand human options by reconfiguring the past and transcending it through creative improvisation. For such cultures, the past shapes the present and the future, but the present and the future also shape the past. Some scholars feel responsible enough to the present to subvert the future by correcting the past; others are as willing to redefine, perhaps even transfigure, the past to open up the future. The choice is not cognitive, but moral and political, in the best sense of the terms.

State, History and Exile in South Asian Politics: Modernity and the Landscape of Clandestine and Incommunicable Selves

The Nation-State

Like other similarly placed countries in the South, India—perhaps the whole of South Asia—relates to the global political-economic system and the global mass culture of our times mainly through its modern political self. When India resists these global orders, the resistance is articulated and legitimized by this self; when India opens itself up for globalization, that opening up and the zeal that goes with it, too, are mediated through the same self. India's modern self scans, interprets, assesses and adapts to the demands of the outside world, both as an entity that processes the outside world for the consumption of Indians and an entity that processes the Indian experience for outsiders. The world usually knows India as modern Indians, in collaboration with specialist western scholarship on India, have constructed it. Orientalism is frequently a joint 'dream work' where the psychological defences and cultural 'armour' of the West are matched by the self-representation and self-engineering of the modernizing non-West.

Because these processes tend to get telescoped into the personalities of the social actors involved, the modern Indian is usually in dialogue with himself or herself when seemingly in dialogue with the rest of the world. From the social and religious reformer Rammohun Roy (1772–1833), popularly known as the father of modern India, to the film-maker Satyajit Ray (1920–92), probably the last larger-than-life figure India's encounter with the colonial West has produced, even the most ardent modernists have had to engage in that dialogue, often with mixed results.[1]

[1] Ashis Nandy, 'Sati: A Nineteenth Century Tale of Women, Violence and Protest', in *At the Edge of Psychology: Essays on Politics and Culture* (New Delhi: Oxford University Press,

Sometimes this dialogue has to be established, through a tremendous effort of will, almost as an exercise in self-creation. Satyajit Ray has described in painful detail how he, as an urbane, highly westernized Indian, discovered the Indian village while making a film trilogy that was to paradoxically become, for the world cinema, the last word on the Indian village. As this example itself shows, such implosive dialogues may be anguished, but they also allow enormously creative use of the experience of living in two cultures.[2]

In politics, the most remarkable part of this dialogue with the self is how little the modern Indian self is dependent on or in conversation with what is commonly believed to be the traditional Indian definitions of state, political authority, or political leadership. Despite the immense fascination with Kautilya, within India and outside, the *Arthashastra* has not manifestly influenced the contemporary Indian's political self-definition. The political history of ancient or medieval India and the conventions of statecraft unearthed by that history have influenced Indians even less. Though a galaxy of Hindu, Buddhist, Muslim and Sikh dynasties ran large empires and though the histories of some of these dynasties have been grist to the mills of national and subnational chauvinism in recent times, on the whole, they too have not left any significant memory traces behind. Ashoka is a more living presence in contemporary Sri Lankan politics than in Indian politics. Though the names of Rana Pratap and Guru Govind Singh are ritually invoked by Hindu nationalist propaganda, no recent, mainstream, Indian politician has been influenced in the least by any of these worthies. Even as metaphors, these figures have been marginal to contemporary Indian public life. (The case of Shivaji is slightly different, because he has become identified with regional and non-Brahminic caste pride in Maharashtra.) If the cadres of the Hindu nationalist parties bring up these names once in a while in the service of their moth-eaten, nineteenth-century, colonial interpretation of Hinduism, other modern Indians reject them as parts of a cultural baggage that deserves to be respected only from a safe distance.

Apart from the colonial state, the only other state that has left some memory traces behind is the Mughal empire. That is partly because

1980), pp. 1–31; and Ashis Nandy, 'Satyajit Ray's Secret Guide to Exquisite Murders', in *The Savage Freud and Other Essays in Possible and Retrievable Selves* (New Delhi: Oxford University Press, and Princeton: Princeton University Press, 1995), pp. 237–66.

[2]Ashis Nandy, 'Satyajit Ray's India', *Deep Focus*, 1996, 6, pp. 32–8; and Ashis Nandy, 'The Decline in the Imagination of the Village', in Vinay Lal (ed.), *Dissenting Knowledges, Open Futures: The Multiple Selves and Strange Destinations of Ashis Nandy* (New Delhi: Oxford University Press, 2000), pp. 176–85.

during the early years of the Raj the style of governance and the culture of politics (especially the frame of legitimacy) were recognizably Mughal in some respects and they were designed to be so.[3] Till the middle of the nineteenth century, the British in India were not only sometimes called 'Nabobs', they continued to rule India with one eye on the conventions of the Mughal empire, the other on European ideas of statecraft. Even the official language of the Raj was Persian for about seventy-five-years. The culture of the state for a long while after that reflected not merely the influence of important currents of British political thought, but also the culture that had crystallized during the first seventy-five years of the Raj. Bernard Cohn's work on the 'codification of ritual idiom' under the Raj has a tacit narrative dealing with this bifocal vision: how the British defined themselves in India and how they sought to link this self-definition to the idea of the state in the ruled people. For instance, the Darbar of 1911, Cohn suggests, replicated the Mughal court rituals in many ways and sought to derive consent for the Raj by systematically invoking Indian ideas of rulership.[4] The coronation of King George V was simultaneously a Mughal coronation.

However, by the 1860s, this indigenous Mughal imperial culture was being cornered and pushed underground by an increasingly assertive Utilitarian ideology of the state which linked with wider demands and expectations from the state in the more articulate, politicized sections of the Indian people. It is this second concept of state that has evolved gradually into a quasi-Hegelian imagination in contemporary India, with two identifiable features. First, the image of the ideal state is still heavily dependent on nineteenth-century Anglo-Saxon texts on the state and their social evolutionist legacy and, second, that dependence has been defined much more by texts than by the practice of statecraft in Europe. As a result, the ideal state in modern India still carries with it a touch of purism and a certain fear of clumsiness, ambiguity and the dirty imprint of life. At the same time, there is, paradoxically, a continuous defensive

[3]So that even today, remembering the Mughal culture remains a way of going ethnic that the heritage of the Raj defines as elegant, authentic and safe. This is another way of reading Mukul Kesavan's work on the 'Islamicate' frame of Indian popular cinema. Mukul Kesavan, 'Urdu, Awadh and the Tawaif: The Islamicate Roots of the Hindi Cinema', in Zoya Hasan, (ed.), *Forging Identities: Gender, Communities and the State* (New Delhi: Kali for Women, 1994), pp. 244–58. Following Marshall Hodgson, Kesavan distinguishes between the Islamic and Islamicate, the latter standing for 'the social and cultural complex historically associated with Islam and the Muslims, both among Muslims themselves and even when found among non-Muslims', p. 246.

[4]Bernard S. Cohn, 'Representing Authority in Victorian India', in *An Anthropologist Among Historians and Other Essays* (New Delhi: Oxford University Press, 1987), pp. 632–82.

attempt to define statecraft as a dirty, hard-eyed, masculine game of *realpolitik* which Indians, especially overly idealistic, romantic Indian critics of India's external policies and nuclear and security choices, cannot fathom.

Also, during the period when India's modern political identity was being formed, the only real-life experience with the state to which modern Indians were exposed was the imperial British-Indian state. Hence the idea of the state that dominates modern India is that of an imperial state run, naturally enough now, by modern Indians well-versed in Anglo-Saxon theories of the state. Statecraft means for many Indians a centralized command structure; a condescending welfare system for the poor and the powerless; an apparatus for impartial arbitration among permanently squabbling tribes, castes, religions, language groups and regions; and for the slow and steady inculcation into citizens of the spirit of Baconian science. Hence also the modern Indian's almost desperate belief that he or she stands between the wolves in the global nation-state system and the vulnerable sheep—in the form of the irrational, uniformed majority of the Indians.[5]

The picture does not change dramatically even when religious chauvinists begin to speak of a Hindu state. That state, too, remains quasi-Hegelian and it, too, is associated with deep fears that the ordinary Hindus would not be able to sustain it. In fact, the hatred for Muslims among Hindu nationalists is matched only by their contempt for the Hindus. They would like to herd the Hindus, too, like cattle, towards the beatitude of a well-defined nationality, hitched to a national security state modelled on the pre-World War I European concept of the state. Hindu chauvinists are plaintively waiting for a Hindu Bismarck to emerge who will forge a nineteenth-century nation-state to liberate semi-westernized Hindus from the non-Hindus on the one hand and the infra-Hindus on the other. Even the ideology of Hindu nationalism, which is supposed to back up such a state, is pathetically dependent on European nationalism of the kind popularized by Johan Gottfried von Herder (1744–1803) and Giuseppe Mazzini (1805–72), who wrote of culture as the soul of a people and whom many Hindu nationalists in colonial times adored as much for their ideological fervour as for their maudlin tone.[6]

A more clinical way of describing the situation would be to say that

---

[5]See, 'Culture, State, and the Rediscovery of Indian Politics', pp. 16–33 above.

[6]For some idea of the ambivalent meaning that Herder at least has acquired in our times, see Pierre Birnbaum, 'From Multiculturalism to Nationalism', *Political Theory*, 1996, 24(1), pp. 33–45.

modern Indians have stabilized their modern self by internalizing the colonial ideology of the state they confronted in the nineteenth century. Such a self has limited space even for the new currents of political culture— especially new editions of some other less-known ideas associated with the state in Europe and North America, which have allowed them to partially transcend the gory history of wars and conquest in recent years. The frozen concept of the state for modern Indians includes within it not only indigenized European ideas of nationality, nationalism, progress, rationality, and secularism, but even a unique concept of a desirable society, built mostly on once-popular ideas of European thinkers, and their tropical editions prepared by important Indian public figures. To give random examples, the influence of Bertrand Russell, H.G. Wells, Harold Laski, Christopher Caudwell, Maurice Cornforth, and Rajani Palme Dutt have survived much longer in the warmer, grateful climate of the tropics than in the colder, forgetful intellectual environment of Europe and North America.

Such an imagination of the state includes a reactive component. Many Indians have, over the last hundred years, worked hard to establish that Indian cultures had traditionally included each of the cultural prerequisites required for the sustenance of a modern state in India— from Baconian rationality to post-Reformation secularism. Once these previously repressed or cornered themes are rediscovered and revalued, their argument goes, whatever little contradiction between traditions and modernity exists in India will dissolve, as has reportedly happened in countries like Japan.[7]

In this way of looking at the past, British rule was implicitly a God-sent instrument to modernize India and retool the natives, and such modernization had to involve the jettisoning to the 'dysfunctional' and 'degraded' aspects of heritage as a liability. Various brands of religious and ethnic nationalists have done one better. Their model being European nationalist thought, they have actually tried to subvert the organizational frame of the heritage and reconstruct it according to the needs of a modern nationality. If the record of the Hindu Mahasabha and the Rashtriya Swayamsevak Sangh looks abysmal in the matter of India's freedom struggle, it is because Hindu nationalism discovered quite early that silence, even if not direct collaboration with the colonial rulers, paid handsome political dividends and left it free to pursue its agenda against the minorities on the one hand, and nonmodern and non-modernizable

---

[7]The best-known effort along these lines is Deviprasad Chattopadhyay, *Lokayata: A Study in Ancient Indian Materialism* (New Delhi: People's Publishing House, 1959).

Hinduism on the other. The record of Muslim nationalism in South Asia, of the kind represented by Syed Ahmed Khan, mimics in many respects that of its sworn enemies among the Hindus.[8]

All these responses are probably contextualized by the growing salience of what can only be called a historical or historicized self in Indian public life.

The Enterprise of History

The first few generations of British administrators and English-educated Indians produced a substantial volume of historical work on India. Though historical scholarship (or at least something akin to that) was not entirely unknown to either Islamic or Hindu traditions, the history the colonial historians produced was disjunctive with the constructions of the past the South Asians knew. It was history as it was conceptualized and institutionalized by the European Enlightenment. In any event, in South Asia history itself had never enjoyed the absolute or deep legitimacy it had in modern Europe.[9] Nor did it enjoy or seek, in its pre-modern forms, a monopoly on interpretations of the past. Most South Asians used other ways of constructing the past; European-style history to them was a new technology of organizing memories and a new form of consciousness that seemed to negate many traditional categories of thought and much of the traditional moral universe.

It is not clear what kind of legitimacy these new histories came to enjoy in India outside the modern sector. They certainly did not remain only school and college texts; nor did they substitute other forms of memory in even the middle-class families that opted for modern education, and noisily and aggressively began to lament the absence of

[8]Shan Mohammad (ed.), *Writings and Speeches of Sir Syed Ahmad Khan* (Bombay: Nachiketa, 1972). I have in mind particularly those comments of Sir Syed which reek with contempt for the 'people of low rank' and 'humble origin' (see for instance, ibid., p. 208).

[9]See, 'History's Forgotten Doubles', pp. 83–109 above. Recently, the argument has been ventured that there are no universal, timeless principles dividing historical from ahistorical societies. Kerwin Lee Klein, 'In Search of Narrative Mastery: Post-Modernism and the People Without History', *History and Theory*, 1995, 34(4), pp. 275–98. That, however, is like saying that no culture has timeless attributes. However, cultures change and yet remain identifiably the same cultures. I believe that it is likewise possible to say that while the principles of separation might change, cultures may still remain different. Perhaps the problem arises because the 'double plot' which Klein speaks of takes into account local and global histories, but not the local meanings of global histories, when the politically and intellectually challenging act may be to make that tripartite division, so as to empower competing versions of global history and, implicitly, universalism.

historical memory in Indians.[10] It is true that many modernized Indians thought they had shed their past and chosen to live with a truncated self that had banished the ahistorical. But next to them lived other Indians, often in the same household, who led a life informed with rich but non-historical modes of constructing the past—with living myths, legends, epics and folkways. They also presumably had their own non-historical 'theories' of what the historical mode meant or did.

The passions that attached to history among historically minded Indians were, however, not the same as those attached to the discipline in the by-now more fully historical societies of the West. Nor was it the same as the attitude to history of those outside history. The newcomers to history implicitly saw history as a new kind of epic or a moral myth that had to be constantly reaffirmed to fight the wretched state of Indian society. Enemies of history increasingly began to look to them like enemies of the Indian people. One is tempted to venture the proposition, in the context of the experiences in recent years, that one of the main sources of Hindu and Buddhist chauvinism in South Asia lies in the repressed, extra-historical attitude to history that survives in South Asia's historical self. In Pakistan, the same dynamics have come to inform the production and distribution of official history in a consumable form in recent decades.[11] The newly-historicized South Asians have brought to history the passions they had traditionally associated with epics and legends. History, while historicizing the world, dehistoricizes itself. The passions that underlie history, therefore, remain unnegotiated and begin to use history as a massive defensive shield and a new justification for violence and expropriation. The absence of self-reflexivity of Indian historians themselves and their tendency to prioritize history over life in the name of objectivity, neither an uncommon trait in the global culture of history, have contributed handsomely to the new, violent uses of history in India.

The idea of history, it should be obvious from the foregoing, has linked up with not merely the new idea of the state but also its various components. Among them are the emerging concepts of the national state, nationalism and national security; the theory of progress as concretized in the ideas and processes of development; secularism, especially its vari-

[10]See Vinay Lal, 'The Perils of History and Historiography. The Case, Puzzling as usual, of India', *Journal of Commonwealth and Postcolonial Studies*, Fall 1995, 3(1), pp. 79–112; and 'The Discourse of History and the Crisis at Ayodhya: Reflections on the Production of Knowledge, Freedom and the Future of India', *Emergence*, 1993–94, (5/6), pp. 4–44; also, 'History's Forgotten Doubles', pp. 83–109 above.

[11]Ayesha Jalal, 'Conjuring Pakistan: History as Official Imagining', *International Journal of Middle East Studies*, 1995, 27, pp. 73–89.

ous South Asian, Left Hegelian versions; and a distinct Baconian concept of scientific rationality brought into public life as the final justification of all the other components.[12] When modern Indians, irrespective of their ideological postures, opted for the Utilitarian—and imperial—concept of the state, they also had to own up European history as more relevant to Indian futures than the unreliable, scrappy accounts of the past in India. They did this so systematically that some thinkers came to feel that India's history had been stolen and that the country was being forced to live on borrowed history.[13]

This emergence and acceptance of the historical self, then, got quickly intertwined with the making and unmaking of Indian pasts and the telescoped presence of European history in these attempts to ensure the reconstruction of India's past along historical lines. This came in two versions. Either India's historical past was made to look like a belated replication of European history or it became, as in the various Left Hegelian doctrines, all of India's past and, hence, a point of departure for all social criticism. (So that in social and political analysis, the categories and the narratives could come from the First World, while the conclusions drawn and the prescriptions offered could apply to the Third World.[14]) All other memories related to the past were pushed out of serious intellectual consideration in modern India and were kept open for the use of rustics, women and children, creative artists, the illiterate, the insane and the superstitious.

The self that emerges from the crucible of history has different features from that of the self that emerges from the crucible of myths, legends and epics. In both cases the self has to cope with memories, but the

[12]Some of these links have been acknowledged by historian Dipesh Chakravarty. Dipesh Chakravarty, 'History as Critique and Critique of History', *Economic and Political Weekly*, 14 September 1991, pp. 2262–8.

[13]For instance, this was Rabindranath Tagore's reading of Indian nationalism. Rabindranath Tagore, *Nationalism* (1917) (reprint, Madras: Macmillan, 1985). Also, Ashis Nandy, *The Illegitimacy of Nationalism: Rabindranath Tagore and the Politics of Self* (New Delhi: Oxford University Press, 1994).

[14]This is not merely a South Asian disease. Any serious Afro-Asian scholar who has read the ethnophobic, crypto-racist histories produced in Europe and North America by some of the most respected figures in contemporary radical thought—from H.G. Wells to E. Hobsbawm—will immediately know what I am saying. In all these works, 'agency', social creativity and transformative politics are monopolized by the northern hemisphere, not to speak of the analytic categories that structure the work. H.G. Wells, *A Short History of the World* (1922) (London: Pelican, 1965); E. Hobsbawm, *Age of Extremes: The Short Twentieth Century, 1914–1991* (New Delhi: Viking, 1995).

historical self configures memories differently from the way the ahistorical self does.

In the first case, memories are available for scrutiny, for tests of reliability and validity. The scrutiny is usually mounted from the vantage ground of what can be called distant, dispassionate objectivity, for such objectivity is supposed to guarantee the truth value of propositions about the past. (The idea of truth used here is that of modern science, not that of the moral philosopher or cultural or 'holistic ecologist' who might leave some scope for nonmaterial truths in a model.[15]). Memories that fail the scrutiny are in effect declared non-memories or anti-memories, and either banished from history or studied clinically as rumours or stereotypes, or handed over as fantasies to artists and writers for creative use. If some individuals and groups nevertheless insist on retaining or returning to these memories *in* history, they can do so, but others, if spiteful, would call such history pseudo-history, or, if they are generous, myths or fantasies. There *are* persons or communities in the modern world which insist on living with 'unreliable' and 'invalid' history.[16] These individuals and communities usually end up as case histories for psychiatrists and researchers in social pathology.

But there are other persons and groups outside modernity who live with selves that originate and are grounded in ahistorical modes of constructing the past—in legends, myths and epics. None of these can be particularly easily fitted into the clinical format, even though some first-generation, over-enthusiastic psychoanalysts did try to do so at one time. Sometimes, when return to childhood and unencumbered, creative innocence become an important cultural theme (as in the late 1960s and early 1970s), such persons and groups can even be seen as paragons of normality, creativity and transcendental awareness. The epithets 'primitive' and 'ahistorical' may then begin to carry an ambivalent load in historical societies where they may occasionally provide a respite from the psychological closure the historical consciousness has come to represent.[17] Otherwise, the effort is usually to separate the historical self

---

[15]For a brief introduction to the 'historical' battle over the disputed mosque in Ayodhya, in which both sides claim scientized history to be their ally, see Lal, 'The Discourse of History'; also, 'History's Forgotten Doubles,' pp. 83–109 above.

[16]I use these two terms in the sense in which mathematical statisticians use them when assessing new psychological, political, or social measures such as attitude scales or personality inventories.

[17]Post-modernism, whatever may be its other merits or demerits, can be read as the formalization of this awareness and, thus, as a successful attempt to locate the world capital of dissent in the West by appropriating the available nonwestern critiques of the West.

from its ahistorical contexts. (The ongoing debate on the personality and biography of Jesus Christ in western Christendom, for instance, parallels, similar efforts that have been going on since the middle of the nineteenth century in the case of Hindu gods and goddesses.)[18]

Configuring the historically-grounded self in an ahistorical society, however, acquires a second-order complexity where such a self does not get the 'normal' consensual validation from either the community or the larger culture. Such a self has to work on limited or partial endorsement from the scraps of historical selves constructed in the modern sector, often by psychologically uprooted, atomized individuals and small sect-like professional groups. History in India is basically a modest enterprise with a limited reach; it is not the entire constructed past. It has to compete with other such constructions and can either triumph over them or lose out to them.[19]

Uprooting and Its Compensations

The concepts of nation-state and history, when wedded to the urban–industrial vision and conventional development, is a potent concoction. It becomes a complex of ideas particularly appealing to persons and groups experiencing uprooting, breakdown of communities, and inner exile. Even more dangerous, the combination is presumed to work better when it operates on the assumption of a cultural *tabula rasa*, authenticates forms of cultural intervention that ensure the decline of communities, and encourages the emergence of fully autonomous, unencumbered individuals. It is this combination that is turning India and its neighbouring countries—like other old cultures trying to redress their record of victimization by catching up with the developed societies, according to dominant contemporary ideas of success—into a region of the territorially or psychologically uprooted. The ideas of nation-state and history in this respect have begun to play new, more important political–psychological roles in South Asia.

There is nothing spectacularly new in the situation. Most old-societies-turned-young-nation-states learn to live in a world dominated by the psychology and culture of exile. For some, the twentieth century has been

---

[18]Ashis Nandy, 'A Report on the Present State of Health of the Gods and Goddesses in South Asia', in *Time Warps: The Insistent Politics of Silent and Evasive Pasts* (Delhi: Permanent Black, 2001), pp. 129–56.

[19]Ibid. There are examples of this clash also in Ashis Nandy, *The Intimate Enemy: Loss and Recovery of Self Under Colonialism* (New Delhi: Oxford University Press, 1983).

a century of refugees.[20] Others like Hannah Arendt have identified refugees as virtually a new species of human being who have come to symbolize the distinctive violence of our times. Refugees as contemporary symbols, however, proclaim something more than a pathology of the global nation-state system. They also represent a state of mind, a form of psychosocial displacement that has become endemic to modernizing societies. One does not even have to cross national frontiers to become a refugee; one can choose to be seduced by the 'pull' of self-induced displacement rather than be 'pushed' by an oppressive or violent system at home.[21] It is this changed status of territoriality in human life that explains why, in immigrant societies like the United States, the metaphor of exile is now jaded. Some have already begun to argue that human beings need not have a 'home' as it has been traditionally understood in large parts of the world, that the idea itself is a red herring.[22] While the idea of exile begins to appear trite in intellectual circles, an increasingly large proportion of the world is getting reconciled to living with a labile sense of self. Exile no longer seems a pathology or an affliction. Displacement and the psychology of exile are in; cultural continuities and settled communities are out; there is a touch of *ennui* about them.

In societies such as China and India, which many insiders and outsiders were accustomed to view as relatively stable and unchanging, adjustment to the culture of exile can be particularly disorienting and unnerving. In India, where the metaphor of 'eternal India' continues to be an important ingredient of the public lexicon, the spread of the culture of uprootedness has produced new cultural dislocations, anxieties and social tensions. Yet, many aspects of uprooting in South Asia remain invisible. We have not yet noticed, for instance, that the psychology and culture of displacement, as opposed to its sociology or politics, is becoming a serious presence in the South Asian landscape and elements

[20]Nicholas Xenos, 'Refugees: The Modern Political Condition', *Alternatives*, 1993, 18, pp. 419–30.

[21]This is not to estimate the push but to recognize that voluntary emigration is only another kind of uprooting, and the difference between it and enforced emigration would not have been pronounced in systems suffering from chronic discrimination, exploitation and the early rigours of development. The last-named ailment is painful to acknowledge, though it has been known and feared since the days when it did not have its present meaning. See Karl Polanyi, *The Great Transformation* (London: Victor Gollancz, 1945).

[22]Aviezer Tucker, 'In Search of Home', *Journal of Applied Philosophy*, 11(2), pp. 181–7. 'Our actual home,' Tucker argues, 'is the result of our efforts to reach our ideal home, departing from our natural home ... we may change our homes often throughout life, with changes in tastes, circumstances, and emotions ...' (pp. 181, 183).

of South Asian public life are readjusting to the culture of the uprooted. However, politicians everywhere are a superbly alert lot. They never wait for social scientists or psychologists to supply analysis that would guide action. The South Asian politicians have grasped the power and reach of the culture of psychological lability. They have sensed that, even though it is still the culture of a minority, it already offers immense political opportunities, especially in the matter of large-scale mobilization. South Asian politicians, therefore, have refashioned their platforms and campaigns to cater to the passions of the banished and the uprooted.

Paradoxically, this has given the metaphor of continuity a new status in Indian public life—it has become a potent myth. This is precisely because a large proportion of Indians feel uprooted geographically, culturally, and psychologically and, while living with a culture of flux, which they have accepted as the ruling culture, want small, symbolic areas of turbulence-free life of predictability and continuity. These Indians demand psychological security and cultural constancy of a kind that not even a highly stable, isolated society can provide. These demands are honed by the growing evidence of flux all around. In this respect, what the great Partition riots in 1946–8 could not do, despite uprooting more than sixteen million people, massive urbanization and industrialization backed by development have managed to do. Many communities in India are now predominantly, and in some cases entirely, communities of the displaced. Estimates are that one-third of the entire tribal population of India, consisting of at least 200 different tribes, has been displaced, about half of them by development.[23] That is, some tribes are now entirely tribes of refugees, uprooted from their natural habitats, traditional vocations, lifestyles and life-support systems. Their deculturation and disintegration as communities is virtually complete.

Some other communities have been dramatically pushed into urban-industrial life because of the loss or unsustainability of their traditional vocations, social discrimination or exploitation. When India became independent, its urban population was less than 70 million. Today, though the population of urban Indians has risen by only 5 per cent, from 20 to about 25 per cent, in absolute terms it is already around 250 million, larger than all except three countries in the world. We do not have corresponding figures for Indians who have moved from one language area to another, from rural communities to urban slums, from

[23]Smitu Kothari, 'Theorising Culture, Nature and Democracy in India' (Delhi: Lokayan, 1993), mimeo.

rooted vocations to contractual jobs. Many of these first-generation urban Indians show the characteristic psychology of the uprooted and they too have begun to bend the Indian political culture to their needs. Many communities of traditional artisans, especially the Muslims and the Dalits among them, fall into this category. Also, as agriculture gets industrialized, some sections of landless labourers and tenant-farmers, unable to sustain themselves in the villages, are migrating to the cities and assembling there in slums, which are becoming the down-market depots of the culture of exile.

In recent decades, the growing environment-induced displacement in the region has handsomely contributed to the process. Prosperity through large-scale cultivation of cash crops like sugar-cane, and the growing industrialization of agriculture itself has led to demands for mega-dams, diversion or monopolization of water resources, deforestation, drought or rising salinity in many parts of the region. These in turn have led to a deepening sense of dislocation and disjunction with the past. Thus, the Farakka barrage and the destruction of the Ganga has not only led to uprooting and emigration from southwest Bangladesh to India, but also from Bihar and, to a lesser extent, West Bengal to other parts of India.[24]

This is, however, an age of exile in more than one sense. Not only have many communities that looked settled till recently experienced colossal dislocation through migration, war, unbridled urbanization, and mega-development, a large part of the world is now inhabited by people who have experienced or carry within themselves memories of uprooting. Even when we talk nowadays of a global order dominated by one superpower, that power represents, among other things, the culture of the immigrants, the displaced, the decultured and/or recultured. This power, which also dominates the global cultural order, upholds public values that can survive in a society of uprooted. Few will disagree that America *is* primarily a culture of the uprooted. But fewer will admit that it is a culture that must deny that it is atypical. For America sees itself as a model for the rest of the world—as a haven where the poor, the powerless and the discarded of other lands have come and remade their lives voluntarily and produced a lifestyle that now makes transcultural sense. This denial is continuously endorsed by the ruling élite of the southern

[24]For example, Ashok Swain, *The Environmental Trap: The Ganges Diversion, Bangladeshi Migration and Conflicts in India* (Uppsala: Department of Peace and Conflict Research, Uppsala University, 1996), Report 41.

world, constantly talking of catching up with the United States in the distant future.

That self-confident culture of exile now seeks to remake the world in its own image. In fact, the entire post-World War II world and the second half of the twentieth century can be read as an unfolding of the politics of that effort, though the celebration of the effort had begun before the effort had, in the inter-war years. This is not a wholesale criticism of the culture of the uprooted. It is an acknowledgement that, while some of this century's greatest creative achievements might have come from deculturation and the breakdown of communities, some of the greatest pathologies of our times, too, can be traced to the sense of exile and loneliness that has haunted the modern individual. The ambience of the Weimar Republic and the cultural citadels of Europe—Paris, Vienna and London—in the inter-war years, the celebration of loneliness, exile, uncertainty and liminality in lifestyles, literature, the fine arts and cinema—all these did contribute to the closure of the European mind in the 1930s. To speak in terms of extremes, Pablo Picasso (1881–1973) and Albert Camus (1913–60) are the other side of the same cultural process that produced European fascism.

The self that these experiences spawn has a few specific features. In its more integrative form, it takes the shape of what Robert J. Lifton calls the protean personality.[25] There is a certain flexibility and adaptability about it and it seems particularly suited to a situation of flux. In its more problematic form, it tends to underwrite many of the pathologies that have been markers of the twentieth century. It is part of the same story that, while the over-stretched modern self offers a wide range of choices as far as self-construction and self-expression go, it cannot adequately protect self-consistency and self-continuity. That consistency and continuity have to be sought through specialist options—psychotherapy, movements for religious or spiritual self discovery, millenialism in politics and, above all, ethno-religious chauvinism and nationalism.

India has chosen to confront its overstretched modernity mainly through ethnic chauvinism and ultra-nationalism. Few recognize the promise of psychological security and 'therapeutic' solace that funda-mentalism and ethnic conflicts offer in modernizing India. Social and political violence can sometimes bind a fractured self within. Those

[25]Robert J. Lifton, *The Protean Self: Human Resilience in an Age of Fragmentation* (New York: Basic, 1993). Lifton does take into account the backlogs—the broken connection—of the protean self but, on the whole, he seems reconciled to this new psychodynamics of self.

living with a dislocated cultural self-definition, precariously perched on a labile sense of the self can, for that very reason, continually seek a national, religious or ethnic community to restore a sense of cultural—and through it, personal—continuity.[26] They may not be open to serious political appeals or to deep analysis of public life, but they are always open to populist slogans and demagoguery, especially of the type that promises new brands of easy pseudo-solidarity, as Hannah Arendt used to describe it. In open societies, based on competitive party systems, politicians seeking to mobilize massified sections of citizens for electoral purposes through centralized communication machines, quickly identify these needs and deploy them in innovative ways.[27]

Not surprisingly, South Asian slums, like their South American and East Asian counterparts, are becoming the ultimate targets of mobilization by every kind of extremist grouping—from ethnic chauvinists to crime syndicates that, like the *cosa nostra*, promise the individual a community and a chance of escape from loneliness and massification. The 'anti-social elements', of whom political analysts and journalists in South Asia talk incessantly as the main actors in caste, ethnic or communal violence, are the fringe of a larger social sector nearer home that the middle classes in the region would like to forget.

The clearest example of this came when the Babri Masjid was demolished. The movement leading up to the event—the biggest of its kind since Independence—had received its most active support from middle-class populations in small towns and cities; it now turned out that a majority in the demolition-squad also came from provincial backgrounds.

History was made that day, but not by metropolitan Indian which was relegated to the level of captive bystanders, released afterwards to deal with the repercussions of the event through either post-facto analysis or communal rioting. Provincial India had upstaged it, and in doing so had only given a small demonstration of its potential.

For, apart from demolishing the Babri Masjid and so peremptorily revising the national agenda, it was also ... bringing forth a new kind of sensibility:

[26]Not only in India, but in Pakistan and Bangladesh too, a high proportion of the leaders of the ultra-nationalist, ethnic chauvinist and fundamentalist groups have a background of uprooting. This is consistent with the emergence of the South Asian diaspora as one of the main sources of support for communal and ethnic chauvinism in recent decades. Strange though this may sound, the diasporic communities are becoming the psychological and cultural counterparts of slums in metropolitan India.

[27]Ashis Nandy, Shikha Trivedy, Shail Mayaram and Achyut Yagnik, *Creating a Nationality: The Ramjanmabhumi Movement and Fear of the Self* (New Delhi: Oxford University Press, 1995).

one that could combine in itself a taste for strident politics, violent films, ostentatious architecture, lewd music, rumour-mongering newspapers and overcooked food.

... From all accounts, Indian small towns and cities had shed their earlier sleepy, half-apologetic air. ...[28]

These newly self-assertive citizens are generally susceptible to the appeals of various forms of nationalism that depend on centralized, mass-media-based communications and mobilizational strategies. India may not be a mass society, but even the process of massification has released new demands and created spaces for ideologies that promise to fill the void that breakdown of communities and 'primordialities' has created. These promises are based on packaged forms of faiths that can serve both as substitutes for faiths seemingly unable to survive in their earlier form under globalized lifestyles, and as political ideologies particularly suited to middle-class mobilization. In both incarnations, the ideologies permit a certain degree of channelization of what would otherwise be free-floating violence constantly seeking new targets.

But apart from its close links with the growing culture of violence, uprooting and exile are associated with a number of personality traits that have been much adored in the literature and folklore of development: greater individual initiative, entrepreneurship and competitiveness. Immigrants are comparatively more pushy, risk-taking and often less burdened by a harsh, repressive conscience and shared cultural norms in their professional and business deals.[29] The refugees created in the aftermath of the Partition, in western India, on whom there are some scrappy data, are more aggressive within the family and outside and their

---

[28]Pankaj Mishra, *Butter Chicken in Ludhiana* (New Delhi: Penguin, 1995), p. 11. The 'earlier, sleepy, half-apologetic air' probably came from the wide consensus that these towns mediated between the rural and the urban, whereas they have now become the phalanx of metropolitan India, reaching into the heart of the countryside and sometimes re-entering metropolitan India as a transmogrified version of its own agenda for the rest of the country. A fascinating invocation of the culture of this class is in Gautam Bhatia, *Punjabi Baroque* (New Delhi: Penguin, 1995), which reminds the reader of Stuart Hall's recent comment: 'We always knew that the dismantling of the colonial paradigm would release strange demons from the deep, and that these monsters might come trailing all sorts of subterranean material.' Stuart Hall, 'When was "the Post-Colonial"? Thinking at the Limit', in Iain Chambers and Lidia Curti (ed.), *The Post-Colonial Question: Common Skies, Divided Horizons* (New York: Routledge, 1996), pp. 242–60; see p. 259.

[29]They are the kinds of people described in that underrated and forgotten book, Stephen Keller, *Uprooting and Social Change: The Role of Refugees in Development* (Delhi: Manohar, 1975).

trust in the interpersonal world around them is low.[30] This aggressiveness and distrust acquire a dangerous edge because the refugees also usually have a stronger sense of invulnerability.[31] One of the unnoticed findings of the once-popular studies of achievement motive as the engine of economic growth were the links between spatial mobility, uprooting and higher levels of achievement motivation.[32] Indeed, to complete the picture of the contemporary ideal of the achieving person, David McClelland did invoke the image of Hermes in the *Homeric Hymn to Hermes*, the Hellenic god who started travelling from the day he was born.

Hermes presumably had a place to come back to, and that myth of a place to return must have been for the displaced a living reality for centuries. In contemporary times, the chances are that such an idea of return, or of a place to return, has primarily a mythic status and is available mainly as a consumable fantasy. Vladimir Nabokov's Russia and Salman Rushdie's India are obvious examples.

The Myth of Return

The basic formulation in this essay can now be further sharpened. South Asia is linked to the global order not merely through its modern political self but, more specifically, through historicized readings of its past and the traumata of uprooting. Both readings and the traumata seek in the ideology of the state and in various forms of nationalism floating around in the market, greater psychological security, stability, and symbolic redress of cultural defeat.

However, that formulation does not say much about how the modern political self in India confronts the panoply of other selves in India, or about the unequal contest among them to shape India's political culture and the nature of transformative politics in the region. This brings us

---

[30]Ibid.

[31]Ibid. Some South Asian readers may remember how an archetypal, new hero in Indian popular cinema stormed into the public consciousness in the 1970s with exactly this combination of traits. He operated at the margins of law, sometimes outside it, but always with a tinge of nostalgia for the earlier, soft, androgynous hero that had dominated the screen for nearly fifty years. See 'Introduction: The Popular Cinema as the Slum's Eye View of Indian Politics', in Ashis Nandy (ed.), *The Secret Politics of Our Desires: Innocence, Culpability and Popular Cinema* (London: Zed Press and New Delhi: Oxford University Press, 1998), pp. 1–18.

[32]David C. McClelland, *The Achieving Society* (Princeton: Van Nostrand, 1961). Everett E. Hagen's attempts to trace economic growth to 'displaced élites' and their psychological state of 'retreatism' can also be read as an early celebration of the culture of the uprooted as the source of a modern political economy. Everett E. Hagen, *On the Theory of Social Change* (Homewood, Ill.: Dorsey, 1962).

back to the issue of a political self that is primarily in dialogue with itself because that dialogue includes a dialogue with the world. True, that conversation with self can be defensive, for it is a conversation partly with those who have been defined either as being on the other side of a monolithic, granite wall of traditions or as masses of poor, culturally deprived, somewhat obstreperous, trainee citizens. Nonetheless it is conversation; the very fact that it takes place gives it a political status of its own.

Programmatically, that conversation goes on at two planes. On one plane, the aim is to bring these others within the fold of the ideology of the Indian state. On the other, the aim is to set them up as 'proxy-selves', by conversing with whom you stabilize your partly individuated, culturally uprooted self. Without these dialogical experiences, modern India's nineteenth-century political self will be even more in touch with the past of Europe than with its present, even more in touch with Europe's construction of India than with India as most other Indians see it or live it out.

To build a political self outside this model is to build partly outside history, science and sanity; it is to start living partly outside modern India, with those already living there as outcasts. That is a painful choice socially and even psychologically. Such scepticism towards the mainstream culture of élite politics demands a different set of identifications, empathy and forms of psychological mobility. It involves the admission that most Indians for most of the time live in another India, and de-recognizing this forgotten majority, in an open society and in competitive democratic politics, is a sure prescription for political defeat and an even surer indicator of the precariousness of the modern self in India. This is a contradiction built into India's political self which nothing, not even the immense power of globalization and unbridled capitalism, can remove. It has to be worked through the way a psychoanalyst and his or her analysand together work through a case *history* of self by 'flattening' or 'dehistoricizing' history to access levels of consciousness that are non-historical or, as the moderns would have it, pre-historical. (As in all clinical disciplines, history has to be coped with and opened up for intervention by converting diachronicity into synchronicity. Intervention on the basis of a case history is never actually in history, it is always in the present. One never redresses history but only surplus suffering at present.) Clinically, history is not a way of structuring the past; it is a way of opening up the present and the future.[33]

These demands are throwing up different concepts of culture in

---

[33]Nandy, 'History's Forgotten Doubles; pp. 83–109 above.

South Asia and challenging the universality of the modern self grounded in the European Enlightenment, not from a relativistic point of view but by venturing alternative forms of cosmopolitanism and universalism.[34] They seem to challenge the Enlightenment's implicit faith that while there can be many forms of relativism, there can be only one form of universalism. These alternative forms can be destabilizing; they challenge the meaning of life of generations of Indians who, under the colonial dispensation, worked with nineteenth-century European concepts of Indian culture and had a much more romantic and optimistic image of the European enterprise on the world stage.[35] These Indians see the growing demands for the renegotiation of terms between culture and modern selfhood as highly destructive, for they seem to negate the modern social and religious reform movements that started in the 1820s and, thus, the core legitimacy of the modern nation-state and the élite who seem born to it. The fact that there has been some erosion in the cultural self-confidence of the European and North American intellectual élite, and some openness to multiculturalism among them, has further unnerved modern Indians. For that, too, seems to endorse the movement of the peripheralized Indians, unexposed or hostile to the modern self, to the centre of the political stage.

As a result, exactly as the historical self in India is contextualized by the passions and interests of the non-historical modes of construction of the past, the modern self too is buffeted by pre-modern, nonmodern or counter-modern categories and passions. Not merely outside, but also within. This is another stratum of political awareness that shapes modernity fundamentally without being much influenced by it.

In Werner Herzog's movie, *Where the Green Ants Dream*, there is a moving sequence where an old Australian aborigine, who does not speak a word of English, barges into the witness box during a court trial, about to

---

[34] Random examples are Vandana Shiva, *Staying Alive: Women, Ecology and Survival in India* (New Delhi: Kali for Women, 1988); Claude Alvares, *Science, Development and Violence: The Twilight of Modernity* (New Delhi: Oxford University Press, 1992); Frédérique Apffel Marglin and Stephen Marglin (ed.), *Dominating Knowledge: Development, Culture and Resistance* (Oxford: Clarendon Press, 1990) and *Decolonizing Knowledge: From Development to Dialogue* (Oxford: Clarendon Press, 1996); Ramchandra Gandhi, *Sita's Kitchen: A Testimony of Faith and Inquiry* (New Delhi: Penguin, 1992).

[35] Even someone as rooted in his culture as Rabindranath Tagore confessed to such an optimism and the disappointment that followed its betrayal by Europe's death dance in the form of two world wars. Rabindranath Tagore, *The Crisis of Civilization* (Bombay: International Book House, 1941).

decide the land rights of Australian aborigines *vis-à-vis* a uranium mining company. The man begins to deliver a long speech in an incomprehensible language. The shocked judge tells the lawyer fighting the cause of the aborigines that he should restrain his client. The lawyer cannot and when he tries to communicate with the trespasser with the help of other aborigines, even they fail. It then transpires that the man in the witness box is the last surviving member of an extinct tribe and nobody in the world understands him.

This moment in the film can be read in two ways. First, it is a moment that stresses the meaningless survival of an individual who cannot share his thoughts with anyone in the world and has to wait for a lonely death to finalize the extinction of a cultural species and a community. It is also, however, a moment that symbolizes the bankruptcy of the dominant consciousness complicit with the process of extinction, a consciousness which does not even know that it is impoverished by the death of a cultural strain or aware of the brutalization unleashed by that insensitivity. Savagery lies not where the indigenous people once stayed or are staying, nor where the dirty work of colonialism or development is done, Herzog seems to suggest, but at the cultural centres of our ideas of cosmopolitanism and impartial justice.

Herzog, who must have passed through the experiences of German reconstruction, mega-development and the Green movement, underscores these readings by a number of cinematic devices. For instance, he sets the stage by painting a totally polluted environment and pock-marked landscape, bearing man-made scars like the victim of some terrible skin disease. Herzog also makes it clear at the beginning as to who have won the battle of the worlds and who rule the world today. Only ideologically motivated, lonely individuals within the system can now sometimes see through it. To do so, they have to be either someone like the ineffective but well-meaning, innocent hero or someone morally repelled by the ruling culture, such as the eccentric anthropologist living as a recluse outside civilization, and the liberal public-interest lawyer. They are the ones who provide scrappy, moving, but also doomed, resistance or dissent.

This flimsy base of dissent in the personal morality of a few atomized individuals is matched by the loveably arcane, dissenting ideology used by the aborigines protesting uranium mining in their ancestral lands, namely their belief that uranium mining will disturb the dreams of the green ants and thus threaten the survival of the world. Herzog's brilliance ultimately convinces his audience that this belief of the aborigines deserves a future other than the psychoanalyst's couch, that it probably represents a higher-order sanity and rationality and probably a new point of departure for transformative politics. Yet, the overall impression remains one of incommensurability and self-defeating kindness on the one hand, and 'inaudible' dissent on the other.

In Satyajit Ray's *Agantuk* (The Visitor), the same social problem is differently posed and handled. Ray, a newcomer to the world of environmentalism and critiques of development in his last years, seems much less aware of what he is doing politically. *Agantuk* is the story of the 'lost' uncle of a typical urban, middle-class family at Calcutta, whom the family knows mainly as an elusive, professional globetrotter. He briefly returns, uninvited, as a suspicious stranger to his family, to upset the steady, predictable rhythm of middle-class conformism. The uncle, who turns out to be a distinguished anthropologist, has by now become a savage critic of modern civilization and its cultural stratarchies. The dramatic high point of the film comes when the uncle suddenly leaves and the paranoiac family finds out that he was not a crook after the family's wealth, but had actually come to will his property away to the family. The family desperately looks for its benefactor and locates him in a village of Santhals, one of the most systematically victimized communities in India's march towards modernity. The real communication between generations begins when the wife, who was always a little more open to the stranger, joins the Santhals in an uninhibited dance. This time the uncle owns her up because in her attempts to self-transcend, he locates the beginning of self-discovery and a continuation of his own critical self.

There is no devastated landscape or Andre Tarkovsky-like invocation of the terror of soul-killing hyper-urbanity in Ray. The Santhal village, it turns out, is not very far from Calcutta and it survives in poverty, indignity and neglect, but also in simplicity and natural charm. On the other hand, the modern affluence of the urban, middle-class family is not especially conspicuous or consumption-intensive either. To many western and some South Asian viewers Ray's idea of affluence may even look like another less obtrusive version of poverty. There is also a vague, tacit admission in the narrative that the urban middle-class that is being depicted as conformist and myopic is, while increasingly vociferous and dominant, not the whole of India, that the class still constitutes a minority. The divide between the algorithm of urbane bourgeois life and the world of the uncle and his Santhal friends *is* sharp but there is no frontier of incommensurability between the two. When the heroine joins the Santhals in their dance, she is not so much actualizing the dream of her uncle as admitting a previously repressed part of herself. There is certainly no awkwardness about her spontaneity in the rest of the family either.

The community has not been discovered; it has been in some sense restored, even if only symbolically.

In Herzog's film what is a basic incommensurability becomes, thus, a problem of partitioned self in Ray's film. As if Ray, otherwise a fully-formed ideologue of modernity, was admitting that certain possibilities that were open only through the exercise of moral imagination in the case of the Australian aborigines, were open in India through self-excavation and through the ability to work through one's not-so-deep psychological defences. Globalization was not the end of cultures, for as globalization made inroads into the interstices of cultures, so did the politics of cultural self-affirmation and self-exploration.

Exactly as some South Sea Islanders have paid for the blessings of civilization by having syphilis, anthropologist and political activist Fred Chiu suggests, globalized capital has to pay for its expansion by facing the proliferating movements and strains of consciousness—romantic, nasty, utopian, backward-looking, given to excesses, insane. Such affirmation of cultures and identities never restores the past. For the post-globalization affirmation of traditions is different from the reaffirmation of cultures at times when attacks on culture are seen as external, not as attacks insidiously threatening to take over one's household, children and friends and even one's most intimate moments (through standardized textbooks on parent–child relations or by offering consumers a choice of shades and textures in condoms, for instance). This often insecure self-affirmation brings into the world stage a new strain of cultures and identities which lack the easy, less self-aware affirmation of cultures and identities when they are not threatened or when the threats to them are concrete, physical and, to that extent, external. Often the new affirmations bring out or excavate for use traditions and cultures badly contaminated by the principles of dominance and violence that characterize the present global mass culture. The Islam that has come into play in many exiled Islamic communities—among Palestinian refugees, Pakistanis in Bradford in England, Bosnians in Bosnia or outside, or Indians in American campuses—is not the same as the Islam that is a part of everyday life in much of the Islamic world.

The intellectual challenge is to identify the principal characteristics of this reactive affirmation of cultures and identities in South and Southeast Asia in the hope it will also convey something of the common human experience with the politics of cultural self and with the tragedy of lost or stolen memories in other parts of the world.

Terrorism—Indian Style: The Birth of a Political Issue in a Populist Democracy

The war that the United States declared on terrorism in September 2001 was not its first. It had declared such a war in the middle of the 1970s, too, and it should be instructive to have a look at that earlier experience. In a book written towards the end of the 1980s, *Best Laid Plans: The Inside Story of America's War Against Terrorism*, David C. Martin and John Walcott adduced ample evidence to show that, despite all the technological and professional prowess brought to it, the first war against terrorism had been an unmitigated failure.[1]

Has the situation changed since or is the track record of the world's most powerful state, committed to the elimination of political terrorism globally, an exception? Data suggest that the situation has not changed drastically nor has the experience of other nations fighting terrorism for the last five decades been any better. None has succeeded in eliminating terrorism through superior force of arms, efficient intelligence or professional anti-terrorist measures. Great Britain and Israel, though they have sometimes advised other countries on how to fight terrorism, have in their own backyards fought terrorism for decades as ardently and as ineffectively as the United States.[2] Towards the end of

---

[1]David C. Martin and John Walcott, *Best Laid Plans: The Inside Story of America's War Against Terrorism* (New York: Harper and Row, 1988).

[2]India now seems to have become a major target of terrorism and one political scientist has raised the same issue in a different guise. Responding to the argument that the Government of India should not have released terrorists in exchange for hostages, he says: 'Critics are dangerously trivializing the government's difficult choice ... those who take a hard stand (e.g. the U.S. and Israel) have not managed to eliminate terrorism. Have the 37

the first war on terrorism, Brian M. Jenkins of the Rand Corporation asked, 'Will terrorism continue?,' and went on to answer unreservedly 'Yes.'[3]

A look at the global figures show that, during the first war, the number of terrorist acts rose gradually but consistently, from 572 in 1975 to 3089 in 1987—hardly a tribute to the forces of counter-terrorism.[4] In the 1990s, according to the Department of State of the United States of America, the total number of international terrorist attacks seemed to be in decline and usually ranged between 300 and 450, but that is because the Department used a narrower range of definitions.[5] In India itself, the incidence of terrorism in only the state of Kashmir ranged between 1,243 and 5,793 in the 1990s.[6] Reliable recent data are not available, but one knows that while terrorism might have declined dramatically in Punjab, Kashmir has more than compensated for it. There is little chance that India will deviate from the global pattern. Indeed, it seems keen to prove correct the prediction of Marvin J. Cetron and Owen Davis that 'Tomorrow's most dangerous terrorists will be motivated not by political ideology, but by fierce ethnic and religious hatreds. Their goal will be … the utter destruction of their chosen enemies.'[7] At the same time, 'the traditional brand of terrorism—seeking political power through the violent intimidation of noncombatants—will continue to grow at the global rate of about 15 per cent per year.'[8]

Perhaps both the management of terrorism and the current thinking on it need to be revised. It is against this background that one must view the emergence of terrorism as a live issue in Indian politics.

U.S. missiles sent to punish Osama bin Laden ended his thirst for violence? Have the Israelis, for all their toughness in these situations, not continued to wake up to outrage after outrage? We in India have been battering the militants in Kashmir and in other theatres (e.g. Punjab and the Northeast) for the past decades: did that stop the hijackers of IC 814 [the Indian airlines flight highjacked in December 1999]?' Kanti Bajpai, 'Sense in Times of Senseless Violence', *The Times of India*, 2 January 2000.

[3]B.M. Jenkins, 'The Future Course of International Terrorism', in Paul Wilkinson and A.M. Stewart (ed.), *Contemporary Research on Terrorism* (Aberdeen: Aberdeen University Press, 1987), see pp. 581–9; see p. 581.

[4]K.F. Rustomji, 'Coarsening of Sensibilities', *The Tribune*, 23 February 1989.

[5]U.S. Department of State, 'Patterns of Global Terrorism, 1995, 1996 and 1997', Consult for details http://www.globalterrorism.com.

[6]Ved Marwah, *Uncivil Wars: Pathology of Terrorism in India* (New Delhi: Harper Collins, 1995), p. 367.

[7]Marvin J. Cetron and Owen Davis, 'The Future Face of Terrorism', *The Futurist*, November–December 1994, pp. 10–15; see p. 10.

[8]Ibid.

I

Though it made its first hesitant appearance in colonial India in the 1860s, the idea of terrorism entered Indian public life in a significant way only in the aftermath of the first partition of the province of Bengal in 1905. According to some, Brahmabandhav Upadhyay (1861–1907)—Vedantist, Catholic theologian, educationist, and editor of the nationalist publication, *Sandhya*—was the first to make a theoretical case for terror as a possible political weapon in the anti-imperialist struggle. By 1910, urban Bengal, Maharashtra, and Punjab had spawned a number of groups which could qualify as terroristic. They declined in importance only after Mohandas Karamchand Gandhi established his hegemony in Indian politics in the 1920s.

From the beginning, two kinds of public debate took place around the issue. The first consisted of angry exchanges on whether those using terror were or were not actually freedom fighters or revolutionaries, being stigmatized by the imperial regime as terrorists. The second concerned the extent to which some sanction for political terror existed in the traditional Indian way of life. Among the persons passionately involved in the second debate were Gandhi and Rabindranath Tagore.

Neither of the two debates was ever to die down. I mention them here only to warn the reader that the expression 'terrorism' is not unproblematic in India. I use it here only descriptively, without prejudging the final status of the 'terrorists'—from freedom fighters of the Anushilan and Jugantar Samitis in colonial India to Laldenga, Maqbool Bhat and Subhas Ghising—in a future India.[9]

Since Independence, India has experienced five major terrorist movements. Of these, two have been endured by ordinary Indians in complete, and the third in partial political silence. In these three, the Nagas, the Mizos, and lower-middle class, urban, Bengali youth in the Naxalite movement paid dearly for the luxury of defying the Indian state. Despite that they were not able to crucially influence the Indian political scene. Occasional efforts *were* made to bring the issues raised by such rebellions within the mainstream of politics by outsiders. Jayaprakash Narain, for instance, made one such effort in the case of the restive North-East in the 1950s and 1960s. But, for various reasons, all-India electoral politics and the party system did not respond to these efforts. No one could exploit the issue of terrorism to win an election or stop someone

[9]For a systematic general discussion of this issue, see Walter Lacqueur, *The Age of Terrorism* (Boston: Little, Brown, 1987).

else from winning one; the issue remained at the periphery of Indian politics. Terrorism may be the price one pays for democracy, as some experts believe,[10] but Indians apparently worked for a while with a culture of democracy that allowed them to keep terrorism and counter-terrorism out of mainstream politics.

In other words, till recently, the vast majority of Indian citizens did not live with terrorism as an everyday political reality nor did it influence their political choices. Thanks to the limited geographical reach of terrorism and the tradition of self-censorship practised by the national media, especially the newspapers, the majority lived as if terrorism had to do with only the peripheral Indians and the upper echelons of political decision-makers at Delhi. When Nandita Haksar and Luingam Luithuli in their *Nagaland File* in 1984 wrote of the continuous and systematic subversion of human rights in Nagaland during the counter-insurgency operations there, there was pained silence in the ruling circles of India, among political commentators, and in the middle-class culture of Indian politics.[11] There was hardly any serious review or public discussion of the book. No one, except probably for Jayaprakash Narain again, took political terrorism seriously.

It was unimaginable in 1984 that the almost perfectly integrated Sikhs—who, like some other minorities in the country such as the Jains and Parsees, never thought of themselves as a minority and were proud to call themselves India's number one community—and the dreamy-eyed, non-martial Kashmiris, 'mired' in their *Sufiana*, would one day, make terror central to Indian politics.

The new salience of terrorism has come at a time when a sizeable section of the Indian populace has begun to think of India primarily as a nation-state and secondarily as a civilization with its own political language and values. This 'coincidence' has ensured the import of concepts, styles of management, and technologies of counter-terrorism from countries which Indians see as 'advanced', democratic polities. Many of these concepts, styles, and techniques, generated in culturally very different situations, have gradually become popular and even unassailable in modern India.[12]

[10]'Terrorism Democracy's Child' (Interview with Joseph Goldberg), *The Statesman*, 4 September 1987.

[11]Nandita Haksar and Luingam Luithuli, *Nagaland File: Question of Human Rights* (New Delhi: Lancer, 1984).

[12]Ashis Nandy, 'The Discreet Charms of Indian Terrorism', in *The Savage Freud and Other Essays on Possible and Retrievable Selves* (New Delhi: Oxford University Press, 1995), pp. 1–31.

In this diffusion of knowledge, the mass media have played an important role. The media have sold these concepts, styles and technologies as universal, gradually standardizing the diverse Indian responses to and interpretations of terrorism.[13] Partly as a result, there is now a widespread, articulate, political demand in India that policy-makers battle terrorism uncompromisingly and visibly, according to the received wisdom about counter-terrorism and statecraft. Such battles may or may not be within the bounds of law and common norms of civility—but a very sizeable section of urban, middle class, newspaper-reading Indians no longer cares.[14] This section is now numbed not only by the spread of various forms of political crimes and venality, but also by the lure of dominant, romantic ideas of political realism. These ideas, however well-packaged and acculturated, disrupts the 'natural' linkage between a society and its politics. The resulting gap may sometimes be immensely creative and generate spaces where politics ceases to mirror the society, acquires autonomy, and opens up the possibility for new experiments in reorganizing aspects of the society. However, in India the gap has now begun to narrow the range of available political options in relation to terrorism.

In this context I shall ask—merely ask—if India, which has faced problems of politically-less-conspicuous terrorism over decades, would

[13]Intimations of this kind are available in a number of examples, such as Raj Chowdhary, 'Tackling Terrorist Tangle', *The Indian Express*, 16 September 1989; and Satyapal Dang, 'How Serious is the Government About Fighting Terrorism?' *The Telegraph*, 16 September 1989. See also Sankar Sen, 'Handling a Hostage Situation', *The Telegraph*, 2 September 1988; 'International Terrorism: Are Only Laws Enough?', Ibid., 8 October 1988; and 'Many Anti-Terrorist Laws, but no United Action', ibid., 10 October 1988. Ajit S. Gopal, 'Computers to Fight Terrorism', *The Times of India*, 28 June 1988; and 'Fighting Terrorism', *Hindustan Times*, 29 December 1989.

Only slightly less predictable are the pathetic attempts to explain the growth of terrorism in India in terms of standard economic and class analysis. See for example Yogendra Bali, 'The Economic Roots of Terrorism', *The Times of India*, 7 September 1989. HT Correspondent, 'Easy Money Lures Teenagers to Terrorism', *Hindustan Times*, 4 September 1989 and 'Easy Money Lures Teenagers to Terrorism', *Hindustan Times*, 4 September 1989.

[14]There has been hardly any reaction to exposés that would have shaken the political community in the country some years earlier. For example, the reader may remember the absence of any reaction to Naveen S. Garewal, 'Evidence Surfaces Against Police: Watery Grave for Punjab Militants', *The Pioneer*, 26 March 1992. Nor has there been any public reaction to accusations, perfunctorily denied by the police, that a police officer killed four relatives of a top terrorist in cold blood. Anikendra Nath Sen, 'Combating Punjab Ultras: Arms Alone are Not the Answer', *The Times of India*, 22 October 1991. This despite respected police officers like Ved Marwah claiming that punishment of guilty security personnel 'has a salutary effect' on their morale and discipline. Balraj Puri, 'Human Rights Key to Kashmir Policy', *The Times of India*, 11 February 1991.

be justified in looking at the problem from a different vantage ground that gives less importance to the available global expertise and understanding of the problem and, instead, seeks to rediscover the cultural and social continuities that contextualize the problem. The rest of the essay can be read as a possible response to such a question.

II

NY [New York] shocked over police torture of boy

—News headline in *The Times of India*, Delhi, 9 May 1985.

Arrested extremist's injuries tell a tale

—News headline in *The Indian Express*, 9 May 1985,
reporting police torture of alleged terrorists at Delhi,
not printed in *The Times of India* of the day.

Publicity to the terrorist is like oxygen, Margaret Thatcher's well-known saying goes. And most experts on terrorism agree.[15] Yet, few are comfortable with the obverse of the formulation—that modern terrorism and counter-terrorism have become consumption items for the media-addicted, excitement-starved middle classes.[16] Even fewer will accept that terrorism can now be advertised, sold and purchased as a political spectacle and as a commodity for television, the newspapers and commercial films. That terrorism, too, may be used as a handy excuse for bad governance or an easy escape for a middle class unwilling to face up to the consequences of its demands for a particular form of statecraft and social delivery system. Publicity for terrorism is also like oxygen to the uprooted and decultured, seeking in the modern state and nationalism new forms of social solidarity and a sense of belonging.

In this sense, the emerging mass culture in India has at last acquired the capacity to sustain modern terrorism. It can now provide, through the 'right' kind of media coverage, the Indian middle classes with a delectable *frisson* which thrills but does not kill, especially at a distance

[15]See Nawaz B. Mody, 'Terrorism and the Media', in S.C. Tiwari (ed.), *Terrorism in India* (New Delhi: South Asian Publications, 1990), pp. 176–89. See also Rajiv A. Kapur, 'Fighting the Terrorist Design: What the Press Can Do?', *The Indian Express*, 15 August 1987. Jenkins, in 'The Future Course of International Terrorism', identifies the growth of the media as one of the key factors in international terrorism.

[16]See for example Michael J. O'Neill, *Terrorist Spectaculars: Should TV Coverage be Curbed* (New York: Priority Press, 1986); also Ved Marwah, 'Hostages of Terrorism', *Hindustan Times*, 12 December 1991.

from the places where the action is. That is why when an upright retired
police chief raises his voice against this emerging political culture, it
falls flat on the newspaper-reading public:

When I hear retired bureaucrats pleading for hard measures to save Kashmir, in
fact murderous assault on our own people, I am reminded of that valiant group
of men whose youthful exploits brought honour to us, and I wonder what has
happened that has changed our approach so much ...

In 1965, I saw the massive support the Kashmiris gave to the Indian Army
in driving out the infiltrators. Have we forgotten that so quickly because of the
communal propaganda that has raged in this land? Have we also forgotten
how the Kashmiris stood to a man behind the Indian Army in 1971? ...

I have seen copies of the holy Koran being thrown in the latrines of Srinagar
to cause a riot. But there was no provocative reaction. Bombs were thrown in
temples but the dead were taken away quietly. All these made the Kashmiris—
both Hindus and Muslims—firm in their determination to stay together.[17]

The toughest analyses and the most violent prescriptions for terrorism
in the South Asian democracies—I have in mind mainly India, Pakistan
and Sri Lanka—come not from the states concerned. They come from
statist journalists, their ready clientèle among newspaper-readers and
television viewers, ambitious retired bureaucrats, and from expatriate
South Asian nationalists in the First World. Indeed, the entry of terrorism
as an issue in Indian politics has been accompanied by a steady growth
in the influence of the media, the Indian diaspora in the West, and those
whom sociologist D.L. Sheth calls Resident Non-Indians, Indians feeling
marooned in India, pining for an India that would faithfully duplicate
the developed societies in the North.

Politically, this combination of internal and external 'exiles' has
become particularly potent. They now constitute virtually a separate
ethnic category. Their uprooting from local or regional cultures of India
is accompanied by a search for a modernized pan-Indian consciousness,
and they usually turn out to be ready buyers of the packaged ideology
of state available, at a heavy discount, from the warehouse of ideas of
nineteenth-century Europe. This ideology they then resell to the Indian
middle classes as the latest and most fashionable product in the
international market place. Indian terrorism and counter-terrorism are
now getting caught in this mass culture and the marketable, export-
quality Indian nationalism which goes with it. I mention both terrorism
and counter-terrorism because the standardized mode of dissent from
the pre-packaged ideology of counter-terrorism is often a pre-packaged

[17]K.F. Rustomji, 'A Case for Soul-Searching', *The Indian Express*, 4 November 1991.

ideology of ethnic or national separatism backed by an ideology of political terror. Some years ago, writing on the aborted peace march organized by the Jammu and Kashmir Liberation Front to the India–Pakistan border, Balraj Puri said:

But, above all, the JKLF's abortive march demonstrated the limitations of arms as a deciding factor in shaping the course of events in Kashmir. For the JKLF asserted its strength through what it called a peace march against the might of the Pakistani state. ... Within the valley it re-established its edge over its better armed pro-Pakistan rivals. This proves once again that the battle of minds in Kashmir is as important as the battle of arms.[18]

It is unlikely that Puri's comments were taken seriously by either side; in the culture of terrorism and counter-terrorism, non-violence has to be justified at every step, not violence. As if violence always succeeded.

The result is the appearance of an odd double bind in Indian politics, probably in all South Asian polities. Terrorism frequently speaks the language of religion and ethnicity, but the future political order of the community—for which the terrorism is supposed to create a space—has usually nothing to do with the traditional concept of public life in the community. The vision that motivates terrorist activities in South Asian societies is usually only a pale copy of the idea of the state that motivates the forces of counter-insurgency. No wonder that, after a while, both the larger community and separatist groups come to share a common ideology which can best be described as a subcategory of the presently dominant global mass culture.[19]

When this shared culture of the terrorist and the counter-terrorist becomes all-pervasive, terrorism becomes part of a country's everyday culture of politics. Then the only way out is tiredness with the violence and insecurity on both sides. Till then, the country remains Lebanonized.

These encounters of India's middle classes with organized political terror and the unfolding adventures of the Indian state—all the way

---

[18]Balraj Puri, 'Lessons Offered by JKLF's Abortive March', *The Times of India*, 11 March 1992.

[19]As a consequence, the same symbols of mass culture are shared by contending forces. I am told that a large number of children born to Sri Lankan Tamils have been given the name Rambo after political terror became a staple diet in the country. And at least one noted, retired, Indian police officer once claimed that in Punjab, during the days of militancy, the real ego-ideal of the young Sikh terrorists was not any mythological Sikh hero but the mythopoeticized international terrorist, Carlos. The articles captured by the police from the Punjab terrorists has varied from hideout to hideout, but in most of them the police have found at least one leather jacket.

from Nagaland to Punjab to Kashmir—have helped the Indian middle classes to develop, in recent years, an attractive, home-brewed, hard-state oriented, consensual, 'rational' theory of political terrorism that is directly relevant to the fate of civil society in India. Indian journalists, highly self-conscious representatives of middle-class political opinion and stereotypes, have also found it expedient to swallow this theory. The theory is now a major input into the Indian electoral process and into the culture of Indian politics in general. To the extent it is a by-product of the shared culture of terrorism and counter-terrorism, and shapes the experience of terrorism as it filters through the mass media, the culture of terrorism in India now feeds on itself.

The uncritical acceptance of a hard-state oriented theory of terrorism has created political demands that no state in the world can live up to. For the theory vends the idea of an ideal counter-terrorist state that is actually a mythical state, but goes by the name of one real state or other. Sometimes that ideal is called the United States, sometimes Israel, and sometimes, unbelievably, Great Britain.[20] The myth, like all myths, springs not from empirical data but from deep emotional needs. If some states have done well in economic growth or in building powerful military machines, the argument behind the myth goes, they must also have done well in fighting terrorism.

Such mythification opens up two possibilities. It creates a direct, open demand for forms of expertise and awareness that only the modern Indian can provide. It also helps many to cope with the deep ambiguities arising from the problems of living with a modern nation-state in a deeply traditional, post-colonial society. In such a society, traditions remain strong, but so do the memories of the humiliation and domination by aggressive, 'virile' outsiders.

Modern Indians use this contradiction to set themselves up as a vanguard trying desperately to protect the rest of the society—seen as muddle-headed, effete and irrational—from the hazards of living in a conspiratorial global system of nation-states. After a time, such moderns come to believe this themselves, and begin to depend on a hard-boiled law-and-order approach and on a rather pathetic faith in the coercive power of the state. The expertise that the articulate middle-classes and journalists claim is partly a rationalized version of this ambivalence

---

[20]When, after many years, Israel was recognized by India, there was widespread feeling in India, expressed publicly by the country's defence minister, Sharad Pawar, that the way had been cleared for 'drawing on Israel's successful experience' of curbing terrorism. See Ziaul Haq, 'Israeli Method' (Letter to the Editor), *The Times of India*, 4 March 1992.

towards the rest of the society, and partly a justification of the violence which results from the attempt to live with the self-created myth of the perfect counter-terrorist nation-state. Even something like planned systematic torture can then look to this sector a necessary domain of professional expertise.[21]

When, however, due to some external event, larger sections of the people get infected by the anxieties of the middle classes—as happened when Mrs Indira Gandhi was assassinated in 1984—it becomes a live political issue as well as ideology. Parties and persons are then judged by a large section of the Indian electorate according to rigid, stereotypical thinking about terrorism. This makes it even more difficult to initiate political processes which may appear to compromise not so much the security as the majesty of the Indian state.

In this respect, two elements in what we have called a packaged ideology pose their own distinctive political problems.

The first element is a process which reifies nationalism to separate it from the living Indian. So even the limited creativity of some southern forms of nationalism—a creativity one implicitly acknowledges when one speaks of national liberation movements in Asia or Africa—is lost. What one gets instead is merely a local copy of the standard form of nationalism globally available, the form that Ernest Gellner and others go to town with.[22] This nationalism demands commitment to an abstract idea of the nation and begins to view the real people who constitute the nation as expendable. When Mr Bal Thackeray, the Shiv Sena supremo, declared some years ago that the Kashmiri Muslims, if they desired, could migrate to Pakistan leaving behind Kashmir in India, he was illustrating, rather elegantly, the process I am identifying. It is significant that Thackeray's comment, though widely reported in the Indian newspapers, did not create much of a stir. I like to believe that the comment was dismissed because it was thought to be insane, but I suspect that it was dismissed as the over-statement of an eccentric political maverick who nonetheless had a point.

Underlying Thackeray's proposition is also the assumption—widely shared by urban, western-educated Indians—that these fractious Indians are usually not up to the mark as citizens of a great country. Indeed, there is a widespread belief in this section that the country would collapse as a nation-state but for those who have acquired expertise in modern statecraft and have the right kind of exposure to global institutions. Given

[21]See for instance Sadhna Mohan, 'Break Him', *The Pioneer*, 1 March 1992.
[22]Ernest Gellner, *Nations and Nationalism* (Oxford: Basil Blackwell, 1983).

that the support base of Indian ultra-nationalism is often the quickly expanding middle-class, particularly those sections of it that have experienced the erosion of community ties and cultural uprooting, this image of the irresponsible, quarrelsome Indian usually accompanies deep self-doubts and absence of self-esteem.

For example, the Bharatiya Janata Party (BJP) in India has a large support base among the urban middle class and its leadership also has a good record of resistance to the suspension of civil rights during the Emergency of 1975–7. Yet, once the party moved closer to power in 1989 and faced the problem of terrorism in Kashmir, it did not recommend anyone from its own ranks as a candidate for the Governorship of Kashmir, though its voice mattered at that stage among the decision-makers. The party chose to support the former governor of Delhi, Jagmohan, who, though now a BJP functionary, had once been one of the strongmen of the Emergency, at whose hands the BJP claims to have suffered itself then in Delhi. The argument, presumably, was that Jagmohan knew statecraft and crisis management better than the semi-modern, Hindi-speaking riffraff who constituted much of the BJP leadership.

Such self-abnegation finds expression in other ways, too. Thus, there are daily exhortations in the national newspapers, to the police and other security forces, to be tough and ruthless with the terrorists. The same newspapers also daily print long stories on the corruption, inefficiency, nepotism, greed, and mindless violence of the police. But they usually suspend their scepticism and even censor their own news coverage to promote the faith that, when it came to terrorism, the corruption, inefficiency, bias, greed, and violence of the law-enforcing agencies magically evaporate: As if the main function of the agencies was not the containment of terror but the containment of the anxieties about terrorism that plagued a section of citizens.

The other element in the middle-class folk theory of terrorism is an undying faith in professional counter-terrorism. Soon after two Indian Airlines planes were hijacked in India in 1984, newspapers began to publish a series of stories on anti-terrorist measures in the West, most of them allegedly resounding successes. India's premier national daily even published an article on how the EI Al airline of Israel had turned its planes into flying fortresses, totally protected against terrorists. The paper did not mention what the accountants of EI Al thought of the measures—whether they had found that flying fortresses were a popular mode of travel among the paying public. Other papers published pleas for the import of technology for the detection of liquid bombs and fire arms that evaded standard metal detectors, even without any hard evidence that the hijackers had carried such weapons.[23]

It is an open question whether Rajiv Gandhi's popular image as a person wedded to high technology did not transfer to his image as a prospective fighter against terrorism and contribute to his victory in 1984. Certainly Mr Gandhi himself thought it did; he made the containment of terrorism a major plank in his election manifesto and campaign in 1989, too, this time with less dramatic results.

Such professional counter-terrorist measures have not been especially successful in India, even though the opponents are often less-than-professional, unpredictable youth. This combination underpins another psychological process in Parliament and the press. Total professionalism, perfect intelligence, and technical mastery are attributed to the terrorists, their sponsors and trainers. No scope is left for spontaneous, unorganized, popular upsurge against the state, which gradually becomes violent, organized, and begins to involve foreign support.

The ideas of training and the supply of weapons become crucial factors in such a context, even though the huge majority of instances of terrorist violence in India in recent years have been backed by local technology and indigenous knowhow. Despite all the accusations of arms supply by Pakistan, it is an open secret that a detailed scrutiny of the sophisticated weapons seized at the Golden Temple, Amritsar, after Operation Bluestar in 1984 showed that 90 per cent of the weapons were of Indian origin, mostly stolen or obtained through bribery from the army.[24] Nevertheless, in each case of terrorist action, allegations of a foreign hand have been taken very seriously, not merely by the policy-makers, who understandably have a vested interest in underplaying corruption in the law-enforcing agencies, but also by the newspaper-reading public. At some plane, there are deep doubts in many Indians that simple, rural, unskilled Indians can pull off their terrorist acts without any transfer of technology from dedicated, sophisticated, professional, outside conspirators against the Indian state.

Some other countries in the region have taken this part of the story to its logical conclusion. The Sri Lankan regime in its anti-terrorist campaign began by reposing its faith in modern professionalism as represented by British and Israeli experts and, later on, the Indian army. If outsiders

[23]Nandy, 'The Discreet Charms of Indian Terrorism.'

[24]N.K. Saxena, 'One Aspect of Terrorism in India: Subordination of Law and Order to Politics', in Tiwari (ed.), *Terrorism in India*, pp. 157–62; see. p. 161.

could plan and engineer terrorism, outside expertise had to be mobilized to fight such terrorism successfully. The Sri Lankans never stopped to ask why, if the British, Israeli and Indian expertise was that good, terrorism had not been rooted out from Britain, Israel and India. Britain has been fighting terrorism for eighty years; Israel for forty. The Indian record in this respect might turn out to be a little better for a reason that I shall now briefly touch upon.

III

There is another series of forces operating in Indian politics which bear no relationship to the dominant reading of terrorism in the world or to the dominant culture of the Indian state. They survive—and are tolerated—as part of the Indian concept of unavoidable cultural politics, as a compromise with anti-national forces, or as instances of the political hypocrisy of compromised leaders or the public posturing of misguided, insufficiently patriotic, public figures like V.M. Tarkunde and V.K. Krishna Iyer who lead India's dispersed, noisy, dedicated, but only occasionally effective, human-rights groups.

These processes are sanctioned by a vague awareness that the security apparatus of the state is not an automatic antidote to terrorism. The Indian state might not have learnt its lessons, but the wily Indian politicians have noted that even a small minority like the Nagas, about one-fifth the population of the city of Delhi, engaged the army for more than thirty years. This, despite the wholesale killings, arson, rape and other forms of vandalism by the army and the para-military forces. Roughly the same thing can be said about the Mizos and will almost certainly be said in the future about the Kashmiris.

Implicit in this knowledge is the awareness that politics does not always succeed, but the success rate of politics is better than that of the military might of the state. This is not residual Gandhism in Indian public life, but the persistence of a hard-nosed political judgement. That judgement operates, not with a pure theory of political morality, but with the practical wisdom that if non-violence has not worked in human affairs in most cases, violence has not either. For, 'by definition, terrorism works when the target of terrorism acts in such a manner that it either loses public support for its political position or it lessens its own political capabilities. Terrorists cannot weaken the hated political authority by their own actions.'[25] There is also the corresponding assumption that,

---

[25]N.O. Berry, 'Theories on the Efficacy of Terrorism', in Wilkinson and Stewart (ed.), *Contemporary Research on Terrorism*, pp. 293–306, p. 293.

while war may or may not be another form of diplomacy, terrorism *is* an alternative form of negotiation and the challenge is not to allow a terrorist movement to turn anti-political. For as long as such a movement remains within politics, it can always be won away from its apolitical utopia.[26]

Thus, Mizoram had, as part of a political settlement, a chief minister who was till a few years earlier the head of a rebel army fighting the Indian state. When the insurrection in Mizoram ended with an arms surrender, Indian politicians and newspaper-readers chose to forget the earlier role of chief minister Laldenga. They appeared to accept that internal terrorism was the instrument of the politically weak, and Laldenga's terrorism had died a natural death with his political empowerment.[27]

These two axes—uncritical conformity to a textbook concept of the nation-state or to what I have elsewhere called the universal sociology of statecraft, and an unrecognized, indeed disowned awareness of a latent culture of politics—define how, at any given time, Indians respond to the politics of terrorism.

In their 'less self-confident' days—when they were unsure of the universal rules of managing nation-states and about being able to run the Indian state by adhering strictly to these rules—the Indian élite had better access to the latent co-ordinate and felt less embarrassed to own it up. The textbook concept of the state existed side by side with even some tolerance of other, culturally more rooted concepts of statecraft and even for the idiom of separatism. In the 1950s, for instance, the Dravida Kazgham (DK) and Dravida Munnetra Kazgham (DMK) politicians in Tamil Nadu were such successful separatists that, mainly with the likes of them in mind, Selig Harrison wrote a book virtually predicting the

[26]Perhaps that is why many Indians, despite their rhetoric, have often taken their terrorists less seriously than their blood-curdling public proclamations on terrorism would suggest. In 1993 one admirer of the Bharatiya Janata Party, supposedly committed to a hard state, hijacked an Indian Airline plant at Lucknow and agreed to surrender if the then-leader of the opposition and now prime minister, Atal Behari Vajpayee, appealed to him. Vajpayee did not seem unduly mortified and obliged his admirer with much fanfare. This was not the first such instance. In 1978 two persons owing allegiance to the Indian National Congress, Devender and Bhola Pandey, had hijacked an Indian Airlines plane on its way to Varanasi. Their demand was release of the former prime minister Indira Gandhi, another votary of the hard state, who was then being tried for subverting civil rights in 1975–7. She apparently appreciated the gesture. Both hijackers were subsequently given Congress party tickets and elected to the U.P. State Legislative Assembly.

[27]On terrorism as a strategy of the weak, see Alex Schmid, *Political Terrorism: A Research Guide to Concepts, Theories, Data Bases and Literature* (New Brunswick: Transaction Books, 1983); and Berry, 'Theories on the Efficacy of Terrorism.'

disintegration of India.[28] They rose to the higher echelons of politics from a background which included the burning of the Constitution and the Indian national flag in public. Some of them had even taken part in public demonstrations in which the idols of Rama and Lakshmana were beaten with sandals in the main thoroughfares of Madras. Yet they ended up as pillars of the Indian establishment, voluntarily giving up the secessionist platform. And as if to prove that the Laldengas and the C.N. Annadurais were no exceptions, Farooq Abdullah, who is said to have once gone to the United Nations as part of a Pakistani delegation and also once carried a British passport went on to become another pillar of the Indian establishment. When he was called anti-national by the Congress-I some years ago—this was before the Congress-I began to call all critics of Farooq anti-national—almost the entire opposition and a large section of the Indian press vehemently protested. Farooq Abdullah had 'reformulated' his past; so had the other parliamentarians and most politically articulate Indians who had been his critics earlier.

Yet, if one forgets specific cases and looks at the middle-class folk theory of politics, things were not very different during the early days of Annadurais and the Abdullahs. Even in those days, many analysts saw political dealings with such figures as dangerous compromises with the dignity and power of the Indian state, not as indicators of the political acumen of those running the state machine. The only difference was that few politically articulate Indians then expected the Indian state to work as a 'proper' state; they expected it to make compromises with the various forms of 'primitivism' for its survival.

Second, there is a latent awareness in many of those directly fighting terrorism that state violence has its limits and by itself cannot solve the problem of terrorism. Often this awareness comes out into the open when the person concerned retires or leaves the battlefield for safer and less glorious pastures. Thus, retired police commissioner of Punjab, J. Ribeiro, had during his stint in Punjab kept many of his admirers vainly waiting to see peace return to Punjab through his strong-arm methods.[29]

---

[28]Selig Harrison, *India: The Most Dangerous Decades* (Princeton, NJ: Princeton University Press, 1960).

[29]Chandan Mitra, 'Ribeiro Retires in Uncertain Glory', *The Times of India*, 3 October 1989. There were reportedly 250 important terrorists when Ribeiro took charge; there were roughly 250 when he left. Only when the incorrigible Kuldip Nayar publicly mentioned the unmentionable, did the Indian public partially admit what they already knew—that the terrorist ranks were not thinning because of continuous recruitment in a frustrated and angry community. Kuldip Nayar, 'No Let Up in Terrorists' Recruitment in Punjab', *The Indian Post*, 27 August 1989.

But after his exit from Punjab, the redoubtable officer spoke an altogether different language. Openly claiming that Punjab was not a law-and-order problem, he said,

You cannot win the war against terrorism till you have the people on your side. ... I would have been a happier person while leaving Punjab if police officers, policemen and Government servants had understood this concept and followed it.[30]

People do not feel that we are on their side.[31]

Ved Marwah, who was security advisor to the Governor of Jammu and Kashmir, once openly said in a press conference that the acts of terrorism in Delhi during 1985–8 were the handiwork of the Sikh victims of the November 1984 riots in Delhi, not those of dedicated professional enemies of India. The band of fanatical terrorists striking the city and those who harboured them had been motivated by the riots, Marwah claimed.[32] Ribeiro has even claimed in an interview that terrorism in Kashmir was a direct product of the pathologies in Indian politics.[33]

There is even some awareness in many Indians, who have otherwise swallowed the dominant ideology of the state hook, line and sinker, that terrorism breeds on counter-terrorism and state terrorism breeds on anti-state terrorism. This includes the knowledge that even when terrorism apparently dies down after a long tenure, it does not really do so, for, by that time, large parts of the state machinery, especially the security forces, and even the public sentiment, have become brutalized and terroristic themselves.[34] In the case of Punjab that brutalization is

[30]'I did my bit in Punjab, says Ribero', *Hindustan Times*, 2 October 1989.

[31]'A Good Innings' (Editorial), *Hindustan Times*, 3 October 1989. See also Mitra, 'Ribeiro Returns in Uncertain Glory', and 'Quiet Exit for the "Supercop"', *The Statesman*, 9 October 1989. Mitra's article claims that the state failed to win the battle against terrorism in Punjab, while the article in *The Statesman* claims that Ribeiro at the end of his term had said privately that Punjab's was a political problem and hence needed a political solution.

[32]'We're Still Paying Price for 1984 Riots: Marwah', *The Indian Express*, 2 August 1987.

[33]Julio Ribeiro, Interview in *India Today*, 30 June 1990. To get an idea of how much of a somersault this was for Ribeiro, see Vinod Mehta, 'Sad, but Ribeiro Has to Go', *The Sunday Observer*, 12 July 1987. Mehta, while admitting his admiration for the police chief's calibre and dedication, insisted that 'in no country in the world has terrorism been wiped out by force.'

[34]See Akhil Gautam, 'What Price a Life', *The Indian Post*, 21 August 1989; Avinash Singh, 'Police Brutality on One More Woman', *Hindustan Times*, 19 September 1989; Naveen S. Garewal, 'Police Hit Squads Run Amuck in Punjab', *The Indian Express*, 14 September 1989; Rahul Singh, 'The Brutalization of India', *The Indian Express*, 11 December 1984; Seema Guha, 'In Lanka, Death is Cheap to Come By', *The Times of India*, 16 August 1989; K.P. Sunil, 'The Midnight Massacre', *The Illustrated Weekly of India*, 8 June 1986.

already patent.[35] Under the leadership of police-chief K.P.S. Gill, terrorists in Punjab were officially wiped out, only to be reborn in the incarnation of a new-look Punjab police.

IV

When terrorism enters a society like India, it is at first restrained by existing cultural codes which continue to guide the terrorists, their opponents and their victims.[36] However, with the expansion of the domain of the modern secular state and a national press, both of which share these codes less and less and are increasingly parts of the culture of the global nation-state system, the cultural compact between the three parties involved in terrorism breaks down and all three begin to operate within a more reified world of ruthless zero-sum games. I have hinted elsewhere that introducing the highly modern, highly professional apparatus of anti-terrorism aligned with modern concepts of statecraft in such contexts could sometimes be counter-productive, for they continuously raise the stakes and further rupture the cultural and psychological bonds between terrorists and their targets.[37]

Also, once the issue is politicized enough to be available for electoral use, the Sri Lankan logic of events takes over. Each party or coalition enters the electoral fray promising a tough posture against the terrorists, secretly hoping that, when elected, it would rein in the security apparatus and open a political dialogue. But as time passes, the dialogue becomes more difficult because a political constituency or vote bank gradually builds up for the tougher variety of counter-terrorism among the urban, newspaper-reading public and among the policy élite. In response, the position of the terrorists also hardens, for they see no chance of a political deal with their opponents. Terrorism is a child of democracy in more senses than one. Thus, the Janata Dal regime in India during 1989–90 did maintain touch with terrorist groups in Punjab, through intermediaries and individuals respected by the anti-Establishment Sikhs, and it did try to open up similar lines of communication with the Kashmir freedom fighters. So did the Janata Dal (S) and Congress (I)

[35]For example, Singh, 'Police Brutality on One More Woman'; Sunrita Sen, 'Inhuman Police Torture on Two Punjab Terrorists', *The Telegraph*, 10 September 1989; Akhil Gautam, 'Punjab Cops Turn Terroristic', *The Indian Post*, 23 September 1989; Garewal, 'Police Hit Squads Run Amuck in Punjab'; and 'Evidence Surfaces Against Police'; Ajit Singh Bains, 'State Terrorism in Punjab', *The Indian Express*, 20 July 1992.

[36]Nandy, 'The Discreet Charms of Indian Terrorism.'

[37]Ibid.

regimes subsequently. But all did so secretly and, one might add, apologetically. It means political disaster for any regime if such contacts have official blessings. Formally, the government's posture has to be one of uncompromising toughness.

Thus, organized political parties in India are now caught in the web of their own slogans and practices. They know that there is some chance of coping with terrorism within a political framework, that slogans such as 'no talks with terrorists' or 'no talks with the terrorists unless they surrender or accept the constitution and give up their separatism', when taken literally, serve to disrupt this political process. They may even know in their saner moments that to sell such slogans to the middle classes, through a tamed section of the media, as indicators of ultra-nationalism and as a cure-all for problems of political violence is dangerous, that the slogans then become a mill-stone round the neck of the ruling regime in a populist democracy and push the rebellious outside the mainframe politics. But the parties can do precious little with their awareness, for they also know that their political survival could be threatened if they articulate this awareness in politically tangible ways.

When Paramjit Singh, the failed assassin of Prime Minister Rajiv Gandhi was caught at Rajghat, New Delhi, on 2 October 1986, the birthday of Mohandas Karamchand Gandhi, the newspapers were full of accounts of him as a hard-core, highly motivated, superbly competent terrorist who had spent years being trained and armed in Pakistan and had done 'systematic planning' and shown 'amazing self-discipline'.[38] The regime, too, enthusiastically endorsed these accounts to gain maximum political mileage from the event. It tried to build up Paramjit as a cold-blooded assassin, rather than a hot-headed, confused teenager. And no one seemed unduly perturbed when national newspapers openly reported that he had been tortured in the torture chamber inside Delhi's Red Fort. In fact, some columnists argued that India could not 'afford the luxury of a "soft" state any longer' and that 'it must harden its heart.'[39] No one even allowed a sense of anticlimax to develop when the same newspapers reported in their inside pages in small print that Paramjit was, like many of the Sikh and earlier Naxalite terrorists, only seventeen years old and had spent all his life in Delhi; that he was a riot victim who

[38] For instance, 'Mystery Shrouds Choice of Weapon', *The Sunday Observer*, 5 October 1986.

[39] K.C. Khanna, 'Protecting Precious Lives', *The Times of India*, 7 October 1986. For the more innocent readers I should clarify that the adjective 'precious' used by Khanna refers not to the lives of the ordinary citizens but to the country's political leadership only.

had lost his closest friend, some relatives and their homes in the state-sanctioned anti-Sikh violence in 1984 and had lived with dreams of revenge ever since.[40] One police officer even volunteered the information, when interviewed a few years later, that Paramjit's was primarily a symbolic act because after firing a shot, when no one noticed, he fired a second shot and was then caught. Evidently, the Pakistanis who had trained and armed him did a bad job of both. Though he reportedly gave a number of stories of how he got his pistol, the one that seemed most convincing was that it was a home-made pistol of the kind usually produced and sold at Chandni Chowk, Old Delhi, for the twelve-bore pistol had a range of only twenty feet, not good enough to reach Prime Minister Gandhi from the distance at which Paramjit was hiding on that fateful day.[41] No national newspaper and very few political analysts mentioned in this context that the 1984 riot and, more than that, the denial of justice to the victims of the riot had removed some of the restraints that had operated in Hindu–Sikh relationships traditionally and enlarged the recruitment area for the likes of Paramjit enormously.

It is an indicator of the ways of Indian politics in recent times that, after a high-level probe into the Paramjit Singh episode, the only tangible step taken was to cut the shrubs in which Paramjit hid at Rajghat.

---

[40]According to another report, he was twenty-two when he was arrested in 1986 and was nineteen when he took the decision to assassinate the prime minister. (*The Indian Express*, 15 June 1987). This would have been more believable if it did not make Paramjit's decision pre-date even the army action at the Golden Temple and the anti-Sikh riots of 1984. Yet another account spoke of him as a twenty-five-year-old science graduate from Sangrur, Punjab.

[41]'Right Pistol, Wrong Range', *The Sunday Observer*, 5 October 1986. The discovery of the nature of the pistol did not stop two journalists from describing with some relish the *machan* or wooden support Paramjit had constructed to rest his gun on for accurate shooting. Pankaj Pachauri and Ajay Bose, 'Blunder after Ghastly Blunder', *The Sunday Observer*, 5 October 1986.

PART THREE

Culture, Voice and Development: A Primer for the Unsuspecting

> It took twenty years for two billion people to define themselves as underdeveloped
>
> Ivan Illich
> quoted by A. Escobar from a documentary

> Development, as in Third World Development, is a debauched word, a whore of a word. Its users can't look you in the face. ... It is an empty word which can be filled by any user to conceal any intention, a Trojan horse of a word. It implies that what is done to people by those more powerful than themselves is their fate, their potential, their fault.
>
> Leonard Frank
> in 'The Development Game'

The Meaning of Culture

In the global public discourse of our times, 'culture' has become an amoeba word. It can take any shape and convey any meaning—from high fashion to obscurantism, from entertainment to class status. Even within cultural anthropology, a discipline self-consciously engaged in the scientific study of culture, there are now dozens of meanings of the word 'culture'. Usually however, when the articulate middle classes and the mass media in Third-World societies talk of culture, they have its two predominant meanings in mind. And, however textbookish and cliché-ridden they may sound, any discussion of culture and development must grapple with these meanings. Meanings today are a form of politics, too.

Culture as Resource

The first meaning of culture comes into play when we go to an art exhibition, stage performance or museum, having in mind a concrete, packaged, distinctive, public expression of a community's artistic self. The meaning presumes that this self can be seen, appreciated and studied by both insiders and outsiders, usually as a leisure-time activity but sometimes, as in the case of public performers and art critics, as a profession. When it becomes a profession and when a professional from a developed society begins to take interest in the artistic and cultural resources of an 'underdeveloped' society, it of course no longer remains a purely artistic performance or art criticism; it becomes ethnomusicology, ethnomuseology or expertise in ethnic arts.

In this meaning, culture is first separated from everyday life and viewed as a form of cultivation or entertainment or as a sum of serious expressive forms. It is then reincorporated into everyday life on the basis of a new set of justifications. These justifications may come in various incarnations. In literature, for instance, they can range all the way from the so-called morally or politically elevating role of art to the critical role of art in some mid-Victorian theories of art-as-a-criticism-of-life to the various neo-puritanic theories of socialist realism.

The justifications often go with an organizational structure which sustains culture as a well-demarcated, circumscribed, social system or area of life, somewhat in the manner in which the political system in a society is sustained. There can be politics in every sphere of life—in education, family, sports, and in arts and culture—but there is nevertheless something clearly marked out and identifiable called a political system. In the same way, culture can be everywhere but the moderns refer to something more specific and concrete when they talk of culture or the domain of culture.

Such demarcations almost automatically disjunct critical aspects of culture from the way of life that sustains it. They are predicated on the assumption that the artist as a producer of culture must self-consciously take a social or political stand, for art itself is not *by definition* social criticism or an alternative form of realism. It has to be used as such. Thus, in India during the last hundred and fifty years, influenced by the main currents of modern thought, some of the country's great national leaders and social reformers have tried to reconcile culture and society mainly at this plane, often showing scant sensitivity to the springs of their own creativity and to the long-term relevance of their own works in their culture. They have viewed art as a means of social criticism and political intervention at the crudest of levels.

Thus, the gifted Bengali writer Saratchandra Chattopadhyay (1876–1938), who can be said to have brought up at least three generations of middle-class Indians and taught them how to think about the problems of their society, considered his novel *Pather Dabi* (1926) a good and relevant cultural product because it was a nationalist novel. (The novel is concerned with a slice of the life of a Bengali revolutionary, and clearly mirrors the author's sympathy for the violent anti-imperialist movement against the British in the early twentieth century.) Many of his readers thought so, too, and the British-Indian colonial regime tried to prove both parties right by dutifully banning the book. However, it is possible to argue that the author's less ambitious story *Mahesh* (1934) had a more long-term relevance to India's destiny because the author in the story may have been less self-consciously political but more subversive of the metropolitan culture on which was predicated the civilizational mission of western colonialism in Asia. In *Mahesh*, he is not trying to be a political activist or socially relevant; he is merely trying to give expression to the experienced suffering of a people deprived of their voice. He does so, almost unwittingly, through an analysis of the politics of culture reflected in the futile, anthropomorphic love of a poor Muslim peasant for his cow, which is only technically not sacred for him. If the colonial bureaucracy had been shrewd enough, it would have banned the story rather than the novel, for a culture of politics is usually built on the critical consciousness reflected in stories such as *Mahesh* rather than on the middle-class nationalism preached in novels such as *Pather Dabi*.

I give this example not to make the facile point that an author's evaluation of his own work may go wrong, but to emphasize two aspects of the concept of culture as a resource. First, that culture as a well-thought-out, socially-useful mode of self-expression may sometimes limit cultural criticism and creative intervention in politics and society. Second, that this demand for social usefulness arises from a concept of culture which disjuncts it from life and then reincorporates it into life on the basis of a new set of principles.

Predictably, modern nation-states and modern mass societies usually find this meaning of culture most acceptable. By separating culture from everyday life and concretizing it—and thus allowing the urban-industrial world to turn it into a consumable commodity—this meaning helps bring a culture within the ambit of the modern market, makes it more manipulable from the point of view of the modern state, and depoliticizes the idea of culture (to the extent that while this meaning does not dissuade one from seeing culture as a possible political instrument, it refuses to acknowledge that culture may be a subversive presence in society).

Culture as Lifestyle

The second meaning of culture is less influential. It is borrowed from anthropology and is a recent acquisition of many Asian and African intellectuals. Now, even in anthropology there are a number of important meanings of the word 'culture', as every textbook of cultural anthropology in its first chapter says. However, the meaning that has entered the public lexicon in the southern world (where, according to Fiodor Dostoevsky, the subjects of the anthropologists live) from the world of anthropology (where the anthropologists themselves have to survive) is the one in which culture refers to the organizing principles of a way of life or a tradition of social living.

Anthropologists stress two methodological points as crucial markers of their discipline: that a culture must be described with the help of native or emic categories (that is, those internal to the culture) and that a culture must be assumed to be by-and-large self-justifying. The latter of course is the well-known principle of cultural relativism. Such relativism, to be fair, justifies not so much individual cultural practices as larger cultural designs, though it also tries to give empathetic interpretations of the former and tends to underwrite the belief that cultures can be criticized only from inside.

As it happens, social life is rarely self-consistent; anthropology itself has had a long, colourful colonial connection, and its emphasis on native categories and the principle of cultural relativism have often coexisted with attempts to classify cultures as primitive and modern, simple and complex, ahistorical and historical, little and great, and so on. These attempts usually have a social evolutionist thrust and they do often manage to hierarchize cultures for popular consumption and for social and political engineering.

Even when anthropologists have consciously eschewed such evolutionism—by learning, adopting, using or giving transcultural meaning to the categories of a culture—they have introduced a new brand of expertise into the global scene. This expertise consists of a new bilingualism that seeks to displace the bilingualism of the natives who learn or are forced to operate within the same bicultural space. After an anthropologist has entered a cultural space, the native's bilingualism—usually an offshoot of attempts to grapple with aggressive modernity in an *ad hoc*, pragmatic, and even comical fashion—begins to look less authentically native, even to those revaluing native categories. Over a period of time, the anthropologist's voice may even become the official, audible voice of a culture protesting against all encroachments on it and that voice may marginalize or silence its 'unofficial', 'lowbrow' native versions.

Culture as Resistance

There is, however, a third meaning of culture, even less well-known and influential—culture as simultaneously a form of political resistance and the 'language' in which such resistance is articulated.

From Mohandas Gandhi to Amilcar Cabral, a galaxy of politically sensitive thinkers and activists have given shape to this meaning of culture.[1] Since 1850 or so in South Asia, many have used this meaning of culture unselfconsciously, without being aware of its ideological possibilities. Thus, for instance, the reaffirmation of Indian culture under the colonial dispensation was often at the same time a protest against political domination, a means of challenging the legitimacy of the domination, and a defiance of the language of domination. Examples range all the way from the spontaneous rebellions of the Santhals in East India in the nineteenth century to Gandhian satyagraha in the twentieth, from the anti-colonial struggles of the Khudai Khidmatgars among the Pathans of northwest India to the more recent Chipko movement in Garhwal in northern India.[2]

Today, this meaning of culture is an uncomfortable reminder to the privileged of the Third World that the victims of history in these parts of the globe do not merely carry with them the experience of man-made suffering, that these victims also have a language in which to express their

[1]For instance, M.K. Gandhi, *Hind Swaraj*, in *Collected Works of Mahatma Gandhi* (Delhi: Publications Division, Government of India, 1963), Vol. 4, pp. 81–208; Amilcar Cabral, *Return to the Source* (New York and London: Monthly Review Press, 1973). Among the few contemporary scholars to recognize this politically crucial role of culture are Henry Reynolds, *The Other Side of the Frontier: Aboriginal Resistance to the European Invasion of Australia* (Harmondsworth: Penguin, 1982); Peter Worsley, *The Three Worlds: Culture and World Development* (Chicago: University of Chicago Press, 1984); Gustavo Esteva and Madhu Suri Prakash, *Grassroots Post-Modernism: Remaking the Soil of Cultures* (London: Zed Books, 1998); and Frédérique Apffel-Marglin with Pratec (ed.), *The Spirit of Regeneration: Andean Culture Confronting Western Notions of Development* (London: Zed Books, 1998).

[2]M.K. Gandhi, *Sarvodaya*, ed. Bharatan Kumarappa (Ahmedabad: Navajivan Publishing House, 1954); Dharampal, *Civil Disobedience and Indian Traditions, With Some Early Nineteenth Century Documents* (Varanasi: Sarva Seva Sangh Prakashan, 1971); Khan Abdul Ghaffar Khan, *My Life and Struggle: Autobiography of Badshah Khan* (New Delhi: Hind Pocketbooks, n.d.); Sundarlal Bahuguna, 'People's Response to Ecological Crisis in the Hill Areas', in Jayanta Bandopadhyay et al. (eds), *India's Environment: Crisis and Responses* (Dehradun: Natraj, 1985), pp. 217–26; and Jayanta Bandopadhyay and Vandana Shiva, 'The Chipko Movement: India's Civilizational Response to the Forest Crisis', presented at the U.N. University Conference on 'The Ganga Himalaya Problem, New Paltz, New York, 4–11 April 1986; Tanika Sarkar, 'Jitu Santal's Movement in Malda, 1924–1932: A Study in Tribal Protest', in Ranjit Guha (ed.), *Subaltern Studies IV: Writings on South Asian History and Society* (New Delhi: Oxford University Press, 1985), pp. 136–64.

pain and a theory of domination by which to explain their predicament, and this language and this theory may exclude their self-proclaimed vanguards, protectors and often even their own westernized leaders and well-wishers.

This exclusion is particularly painful to the moderns. One characteristic of the Enlightenment worldview underpinning modernity is the stipulation that all dissent from'modernity, to qualify as worthwhile, must be expressed in a language consistent with modernity, particularly with the demands of historical consciousness, the theory of progress, and scientific rationality. Culture in the third sense rejects this stipulation and the assumption that the future shape of all human consciousness was decided once for all in seventeenth-century Europe.

Culture in the present sense, thus, is not only the language of resistance; it is itself resistance. It is resistance especially to the oppression which comes packaged as a 'historical necessity', often under the names of such worthy causes as scientific history, technological growth, national security, and/or development.[3] In the second part of this essay I shall turn to that part of the story.

Culture, Victimhood and Voice

Every intervention in the world of culture must be located in the matrix defined by these three meanings of culture. Many working with the first two meanings of culture are perplexed by the hostility towards them of those working with the third. Yet, such hostility is inevitable. To those whom culture is a form of resistance, a person who spends his or her entire life patronizing, promoting or studying culture is not *ipso facto* a protector of culture if he or she has no sensitivity to the new forces of vandalism which have been let loose in many societies by unrestrained urban–industrial growth and mega-technology. The patron must prove his or her credentials by being sceptical towards that part of the national and global ideology which is wedded to the urban–industrial vision and is implicitly anti-cultural. Likewise, a person studying a tribal culture or tribal art does not automatically become a 'culturalist' in the third sense. To qualify, he or she must show some sensitivity to the politics of cultures and the politics of cultural survival.

Secondly, the protagonists of the third meaning are aware that not only can life sometimes be a criticism of cultures, culture, too, can sometimes be a criticism of life, that the unintended dialectic between the two

---

[3] See Ashis Nandy, 'Culture, State and the Rediscovery of Indian Politics' pp. 15–33.

forms of criticism define the basic choices many Afro-Asian intellectuals face today. The main question in matters of culture to them, therefore, is: should one criticize local cultures to strengthen the global nation-state system and the modern sector in the nonmodern world? Or should one use culture as a baseline to criticize the nation-state system and the resource-intensive principles of modern living in the nonmodern societies? The answer depends on which pathology one diagnoses as more fearsome in the southern societies at this point of time—that of culture or that of modernity?

Predictably, the third meaning of culture usually goes with the belief that it is the state sector, located in the modernized parts of Asian and African societies, which suffer from the more vulgar forms of normlessness, and one must seek to restore the normal dialectic of public life in these societies by putting greater and, perhaps, an overdone emphasis on culture-as-protest. Those using culture in the third sense admit that culture-as-protest may sometimes be the 'false consciousness' of the resister whose voice has been taken away and on whom a 'violent silence' has been imposed. After all, the cultural decadence of the defeated is also a fact of life.[4] But those subscribing to the third meaning insist on using the language of this 'false consciousness' because it restores or, at least, revalues the voice of the victims and does not force the latter to express their experiences of suffering in a more 'cultivated' way or through their better-informed well-wishers.

Indeed, many using the third meaning flaunt the fact that culture is partly non-rational and non-material, for the simple reason that the experience of suffering cannot but be subjective. Culture today, according to them, is mainly the victim's version of the truth and this truth recognizes that in the world in which we live, domination and exploitation are increasingly by-products of pathological forms of rationality and ultra-materialism, not of irrationality and idealism. Development, according to some, has become a crucial plank of the first kind of pathology.

Those who consider the languages of modern science and history to be the only languages left for global communication may find this position insensitive to the violence and exploitation that come in the guise of cultural traditions. But to those whom culture is a form of resistance, neither scientific rationality nor historical consciousness seems particularly emancipatory any more. To them, however oppressive cultures might

[4]For example, Collin M. Turnbull, *Mountain People* (London: Pan, 1976); Ashis Nandy, 'Sati: A Nineteenth Century Tale of Women, Violence and Protest', in *At the Edge of Psychology: Essays in Politics and Culture* (New Delhi: Oxford University Press, 1980), pp. 1–31.

have been in the past, it is only by incorporating important aspects of modernity—for instance, the social–evolutionist and racist implications of pre-war biology and the absolute instrumental rationality of post-war technology—that a few cultures have managed to enter the big league of human violence and greed. All this not because cultures are automatically less contaminated by human violence, but because in a world dominated by the language of modernity, human ingenuity has found new sources of legitimacy for social injustice in the dominant language of global communication. Whatever might have been their uses in the past, the languages of the defeated civilizations have become less relevant to the powerful and the rich for the purposes of legitimating dominance. Hence also probably the attraction these languages hold for many social and political activists the world over.

Development, Science and Colonialism

Development has come into the southern world as an analogue of two processes: modern science, wedded to evolutionism and the theory of progress; and modern colonialism, seeking legitimacy in a new civilizing mission.

Development is not merely a process having historical parallels with the growth of science and colonialism, both of which reached their apogee in the nineteenth century. It is an idea contextualized by the ideological frame within which the social changes that we retrospectively call development took place between the seventeenth and nineteenth centuries in the European societies. The ideology of development has come to faithfully mirror the key ideas of the colonial worldview and Baconian philosophy of science, as many in the South have come to experience these ideas, either as beneficiaries or as victims.[5] The origins of development may be in the Judaeo-Christian worldview, in the sense that development has shown a historical correlation with the emergence of Protestantism, especially of the Calvinist variety. But the idea of development is grounded in a concept of science that promises not only absolute human mastery over nature (including human nature) but even human omniscience, and in an edited version of the idea of the white man's burden vis-à-vis those living with 'Oriental despotism' and the 'idiocy of rural life' in the backwaters of Asia and Africa.[6]

[5]Claude Alvares, *Science, Development and Violence: The Twilight of Modernity* (New Delhi: Oxford University Press, 1992).

[6]For a discussion of the evolutionist underpinnings of the mainstream concept of development, see Ashis Nandy, 'The Idea of Development: The Experience of Modern

From science, development has inherited the belief that it is possible to go on increasing the power of human beings over the non-human cosmos, for the world has enough resources to meet not only all human needs but also all human greed. For the ideology of development, this non-human cosmos now includes also the 'subhuman' cosmos—that part of the living earth which can be, for the greater glory of science and the needs of objectivity, ascribed the status of non-living things.[7] From colonialism, development has inherited the idea of a hierarchical ordering of living and non-living beings and the belief that those who are on the higher rungs of history have their right as well as the responsibility to shape the ways of life and the life chances of those on the lower. Even Albert Schweitzer innocently claimed, on behalf of the European civilization, that the Africans were his brothers all right but younger brothers. The basic assumption here is that the developed world has the automatic right and unavoidable obligation to set the pace for the underdeveloped, for what the developed are today, the underdeveloped will become tomorrow, either through their skills in imitation (euphemistically called diffusion of innovations or transfer of technology) or through the generosity of the wealthy and powerful (euphemistically called aid).

The justification for this hierarchy is sought in the analogies drawn between underdevelopment, insanity, immaturity and irrationality, within a conceptual grid that crystallized out as a by-product of the Enlightenment and was neatly picked up by western colonialism and science.[8] The relationships can be crudely summarized as follows:

development: underdevelopment::
sanity (normality): insanity (abnormality)::
maturity (adulthood): immaturity (childhood)::
rationality: irrationality

At this plane, development, modern science and colonialism are not parallel processes, but mutually potentiating forces defining a common domain of consciousness.[9] There is no difference between the way the

---

Psychology as a Cautionary Tale and as an Allegory', in Carlos Mallmann and Oscar Nudler (ed.), *Human Development in its Social Context: A Collective Exploration* (London: Holder and Stoughton, 1986), pp. 248–61.

[7] See for example, Shiv Visvanathan, 'From the Annals of the Laboratory State', in Ashis Nandy (ed.), *Science, Hegemony and Violence: A Requiem to Modernity.* (New Delhi: Oxford University Press, 1989), pp. 257–88.

[8] For more details, see Nandy, 'The Idea of Development'.

[9] A detailed discussion of these themes is in the essays in Nandy, *Science, Hegemony and Violence;* and Alvares, *Science, Development and Violence.*

development experts look at the objects of social engineering, the professional scientists look at the laity, and the colonial powers once laid claim to define the welfare—and in fact, even the concept of welfare—of their subjects. Together they have thrown up a new idea of the social élite who, as secular high priests of the various theories of progress, have faithfully replicated some aspects of European Christendom's passionate fear of the heathens waiting outside the walls to subvert civilization.

Developmentalism

Against this background I shall now examine the four responses to developmentalism that have emerged in recent years, the first visible cracks in the ideology, and the first intellectual and political signs of a post-development era. I do so with full awareness of the power and pull of the ideology of development. The ideology still enthuses the majority of the westernized middle classes and intellectuals in the South. A large majority of the states in the South, too, continue to legitimize themselves in the language of development, even though these states have developed nothing much except themselves and their coercive might.

The first response embraces the conventional idea of development to affirm that modernization is not westernization, and development being modernization, is not western. George Aseniero calls this the response of a new breed of Leibnitzians who believe that we are presently living in the best of all possible worlds and for whom the idea of progress has not yet lost its shine.[10] The developmentalism of these dedicated neo-Leibnitzians does not even have the critical edge of earlier theories of progress, which being the products of a more self-confident age in Europe and North America, allowed at least some criticism of the existing global order.[11]

The response goes with the belief that development, like modern science, has a universal text. If it occasionally shows signs of change when transported over space and time, it is because its core text adjusts to historical and cultural contexts. Such adjustments are, however, more political than intellectual. That is, they are compromises imposed on the universal text of development by sectional interests in a society. Intel-

[10]George Aseniero, 'A Reflection on Developmentalism: From Development to Transformation', in Herb Addo et al., *Development as Social Transformation: Reflections on the Global Problematique* (London: Hodder and Stoughton, and the U.N. University, 1985), pp. 48–55.

[11]Ibid., p. 71.

lectually, the principles of such adjustment can be derived from other parts of the text of development. So, such adjustments or alterations strengthen, not weaken, the paradigm of development in the long run.

It follows that development is the fate of all societies. Some societies may hold up the onward march of history for a short time, but ultimately every society will have to develop through a series of more or less fixed stages. The best that an underdeveloped society can do is to prepare itself to pay the cost of development in as short a time as possible, for everything said, development cannot come free and the countries which are developed have all paid the cost some time or the other during their history.

The response involves two other implicit assumptions. First, the social costs of development cannot be equitably and justly distributed. Unfortunately but inevitably, the weaker sections of a society pay a disproportionately heavy cost for development. However, this should be considered an unavoidable sacrifice imposed on them by world-historical forces. The pain can be reduced by building into development some version of a principle of redistributive justice, but the principle cannot and should not be absolutized; otherwise it goes against the long-term interests of the victims themselves. Second, all societies can be accommodated in the developed world at some future date, for modern science will release unforeseen productive capacities (such as unlimited fusion energy) over the next few decades. In the meanwhile, every society must try to beat the others to enter and/or remain in the big league at all costs.

Critical Developmentalism

The second response assumes development to be a perfectly healthy concept distorted by the political, social and cultural forces shaping or contextualizing it. Accordingly, the pathologies of development are presumed to be by-products that can be fought, even in the godforsaken Third World, through correct political, economic or cultural engineering—to minimize if not eliminate the costs of development to the poor and the powerless. If the problem with development is not its text but the imperfections of societies trying to develop, development can be turned into a relatively painless process for the society's underprivileged if the society is retooled, the assumption goes.

This response admits that in some societies external forces, such as the rapacity of the First World and global capitalism, have linked up with internal forces of inquity and injustice, but it assumes that this link can be snapped.

Implicit in this response is also the assumption that development is only a means of increasing the productive capacity of a society. In the final analysis there cannot be any resource constraint in a technologically-creative and socially-just society. It follows that the nineteenth-century worldview, including the liberal and the socialist visions, needs no extensive revision, for the major pathologies of development—such as unbridled consumerism, ecological insensitivity, and the crudities of middle-class mass culture—will be automatically corrected once the state is captured by progressive forces serving as a vanguard of the people.

Alternative Development

The third response faults the dominant concept of development for being dismissive towards the distincitve cultural configurations of human potentialities and for absolutizing the experience of the developed world as a universal pathway to a monolithic human future. This response seeks to redefine development, to include in it conceptual modules borrowed from a wide range of sources—from humanistic psychology, studies of human creativity and human potentiality, to holistic ecology and Gandhian praxis. The aim is to liberate development from its economistic and historicist straight-jacket, and to relocate it in a non-positivist, more open philosophical grid.

The response grants that the costs of development are intrinsic to development and admits that it is impossible to avoid the sufferings caused by development among the poor and the powerless without substantially modifying the idea of development. The response seeks to make development more culture-sensitive and culture-specific and to resocialize the development community to this new definition.[12] The thriving ongoing grass-roots movements and intellectual currents like sustainable development, eco-development, indigenous, national or ethno-development are all instances of the third response to the five-decades-long experience of development. They have all enriched themselves from the attempts which began in the 1970s to widen the scope of develop-

[12]Random examples are Johan Galtung, *The True Worlds: A Transnational Perspective* (New York: Free Press, 1980); Henryk Skolimowsky, *Eco-Philosophy* (London: Marion Boyars, 1981); and Ramashray Roy and R.K. Srivastava, *Dialogues on Development: Individual, Society and Political Order* (New Delhi: Sage Publications, 1986).

ment to include within it, in addition to economic growth, variables such as social and political development, information expansion, and scientific and technological growth. The growing literature on alternative development has even reconceptualized the needs which development should meet or serve and the institutional fabric within which such needs can be met.

Because this response presumes that development has to be culturally rooted, non-economistic, holistic, and ecologically sensitive, it is politically close to the fourth response described below. However, the third response does have a built-in space for the concept of development, even though the concept is relocated in voluntarism and alternative lifestyles.

Beyond Development

Finally, there is the response to development that believes, partly in reaction to the global experience with development since the 1950s, that the concept as well as the process of development are fundamentally flawed and, therefore, irretrievable. 'Development stinks', says Gustavo Esteva,[13] because whether defined in conventional or in unconventional terms, whether viewed as a concept or as a social process, it is fundamentally incompatible with social justice, human rights, autonomy and cultural survival. Development in all its forms is contaminated by its origin in the structure of repression implicit in the social sensitivities produced by colonial exploitation and by the systematic scientization and desacralization of life and living nature.

This response goes with the belief that, whereas the older forms of violence and oppression have weakened due to the growth of modern consciousness and institutions, new justifications for dominance and exploitation have been built out of contemporary keywords like national security, individualism, secular statecraft, socialism, scientific and technological growth, and development, at least some of which could be once considered emancipatory. Exactly as organized religion and nationalism could once be used for justifying violence and injustice, development, too, can be used to justify the imposition of unequal sacrifices by impersonal agencies like the market and the state on the weak, and to extract the usual surplus from the usual sources. Seen thus, what is happening to

[13]Gustavo Esteva, 'Regenerating People's Space', *Alternatives*, 1987, 12(1), pp. 125–52; see pp. 135, 137.

the life-support systems and cultures of the victims of development to-day is not too different from what happened to the victims of colonialism in the nineteenth century and what has been happening to the victims of modern science and technology in the twentieth.

Obviously, this response goes with the belief that development is incompatible with democratic governance; that it has much in common with modern authoritarianism and tends to legitimize police states, as has been repeatedly shown by virtually all the states which have developed dramatically during this century. From imperial Japan to the Shah's Iran, from army-ruled Pakistan, Thailand, Taiwan, the Philippines and Brazil to Singapore and South Korea under 'controlled democracy', it has been the same story. It is the story of what Herb Feith so appropriately calls 'repressive developmentalist regimes' trying to sell their developmental performance as a substitute for democratic politics. Even societies which have tried to work out more humane forms of development, such as India and Sri Lanka, have fallen prey to the lure of 'pure' development in recent years and have become increasingly willing to pay the social and political costs of such purity.[14] These societies are now more prone to ignore the rights of their minorities and dissenters and more dependent on the coercive power of the state to cope with the unpleasant political by-products of development, such as the protests of the uprooted, the disinherited, and the marginalized.

This fourth response insists that when development becomes incompatible with cultural traditions, the latter should have priority over the former. Not because such traditions are ever perfect but because they are close to the ways of real-life people and are more accessible to and more restrained by participatory politics and the democratic process. Those looking beyond development believe that a culture, especially when it is nonmodern, has no business to become a handmaiden of development nor does it have any responsibility to alter its priorities to accommodate development. Development is merely one way of changing a society; it should not be allowed to hegemonize the idea of social change. There have been other pathways to a desirable society before the idea of development entered the world stage and humankind is quite capable of conceptualizing new, post-developmental modes of social change in the future; there is no reason for every society to compulsorily pass through the stage of development before moving into the postdevelopment world of the future.

---

[14]A more detailed discussion of this theme is in 'Development and Violence', pp. 171–81 below.

A Cultural Critique of Development

The four responses show that there is now a heightened awareness of something being wrong with the state of development. Even those who think of development only in terms of the first two responses are no longer fully convinced that only misguided radical activists, fanatic environmentalists and dyed-in-the-wool obscurantists are resisting development.

Those associated with the last two responses are the ones more sensitive to the relationship between development and culture. There *is* a concern with culture even among those who read development as a universal text. After all, they have often studied what they consider to be the common flaws in the cultures of the South impeding development and their basic premises. But that concern is primarily the concern of cultural engineers, to whom culture is something that facilitates or retards the 'secondary modernization' of the Third World.[15] To these engineers, the major nonwestern civilizations are like continents of darkness waiting to be broken into the modern world; they are not terribly unhappy that many of the smaller nonmodern cultures are fractured today or are crumbling. Strong believers in nineteenth-century Europe's word image, these partisans of development are waiting for the emergence of a single, homogeneous, fully-developed world, with a touch of cultural diversity thrown in for the sake of entertainment or variety.

The third and fourth responses to development are the ones that have provoked serious enquiries into the relationship between development and culture. From the third response have emerged the outlines of theories of development grounded in cultural definitions of a good life and global well-being, and ideas of development that explicitly take into account the constraints on resource use, and the ideas of commons that grow out of cultural traditions.[16] However, these theories and ideas, though they

[15]The major developmental schools of this genre in the post-war era have mainly drawn upon the Parsonian worldview. Some random examples are D.C. McClelland, *The Achieving Society* (New York: Van Nostrand, 1961); Everett C. Hagen, *On the Theory of Social Change* (Homewood, Ill.: Dorsey, 1963); Alex Inkeles and D.H. Smith, *Becoming Modern: Individual Change in Six Developing Countries* (London: Heinemann, 1974). For a good assessment of the literature relating to this theme in political sociology, see Leonard Binder, 'The Natural History of Development Theory', *Comparative Studies in Society and History*, January 1986, 28(1), pp. 3–33.

[16]For instance Sulak Sivaraksa, 'Buddhism and Development', in Mallmann and Nudler, *Human Development*, pp. 233–47; W. Lambert Gardiner, 'On Turning Development Inside Out or (Better) On Not Turning Development Outside-In in the First Place', ibid., pp. 63–90. For a good summary of the literature on alternative development, see Bjorn Hettne, *Development Theory and the Third World* (Stockholm: Sarec, 1982)

have enriched the understanding of development, often have little to say about the way the modern nation-state in nonmodern cultures presides over the oppressive aspects of development. Not that the theories of alternative development do not have a critique of the mainstream theories of state, but the critique rarely extends to the modern concept of the nation-state and to the way the global nation-state system reduces all experiments with alternative development to the status of peripheral, dissenting voices or esoterica—in effect, into forms of ornamental dissent, by tolerating which one establishes one's democratic credentials.

Two other features of development limit the theories and ideas thrown up by the third and fourth responses. First, development, when it revalues aspects of culture traditionally latent or peripheral, usually ends up by underwriting the psychological demands of modernity—hard this-worldly individualism, unrestrained achievement needs, aggressive competitiveness, priority of productivity principle over the expressive ones, acceptance of a mechanomorphic view of nature, and so on. These traits were not unknown to the nonmodern cultures in pre-developmental times. However, there were elaborate cultural checks on the expression of the traits. The idea of development has produced, probably for the first time, a philosophical baggage that unconditionally endorses these traits and institutionally balances the Baconian and Hobbesian impulses. The balancing is done through a carefully built reward–punishment system, the key monitors for which are the market, the state, and the media.

By removing all restraints on these traits, the idea of development has not, as is commonly believed, turned the spiritual East materialistic, but it has destroyed the delicate balance between the soft materialism of everyday life and the hard materialism that ignores the fate of the life-support systems dependent on a naturalistic, often-unstated environmentalism that undergirds many cultures.

Put simply, development does not annihilate cultures; it merely exploits cultures to strengthen itself. That is why, once the idea of development has been internalized by a culture, the internal contradictions produced by development within the society begin to work in favour of the process of development and systematic cultural self-destruction. Defying the growing intellectual fascination for different cultural styles of development, development in the real world has everywhere shown the same social patterning. It has proved itself to be a powerful unifying process in the contemporary world, one which taps some of the basic human motives and aspirations. At this plane, and perhaps only at this plane, the universalist assumptions of the mainstream development theories seem to have a secure foundation in human experience. Only, this universalism ignores the fact that these motives and aspirations were ones that some of the major civilizations of the world had carefully kept under check. The checks were as 'universal' as the predispositions they checked. Let me give an example.

Ethology and comparative psychology suggest that both co-operation and competition are universal human traits. But it was by over-stressing co-operation that many traditional cultures kept in check human competitiveness. Dissenting sects and subcultures within these cultures admitted the deep psychological roots of competition; they were not propelled by any 'innocent' faith that competition could be totally eliminated. But often they also had the institutional awareness that co-operation, not competition, needed to be over-emphasized for co-operation to have a reasonable run in human affairs.[17]

Operating from within extremely narrow philosophical visions, many modern knowledge-systems have read such one-sided emphasis on certain traits as either hypocritical or naïve. These systems have no clue to the reasons why, once the idea of development enters a society and the traditional checks on competition and other allied virtues like individualism and consumerism are removed, development begins to reproduce its universal pattern faithfully. As Dennis O' Rourke's moving documentaries suggest, in the short run, development may show some tolerance of cultures, ideologically it may even be committed to such tolerance, but in the long run development cannot but turn ethnocidal.[18]

Second, despite the efforts of environmentalists and others concerned with the survival of cultures, development introduces into a society a new hierarchy of knowledge. Sometimes for a short while some of the traditional knowledge-systems may enjoy symbolically a high status in a developing society—traditional medicine in Maoist China and Islamic jurisprudence in army-ruled Pakistan, for instance—but in the long run,

[17]See Deviprasad Chattopadhyaya, *Lokayata: A Study in Ancient Indian Materialism* (New Delhi: People's Publishing House, 1973); D.D. Kosambi, *Myth and Reality: Studies in the Formation of Indian Culture* (Bombay: Popular Prakashan, 1962). Recently, while exploring the culture of Victorian cricket, now the national game of a number of ex-colonial societies, I came across a description of the game in a South Pacific island. While elsewhere in the world the game is becoming more brazenly competitive, in this island's version of cricket, a match between rival tribes has to serve as a substitute for traditional inter-tribal competition and/or feud and—here lies its distinctiveness—has always to end without a winner or loser. I invite the reader to ponder if this illustrates Polynesian insensitivity to human competitiveness or a higher-order sensitivity to the power of human competitiveness and the need to contain it.

[18]Dennis O'Rourke, *Yap—How Did They Know We'd Like TV?* (documentary film, 1980); and *The Shark-Callers of Kontu* (documentary film, 1982).

all the incentives are re-aligned to knowledge compatible with development. So, even though in the short run the various systems of knowledge—traditional and modern—may seem to be peacefully co-existent, in the long run, the older ecology of knowledge is destroyed. Not merely because the modern systems and those allegiant to them are intrinsically intolerant of other systems operating from fundamentally different premises, but also because, in a developing society, knowledge commensurate with development acquires dominance as well as prestige, and such knowledge begins to ignore or corner knowledge irreverent or extraneous to development. Wherever development has come, positivist science and mega-technology have come, too. So have ideas of the absolute priority of the human over non-human living nature, the impersonal over the personal, the experimental over the experiential, the productive over the expressive, and the monetized over the nonmonetized. In the context of India, Francis Zimmermann has spoken of the counter-systems within a system of knowledge which reproduce competing and/or incommensurable systems of knowledge as a check against the destruction of any of the systems. The experience of a number of cultures shows that, in the long run, many majestic but politically-undefended systems of knowledge end up as transient counter-systems within the dominant modern systems of knowledge.

In other words, in nonwestern societies trying to develop—actually, it is doubtful if societies try to develop, mostly their regimes and élites do—the positive sciences have broken out of the limited sphere within which they were housed in earlier times and have established close links with the state sector and the middle-class consciousness that sustains the culture of the state. Against such sciences, the various fashionable non-positivist critiques of positivism, the various movements for intermediate technology and for a socially-responsible science have proved to be minor irritants. Despite such criticisms and movements, these sciences, using the coercive might of the state, have occupied much of the available political space. Simultaneously, modern science in general has become the organizing principle and ultimate standard of knowledge and has begun to dominate the spirit of the society; those who cannot organize their experiences into standard formats accessible to modern science and positivist consciousness—usually they are the marginals and dissenters—suffer the most from what can be called 'developmental terrorism'.

Development as a State of Mind

Like war, development, too, begins in the minds of men. If it has to be altered or jettisoned, that, too, must begin in the minds of men. But once development is institutionalized in a society, like war, again, it becomes nearly impossible to exorcise it. It becomes a form of rationality, and begins to cannibalize alternative forms of social intervention. So that the remedies for the ills of development are increasingly seen to lie either in more development or in an edited version of development. That is why development may have begun as one particular form of social change among many but has become an identifiable way of life that must, by its very nature, help other ways of life incompatible with it to die a natural or unnatural death. This is the trap in which the developmentalists and much of the development community are now caught.

In this world of development, officially there can be no legitimate dissent. For the idea of dissent imputes some minimal sanity and good faith to those who differ from the establishment, whereas the official language of development makes no such imputation to those who differ from the core concepts of development and to those who do not grant any moral status to the advocates of development. Unofficially, there *are* dissenters in the world of development, but they are usually dissenters only to themselves. They speak a different language and their voice has no audibility in the public realm. Often, when they belong to small tribes of dissenting communities, they die out before being able to speak out, in oblivion and in silence. When they survive, they do so at the margins of their society, oscillating between fears of extinction and what Nikos Papastergiadis calls the 'violence of silence'.[19]

These dissenters—not the small group of intellectuals who have traditionally opposed development, but the victims of development— have tried often to speak to us through their representatives. However, these representatives, liberals or radicals, have usually represented only those aspects of the victimhood which make sense to the modern world— stark material deprivation or destitution, absence of modern health care, physical dislocation, loss of employment, et cetera. The representatives have had little patience with the victims' ways of life—for instance, physical dislocations leading to the loss of psycho-ecological balance, loss of employment leading to a loss of vocation and art forms and lifestyle, destitution leading to the denial of even the traditional dignity of poverty, and so on.

As a result, the voices of the victims have become even more mute and their links with those who fight for them are weakening by the day. Their sorrows and sufferings are represented in reified, economic terms in international fora and in academic debates in the development

---

[19]On the issue of voice and audibility, an excellent statement is Werner Herzog's *Where the Green Ants Dream* (feature film, 1984).

community. And, in a reversal of the concept of reification, they become the victims of a hard materialism and a form of concretization that presume all economic complaints to be more real than all meta-economic complaints. Above all, they become the victims of systems of modern knowledge which take away from them, the victims, even their right to interpret their own plight in their own terms.

The politics of development begins with attempts to delink the problems of these victims from their interpreters, representatives, and well-wishers within the development community, and, then, empowering both the victims and their categories and theories.

Development and Violence

The problem with the idea of development is not its failure. The idea has succeeded beyond the dreams of its early partisans who never imagined that they had hit upon something whose day had come. Developmentalism has succeeded where western colonialism and evangelical Christianity failed. It has established itself as one of the few genuine universals of our time. It has become an intimate part of every surviving civilization and changed the self-definitions of some of the least accessible societies. Development has converted even the seemingly non-proselytizable.

These changes in self-definition have gone in two directions. First, there has been a rearrangement of the components of the self in the affected cultures. A new hierarchy of preferred traits has emerged in them. In many Asian, African and South American societies, the traditional cultural preferences are now devalued and are a source of embarrassment for the more self-conscious members of these societies. Such preferences are feared as atavistic or retrogressive, even obscurantist. The ruling élites in these societies are now engaged in various forms of cultural engineering to get rid of these qualities while they themselves get integrated into the global cultural order. They are willing to go to any extent to drive their subjects like cattle towards the better world that development promises.[1] A less polite way of describing such self-

---

[1]See Shiv Visvanathan, 'From the Annals of the Laboratory State', in Ashis Nandy (ed.), *Science, Hegemony and Violence: A Requiem for Modernity* (Tokyo: The United Nations University and New Delhi: Oxford University Press, 1988), pp. 257–88; Claude Alvares, *Science, Development and Violence: The Twilight of Modernity* (New Delhi: Oxford University Press, 1992); Wolfgang Sachs (ed.), *The Development Dictionary: A Guide to*

engineering is to call it a mixture of self-hatred and mimicry leading to a new form of political authoritarianism.[2] The mix has become popular even in cultures being glorified the world over as great success stories in the history of development.

The often-violent retooling of the self has gone hand-in-hand with the loss of large parts of the remembered past.[3] In society after society, uncomfortable and allegedly irrelevant aspects of the past are being shed as constructions fit only for the dustbin of history, again with the help of the coercive apparatus of the state and with much of the world looking the other way. Today, only that past is being celebrated which is seen as conducive to modernization and development; only that past is being rued which seems to resist modernity and development. Together, the two 'relevant' pasts constitute history and become, after a time, the only memory accessible to the citizenry. The rest become ahistorical, 'revivalist' myths. So do aspects of the self that are intertwined with that lost past. Violent suppression of that uncomfortable past, and the self associated with it, now enjoys enormous legitimacy as an attack on 'fundamentalism' and new forms of 'Oriental despotism'.[4]

Knowledge as Power (London: Zed, 1992); and 'Culture, Voice and Development', 150–70 above.

[2] Herb Feith's name for such regimes is 'repressive-developmentalist regimes' and his definition would cover a galaxy of 'success stories' in development—from Nazi Germany, Stalinist Russia and imperial Japan to South Korea, Singapore, Taiwan, Brazil, the Shah's Iran, Ayub Khan's Pakistan and, now, Deng's China. See his 'Repressive-Developmentalist Regimes in Asia: Old Strengths, New Vulnerabilities', paper presented at the conference of the World Order Models Project, New York, June 1979 and published in International Affairs, Christian Conference of Asia, *Escape From Domination: A Consultation Report on Patterns of Domination and People's Movements in Asia*, Tokyo, April 1980.

[3] See for instance, the papers in Frédérique Apffel Marglin and Stephen Marglin (ed.), *Dominating Knowledge: Development, Culture and Resistance* (Oxford: Clarendon Press, 1990).

[4] Japan is a neat example; it enjoys unmatched power and autonomy within the world of development but is unable to use them to ensure its own cultural survival. The dominant global consciousness has reconstructed the Japanese tradition as a set of two cultural strands. One consists of a cultural package that has led to Japan's present developmental profile; the other consists of a few cultural accessories and esoterica thrown in for the amusement of Japan's admirers and critics. The former is reportedly the substance; the latter the form that outsiders must master for the sake of predictability or profitability when dealing with Japan. Many Japanese have begun to see themselves through these imported glasses. For them, Japanese history is becoming the history of modernization and the establishment of the development regime in Japan. The rest is relegated to being either folklore meant for the children and the elderly or 'culture' meant for western thriller-writers and tourists. If the present trend continues, it is doubtful if in the next century Japan's past, unrelated to her developmental concerns, will remain accessible to the majority of her own citizens.

Yet, human nature being what it is, all hegemonic visions throw up their own distinctive strains of dissent in the form of counter-visions. Since the 1980s, voices have emerged all over the world against the totalizing thrust of development. These voices seem to carry the awareness that, just when the ideology of development is winning its most impossible victories in global politics, it has exhausted its intellectual possibilities. Many of the most sensitive minds of our times now find the charms of development to be so much tinsel glitter. The details of development now engage mainly the specialists concerned with its pragmatics or management. This loss of intellectual shine has, however, also led to a certain carelessness towards the nitty-gritty of development in the world dominated by the global media and international development experts. The dirty work of development can go on in the backwaters of the world, with many vaguely concerned with the fate of the victims but only a few engaged intellectually and on a day-to-day basis with their fate.

Why this loss of credibility in the world of knowledge when developmentalism is so clearly triumphant in global politics? The reasons are many, but the main ones all centre on the gradual decline in the moral stature of development as an ideology. Many major criticisms of development do have a normative component—such as criticism of the development community's total faith in the global market, impersonal contractual relationships and professional expertise, its commodification of nature, and its näive trust in mega-organizations and mega-technology. In addition, development comes to all societies as part of a package that includes the idea of the nation-state as the prime mover of all social change, a full-blown theory of progress through historical stages, and large-scale massification through urbanization and industrialization. All these are components of a concept of modernity that has a clear moral dimension. If development is, as Arturo Escobar suggests, 'a chapter in an anthropology of modernity,' it cannot avoid the moral evaluation that is being increasingly applied to the modern vision itself. This evaluation has begun to go against development.

One other factor responsible for the spreading intellectual mutiny against the gospel according to the development planners also partly explains the loss of the seductive charms of developmentalism. In the name of individualism, the ideology of development has gradually denuded the idea of the individual of much of its substantive content. With the invention of development, most things that were once a matter of personal initiative and choice have been systematically handed over to agencies making impersonal, contractual, professionalized choices on behalf of the person. The only initiative the person is left with relates to choices from among available consumables offered by the global market. From health care to child rearing it is the same story. As the area of individual choice has shrunk, a false sense of freedom is created because the contextualizing role of the community has been removed from the choice situation. Indeed, atomized in the name of freedom, the person now stands alone against the forces of the global market and mega-technology.

Simultaneously, violence associated with impersonal bureaucratic structures, of the kind Hannah Arendt talked about, has now acquired freer play. As wars, direct use of violence against unarmed populations, torture and blatant violation of human rights become less and less easy to sell, there is an increase in indirect violence, surveillance and destruction of the life-support systems of communities unable to defend themselves by using modern institutional and legal remedies.[5]

These changes have been brought about not through old-style domination—through naked force and open exploitation. The changes have come through the co-optation of crucial segments of the recipient, nonwestern cultures into the developmental community—a new community of scholars, policy-makers, development journalists, readers of development news, development managers, and activists, who together sustain development as a sphere of professional, organizational and entrepreneurial activity. The global system backing the ideology of development has introduced in the recipient cultures new cognitive orders that apparently do not challenge traditions except for their

[5]According to one estimate, 21.6 million people—roughly the population of all the Scandinavian countries put together—have been displaced only by the construction of large dams in India. Gayatri Singh, 'Displacement and Limits to Legislation', in Raajen Singh (ed.), *Dams and Other Major Projects: Impact on and Response of Indigenous People* (Goa: CCA-URM, 1988), pp. 91–7; see p. 91. This estimate, compared to some others, seems to be on the higher side. See Table 5, p. 202.

Another study estimates that of the roughly 70 million aboriginal tribals in India belonging to some 212 tribes, 15 per cent have been displaced by development projects, so that they could themselves be developed and turned into 'skilled human resources'. Smitu Kothari, 'Theorizing Culture, Nature and Democracy in India' (Delhi; Lokayan, 1993), mimeo. At least 40 per cent of all the invisible refugees created by Indian development are by now tribals. This amounts to about 10 million persons. Another 10 million will be displaced by 2010. Walter Fernandes, 'Development-Induced Displacement in the Tribal Areas of Eastern India', (New Delhi: Indian Social Institute, 1994), mimeo. Quoted in Setu: Centre for Social Knowledge and Action, *Development, Equity and Justice: Adivasi Communities in India in the Era of Liberalization and Globalization* (Ahmedabad: Setu, 1999), p. 5.

'irrational', 'easily disposable' aspects. Entering these cultures through well-meaning missionaries of development, preaching to all and sundry an accessible secular heaven on earth, these orders aim at nothing less than establishing an equation between the sustainability of the global development regime and the survival of cultures. So, what can be read as a major threat to the viability of nonwestern cultures is identified as an emancipatory principle updating these cultures for our times and ensuring their survival.[6] Whatever well-intentioned activists and scholars may say, that is the ultimate political meaning of the slogan of sustainable development.

Why is the link between development and violence stronger in the southern world? One reason can be that in the South, among those not fully uprooted or decultured, developmentalism is still suspect. Not because it is seen as a global conspiracy, but because it has been stripped of all geo-ethnic and temporal qualifications in many southern societies by the local modernist élites. In societies where communities have not collapsed and the citizens are not entirely massified, there persists a suspicion of a fully universal, space-and-time transcending sociology of utopianism. For in such societies the privilege of venturing such sociology is given only to religions or theories of transcendence.

Thus, at the very moment the ideology of development seems to have touched something universal in human nature—when from Beijing to Berlin and from Moscow to New Delhi more and more people are taking to the clichéd markers of mass culture as the indices of having made it—some Third-World communities and activist-scholars have persisted in exercising a form of suspicion that is very uncomfortable to those dreaming of a homogenized global mass-culture hitched to a global developmental regime. In doing so they might be speaking also on behalf of other defeated civilizations, including even threatened communities in the superseded West, declared obsolete by the fully modern, reportedly the best-of-all-possible Wests. These activists assume that the struggle against developmentalism is a struggle to reclaim the dignity of cultures that have been turned into a set of experimental subjects, waiting to be sacrificed at the end of a defined set of operations—either to end in a museum or in a university department of anthropology

[6]In his book Arturo Escobar tells that part of the story. See *Encountering Development: The Making and the Unmaking of the Third World, 1945–1992* (Princeton: Princeton University Press, 1995).

or history for a proper *post mortem*. Crucial realities of such cultures have already been excised to ensure—Arturo Escobar says citing Raul Prebisch—the 'doctrinal asepsis' of a fully scientized economics located outside time and space. For development economists, the Third World and its poverty are enabling concepts, which allow them to ply their trade as the resident doctors of our times, specializing in what is allegedly a culturally inherited but curable pathology. They would hate to admit that today's poverty is not an ancient disease that development cures, but mostly an iatrogenic by-product of the healing touch of modernity itself.[7]

Apart from everything else, there is the 'normal' lifespan of an idea. Even the best ideas get dated and, human ingenuity being what it is, even the most emancipatory discourses get transformed after a time into new justifications for violence and exploitation. Even if development had not been a particularly oppressive idea at the beginning, it was bound to become one after being thoughtfully adopted by a series of despotic regimes as the final justification of authoritarian politics. As a product of this political process, the culture of development has to kill off all alternative visions of desirable societies. For the same reason, however, imagining a post-development era has come to represent something more than resistance to a hidden structure of dominance; it now means giving back the savage world the right to envision its own future. Such envisioning, whatever else it does or does not do, promises to de-homogenize nonwestern subjectivities and to repluralize the idea of social intervention and dissent.

This is not an indirect defence of Afro-Asian nationalism or a plea for a return to the idea of the noble savage. It is an attempt to acknowledge that human beings, given long enough time, can convert any theory of emancipation into a new justification for violence and expropriation. Development has now begun to take over from old-style religious conflicts, colonial wars, and racism; it has created new opportunities for a play of those traits that once found expression through standardized channels and justifications of human violence.

One specific issue remains. A painful feature of our times is, I have already hinted, that success in development has usually led to the emergence of

---

[7]Massive poverty in the modern sense appeared, Escobar claims, when the spread of the market economy broke down community ties and deprived millions of people of access to land, water, and other resources. Escobar, *Encountering Development*, ch. 2.

authoritarian politics in Third World societies. One by one the societies that have succeeded in development—or shown signs of doing so—have fallen prey to the very success they have tried so hard to attain, in total defiance of existing theories of democracy and development. This correlation between development and authoritarianism has grown even in open societies like India and Sri Lanka after they opted for more conventional forms of development in the 1990s.

We were told in the past that authoritarianism was due to underdevelopment. Development, we were told, guaranteed democratic freedom, at least in the end. Both those who believed in the socioeconomic prerequisities of political democracy—from Talcott Parsons to David Easton and from Edward Shils to Karl Deutsch[8]—and those who believed in state-controlled economic growth as the sure road to their utopia—from Lenin to Jawaharlal Nehru—saw Oriental despotism as the primary model of authoritarianism. Both expected economic growth to lead the Asian and African societies towards freedom, not away from it. In the 1960s some scholars like Everett Hagen and K.W. Kapp even went as far as to posit a perfectly inverse relationship between the anti-democratic personality and the entrepreneurial man.[9] Even David C. McClelland and company, breathlessly trying to induce economic growth through a higher achievement motive, incidentally produced the insight that the rise in achievement motive in a society before economic take-off usually led to lower levels of power and affiliation motives, and thus to less chances of imperialism and authoritarianism.[10]

The experiences of police states such as South Korea, Singapore, Taiwan, China and Brazil have played havoc with this way of thinking in recent times. It is not accidental that in the Third World, grassroots movements in general and civil-rights movements in particular have increasingly become hostile to the very idea of development. Some of them do not even care whether one means by 'development' conventional development or the new alternative forms of development.[11]

---

[8]See a brief critical assessment of the political development literature and the 'prerequisites' approach in Satish Arora, 'Preempted Future? Notes on Theories of Political Development', in Rajni Kothari (ed.), *The State and Nation Building: A Third World Perspective* (New Delhi: Allied, 1976), pp. 23–66.

[9]Everett Hagen, *On the Theory of Social Change* (Homewood, Ill.: Dorsey, 1962); K.W. Kapp, *Hindu Culture, Economic Development and Economic Planning* (New York: Asia, 1963).

[10]D.C. McClelland, *The Achieving Society* (New York: Van Nostrand, 1961).

[11]For instance, Special Issue on Survival, *Lokayan Bulletin*, October 1985, 3(4–5); Alvares, *Science, Development and Violence*; and 'Deadly Development', *Development Forum*, 9(7), October 1983; Madhya Pradesh Lokayan and Lokhit Samiti, *Vikas ki Kimat* (Ahmedabad: Setu, 1985); Kothari, 'Theorizing Culture, Nature and Democracy in India';

To a second group of scholars, authoritarianism can be a means of development. These scholars do not word their thesis in exactly this form but they cite the examples of Nazi Germany, Fascist Italy, Stalinist Russia, pre-war Japan, the military dictatorships of Latin America, and Maoist China in support of their thesis. In these societies, high-pitched mobilizational politics within a closed polity have been used (1) to enforce consumption-restraints and collective sacrifices, and (2) to justify enhanced spending, in the name of development, on the military, the police and other coercive instruments of the state. James Gregor has analysed one subset of the genre neatly.[12] Cynical and blatantly conservative though his thesis may look, it tallies with the experience of peoples who have been the victims of development and frequently see their rulers and their First-World sponsors choose development over freedom when the chips are down.

There is also the inarticulate thesis—inarticulate because it is implicit in the activism of many grassroots organizations working all over the world in areas such as ecology, cultural survival, and civil rights—that development itself releases authoritarian tendencies after it crosses a certain threshold, and that this is so even in societies seriously trying to combine development and democratic participation. The thesis admits that development has always included authoritarian elements, even in the democratic West. The elements were held in check in western societies by colonialism (to the colonies were exported millions of people marginalized by industrial growth in the West and from these colonies were imported into the West cheap raw materials for development), by restricted franchise (which partly filtered off from the public realm in Europe voices of the victims of development), by the suppression of ethnic groups that were made to pay the price of development through ecological devastation, uprooting and extinction (as with North and South American Indians), or by the export of authoritarianism to crypto-colonies (as the United States has done in South America for many decades). Once these advantages are lost, authoritarianism reveals itself as the other side of development even in developed societies.

Such a point of view recognizes three aspects of development that nurture authoritarianism. First, as democratic participation increases and new channels of social mobility open up in a developing society, it brings

---

Suresh Sharma, 'Development and Diminishing Livelihood' (New Delhi: CSDS, 1985), pamphlet.

[12]A. James Gregor, *The Fascist Persuasion in Radical Politics* (Princeton: Princeton University, 1974); also *The Ideology of Fascism* (New York: The Free press, 1969).

towards the centre of the polity groups previously marginalized. These groups threaten the power of those who control the society and monopolize the benefits of development. Particularly so because development has come to mean in practice the takeover—by the state, the organized sector and the market—of the commons to which traditionally the weakest of the society used to have some access. These commons are then used to produce marketable goods that can never reach the original beneficiaries of the commons. So once some empowerment of the now-displaced beneficiaries of the commons takes place, they begin to pose a threat to the beneficiaries of development.

For instance, a tribe living in a forest may have 'free access' to fuelwood but once the forest is cut down to put up a dam and a hydel plant, the tribe may have no access to the new energy but could, in the process, suffer from uprooting, loss of livelihood, and deculturation. Yet, the very experience of displacement and dispossession may politicize the tribe and make them a threat to the state. Authoritarianism becomes an easy means of containing these new participants in politics and controlling their demands. The containment—A.F.K. Organski calls it the repression of the newly-mobilized sectors and identifies it as the very heart of fascism—is legitimized by the manifest normlessness and crudity of the politics of the new entrants.[13] The middle classes are always appalled by the unseemly style of the lower classes in politics. Authoritarianism often takes advantage of this culture shock to contain political participation.[14] And the slogan of development in such societies legitimizes this containment.[15]

Second, development means sacrificing something of the present for the sake of the future. As development becomes a reason of the state, those who control the state feel justified in imposing these sacrifices selectively, under the guidance of experts. Authoritarianism becomes their technique of extracting sacrifices either from target groups identified

---

[13]A.F.K. Organski, *The Stages of Political Development* (New York: Alfred A. Knopf, 1965).

[14]See Ashis Nandy, 'Adorno in India: Revisiting the Psychology of Fascism', in *At the Edge of Psychology: Essays in Politics and Culture* (New Delhi: Oxford University Press, 1980), pp. 99–111.

[15]The Emergency in India (1975–7) fitted the analysis in copybook fashion. The state violence and suspension of civil rights the Emergency produced came packaged in the rhetoric of development and though occasionally the rhetoric of 'putting democracy back on the rails' was also used, it was the emphasis on development that sought to justify the police-state methods used in areas such as family planning, control of media, and slum clearance. Similarly packaged arguments have been presented at different times by the Marcos regime in Philippines, by the military regimes in Pakistan and Thailand, and by the rulers of Malaysia, Singapore and South Korea.

by the state (in which case the sacrificial sectors on closer examination turn out to be the political dissenters or their support bases) or from those less able to resist making such sacrifices (in which case generally the ideology of 'trickle-down effect' or that of 'market forces' is invoked).[16]

Third, though development in its present sense has been used only since the late 1940s—President Harry Truman was the first to use the term in its present sense—the concept is now retrospectively applied to the 300-year-long process through which developed societies have passed to reach their present state. Development in nonwestern societies is supposed to be a shorter route to that state. Thus, the idea of development has as its underside memories of the violence and exploitation that accompanied the early phases of development in the West, and the idea includes the message that the underdeveloped world should make similar blood sacrifices to develop.

The images of non-unionized workers coming back from work after sixteen hours to rape their own daughters, children below the age of ten working full day in the mills or in high-risk occupations like chimney sweeping, the enclosure movement in England, the women labourers and prostitutes populating the gin alleys—they survive in the western unconscious as an abyss into which the West may slip again if it gives up the ambition of scaling newer and newer heights of prosperity or loses the will to protect its interests aggressively. These anxieties are then projected into the global politics of development. That is why the developed democratic societies are often the first to endorse a military despot elsewhere, particularly if the latter is smart enough to mouth the idiom of development. That is why the Shah of Iran seemed an overly strict schoolmaster to his western admirers, whereas Idi Amin looked like a stone-age monster. The former was seen as a practising developmentalist, even if a misguided one, the latter as an unalloyed Oriental despot.

Finally, development tends to sharpen religious, interregional and ethnic tensions by 'pitting' traditional communities against each other. This does not mean that such tensions did not exist in the past or that the planners provoke them. It means that by giving absolute priority to in-

[16]See for example Ashis Nandy, 'Introduction: Science as a Reason of State', in Nandy (ed.), *Science Hegemony and Violence*.

The idea of the trickle-down effect has had a particularly long tenure in the South. In Third-World societies that have taken the capitalist path to development, the idea often serves the same function as the suspension of democratic rights did in the socialist regimes. In both cases the aim has been to extract economic or political surplus from the population, through the science of development or scientific history, both justifying inequality and violence in the short run in the name of future freedom.

terests over passions, instrumental rationality over visions and worldviews, development converts the rich, multi-layered relationship among communities into a one-dimensional, interest-based, competitive relationship. And it usually does so in a context where it has already introduced massive environmental changes and disrupted the traditional life-support systems of the communities involved.[17] Once such a conversion has taken place, the conflicts between communities are brought into, and negotiated within, the modern political and economic spheres. What was a complex encounter of cultures becomes, thus, a hard-eyed battle for 'concrete', development-related gains. The result is the creation of new opportunities for the state sector to step in as the final arbiter among the communities, in the name of facilitating or monitoring development, or of holding in check violence and primitivism. In the Third World, this arbitration has often been the main excuse or justification for short-circuiting the political process and introducing authoritarian rule.

---

[17]For instance, Vandana Shiva, *The Violence of the Green Revolution* (Penang: Consumers Association of Penang, 1990); also see Helena Norberg-Hodge, *Ancient Futures: Learning from Ladakh* (New Delhi: Oxford University Press, 1991), pp. 122–30; and Joke Schrijvers, *The Violence of 'Development': A Choice for Intellectuals,* trs. Lin Pugh (New Delhi: Kali for Women, 1993, and Utrecht: International Books, 1993).

The Scope and Limits of Dissent:
India's First Modern Environmentalist and His Critique of the DVC

The Damodar Valley Corporation or DVC in eastern India is one of the largest and most ambitious river-valley projects in South Asia. It was built at a time when, in the newly-independent countries of the South, the building of large dams was a matter of national pride and an affirmation of a country's technological autonomy and political equality with the West.[1] In this self-affirmation, the main role was played by the state. Technocrats and planners chose to believe that they were the main actors in the play and urban, middle-class India saw them as such. However, the political establishment usually viewed such technocrats and planners as substitutable functionaries or easily available legitimizers, dutifully providing a comfortable role model for Indian youth.

The DVC is still a massive presence in the eastern Indian landscape, though only four of its eight projected dams have been completed till now and everyone knows that the other four will never be built. Though covering an area of not less that 9,357 square miles and a population of half-a-million, the project no longer appears so august, even to the less technologically minded. Indeed, the appeal of the DVC nowadays resides not so much in its actual achievements as in its being a surviving symbol of the romance of planning and the early, superbly optimistic,

---

[1]From the beginning of the Five Year Plans in 1952 till 1979, the Government of India spent about Rs 200,000 million, a sizeable 15 per cent of India's entire developmental expenditure, on dams and related canals. Of the dams built, 1,554 could be classified as large dams and a hefty 58.37 per cent of them were in Maharashtra and Gujarat alone: *Registrar of Large Dams in India* (New Delhi: CBIP, 1979), quoted in Jayanta Bandopadhyay, *Ecology of Drought and Water Scarcity: Need for an Ecological Water Resource Policy* (Dehradun, U.P.: Research Foundation for Science and Environment. n.d.), p. 11.

techno-scientific vision of Indian nationalism. Built in the 1950s, during the early years of independent India, the DVC is now mainly the pride of an earlier generation of western-educated nationalists. To adapt Jawaharlal Nehru's grandiloquent, now-clichéd description of mega-dams, the DVC remains another of those 'temples of modern India' which has, to spite its committed priests, lost most of its devotees. It is of interest today mainly to archaeologists and temple architects.

Apart from the four multi-purpose storage dams (Maithon, Tilaiya, Panchet, and Konar), the DVC includes, among other things, two barrages (one of them the controversial structure at Farakka), a huge power station at Bokaro and a smaller one at Chandrapura, a well-known fertilizer factory at Sindri, and a few by-now important townships. Together the complex has always invoked—and was designed to invoke—the memory of its better-known counterpart, the Tennessee Valley Authority in Missourie. The American experience actually served as a model for the Indian planners.[2] A book published by the DVC's Chief Information Officer in 1958, the well-known Bengali writer, Amal Home, states:

Sponsoring the DVC bill in Parliament, Shri N.V. Gadgil, the then Minister for Works, Mines and Power, described how the conception of the Damodar Valley Project was inspired by the romance of the TVA, which had ushered in an era of prosperity in the Tennessee Valley by taming the wayward Tennessee river in the U.S.A.[3]

Note the use of the term 'wayward'. It is perfectly compatible with the image of some of the larger, more turbulent rivers in folk tales and memories in eastern India, where rivers are revered as powerful demonic mothers with a touch of wayward, insane violence. They protect and nurture when in a good mood but can turn malevolent and homicidal when not propitiated properly or out of sheer whimsy. That image has not only persisted, but it has powered many contemporary efforts to contain or tame rivers in that part of the world. Asit Sen's Bengali film *Panchatapa* (based on a popular novel by Ashutosh Mukhopadhyay) and even Kamakshiprasad Chattopadhyaya's brief poem, '*Nadi chokh ragrai*', on the dreams that dams can be, both set against the construction

[2]Records of the debates in the Constituent Assembly on the Damodar Valley Corporation Bill reveal the imposing psychological presence of the Tennessee Valley scheme in all plans pertaining to the Damodar Valley. An American expert, W.L. Voorduin, was by far the most important member of the Central Technical Power Board and wrote the main position paper for the Board.

[3]Amal Home (ed.), *D.V.C. in Prospect and Retrospect* (Calcutta: DVC, 1958),p. 7.

of the DVC, are near-perfect examples of the core fantasy that underlay middle-class India's perception of dams in the 1950s and 1960s.

I

Times change. And instead of looking like fearsome, moody matriarchs presiding over the lives of millions, Indian rivers are now more like tired, vulnerable, abandoned mothers facing lonely deaths. It is easy to criticize the DVC today when the TVA itself has come under harsh if not bitter scrutiny.[4] In fact, given that the DVC is in many ways a self-conscious copy of the TVA, its flaws and its failures seem even more glaring today. For they seem to be products of an embarrassing form of mimicry in which the ex-colonial culture of India specialized. Such imitation, however elegant and successful, discomfits many. And there are often reasons to be embarrassed. It is said that the Bhilai steel plant in hot and dusty central India, where the winter temperature rarely falls below 55°F, has a roof modelled on a Russian prototype, designed to withstand heavy snowfall. The DVC may not have acquired anything so impressive, but all around the area covered by it lie evidences of hopes unfulfilled and botched romantic visions of a modern, eastern-Indian utopia. I am told that till the 1970s one could glimpse a few steam launches, lying unused, that had been purchased in the 1950s for the pleasure cruises of tourists, expected to throng the area after the project had been completed. (The idea, one suspects, was borrowed from Nagarjunasagar dam near Mysore. Nagarjunasagar might well be the only mega-dam in the world the entertainment value of which is higher than its value as a source of water and hydroelectricity; the dam is now famous as a backdrop for song-and-dance sequences in commercial Indian movies.)

Two important points, however, should be made here for the sake of those exposed to the growing disenchantment with large projects such as the DVC. First, to adapt the argument of J.K. Bajaj about another controversial dam, Tehri, at the foothills of the Himalayas, the DVC was conceived over sixty years ago in the 1940s, and time has already extinguished much of the passion for such gigantism. If one was planning the DVC today, one would probably consider it a 'worthless exercise ... for nobody takes such risks for such small gains.'[5] In the meanwhile,

---

[4]For instance, William U. Chandler, *The Myth of TVA: Conservation and Development in the Tennessee Valley, 1933–1983* (Cambridge, Mass.: Ballinger Publishing, 1984).

[5]J.K. Bajaj, quoted in T.M. Mukundan, 'The Dams on Narmada and Bhagirathi: Need for a Review' (Madras: Centre for Policy Studies, 1992), mimeo.

however, an entire generation of planners, development economists, engineers, scientists, administrators and even journalists, social scientists, and writers have derived a part of their life's meaning from dreaming, building or legitimizing projects such as the DVC. Now that they face the possibility that their earlier optimism was misplaced and their vision faulty, they frantically defend the optimism and the vision and the meaning of life in which these are embedded. Criticism of dams have become equivalent to criticism of one's painfully constructed self for many.

Second, it is known that for long stretches of its life the cost of maintaining the DVC has been higher than the value of its products economically, environmentally and in terms of energy use. It is also known that direct and indirect state subsidies have made the project a white elephant, and that the energy the DVC produces is almost entirely thermal and not hydroelectric (as the project promised to produce).[6] Yet, certain kinds of criticism of the project have still not been ventured, not because they do not apply or have not been thought of, but because the empirical basis for such criticism has been wiped out by time.

Thus, nobody makes a fuss about the hundreds of communities, many of them tribal, ousted from the areas where the DVC dams were built, even though such criticism is now routine in the case of all large dams.[7] The ease with which land was acquired for the DVC, mainly from cultivators, can be gauged from Table 10.1. Few government initiatives in India have shown such a high rate of success.[8]

[6]Though the DVC has three thermal and three hydel power stations, the former together have a capacity of 1,545 MW and the latter of 104 MW. *A Profile of Damodar Valley Corporation: Forty Years of Service, 1948–88* (Calcutta: DVC, n.d.), p. 4.

[7]Though the issue of displacement came up in the Constituent Assembly during the debate on the Damodar Valley Corporation Bill, compare for instance the low-key debate on the subject and the systematic use of this issue by those opposed to the Narmada Sagar project. Edward Goldsmith, Nicholas Hildyard and Denys Trussell (ed.), *The Social and Environmental Effects of Large Dams* (Camelford, Cornwall, UK: The Wadebridge Ecological Centre, 1984–92), Vols. 1–3; Claude Alvares and Ramesh Billorey, *Damming the Narmada: India's Greatest Planned Environmental Disaster* (Penang: Third World Network/Appen, 1988); Darryl D'Monte, *Temples or Tombs? Industry Versus Environment, Three Controversies* (New Delhi: Centre for Science and Environment, 1985); Enakshi Ganguly Thukral (ed.), *Big Dams, Displaced People: Rivers of Sorrow, Rivers of Change* (New Delhi: Sage, 1992); and Mridula Singh, *Displacement by Sardar Sarovar and Tehri* (New Delhi: Multiple Action Research Group, 1992). Raajen Singh (ed.), *Dams and Other Major Projects: Impact on and Response of Indigenous People* (Goa: CCA-URM, 1988).

[8]This achievement is contextualized by a strange anomaly. When the DVC was built, it was hailed as a major developmental breakthrough because the project was being supposedly located in one of the poorest parts of India. Yet, Bengal at the time was India's richest state and Bihar was only a few steps behind. (Both states are now among the poorest in India.)

The people uprooted by the DVC, according to unofficial estimates about 150,000 strong, are now scattered.[9] Decultured and apparently well-settled, they now seem reconciled to their new life and have already sired a new generation which, like other such uprooted peoples, have learnt to use the dominant idiom of Indian public life. Even when some of them speak of their displacement and deculturation, there is a touch of instrumentality about it. Exposed to and knowledgeable about land prices, market demands, and the world of development in general, they are less unhappy about the fact that they were displaced from their traditional abode and ecological niche than about the paltry compensation they were paid, according to the conventions then prevalent. At least some of them would have agreed with the dedicated socialist planner and influential policy-maker of the period, Pitambar Pant, who once reportedly said in a plan document that India's 'tribal brethren' were expected to make the necessary sacrifices for the future prosperity and happiness of the country.[10] Only they would now like to be paid a hefty compensation as a token of the country's gratitude. Nobody of course

TABLE 10.1: *Land Acquisition—Targets and Achievement (hectares)*

Project	Target	Achieved	Per cent
Tilaiya	10,743	10,743	100.00
Konar	3,734	3,734	100.00
Maithon	10,785	10,785	100.00
Bokaro	673	491	72.96
Chandrapura	764	509	66.62
Transmission & Distribution	101	101	100.00
Hotwar	127	127	100.00
Panchet Tail Pool Dam	–	51	–
Total	35,831	34,361	95.90

Source: *Statistical Handbook 1980–81* (Calcutta: Statistical Branch, DVC, Ministry of Energy 1981), Vol. 19, Table 8.3, Ch. 8.

The value of highly fertile land in the two states was among the highest in the country. Indeed, the politicians probably knew better. Leaders in many other states were said to be jealous about this windfall to the two eastern states in the form of the DVC and its 'natural' by-products for the local politicians and bureaucrats in terms of power, patronage and money.

[9]According to official data, at least 93,874 persons belonging to 21.,310 families and 306 villages were displaced. *Statistical Handbook 1980–81* (Calcutta: Statistical Branch DVC, Ministry of Energy 1981), Vol. 19, Table 8.4, ch. 8.

[10]Quoted by Jaidev Sethi in an informal presentation made on Indian development at the India International Centre, 1989.

asked their tribal brethren at the time they were displaced if they were keen to make the sacrifice nor informed them beforehand of the true dimensions of the sacrifice involved.

In the larger, pan-Indian political culture within which the DVC was built, there was not much audible dissent. There could not be. The building of dams was no mere technological feat. As Shiv Viswanathan argues in the case of the well-known pioneer in the area, M. Visvesvaraya (1861–1962), dam building was also character building in the technological vision implicit in many versions of Indian nationalism. It involved containing and directing untamed, 'natural' energy. Decades ago, when in school, I had gone on an organized tour of the DVC lasting some three weeks along with twenty-five other students of science, engineering, humanities and medicine. A generous Rotary Club of Calcutta had sponsored the trip, and I still remember the enthusiasm and spirit of public service with which the sponsors and the high officials of the DVC explained to the young visitors the grandeur and niceties of the project. There was no doubt or scepticism in the air; no one had one serious critical comment to offer to even vaguely threaten the smooth execution of the master plan of a master project. The attitude of not only the committed business tycoons and plant managers or engineers, but that of the entire development community was that of the clergy explaining the complexities of an apparently ornate ritual to the ignorant but eager laity. Most disagreements to them seemed to arise from innocence and a few from more loathsome motives.[11] Neither that clergy nor its docile laity can now be expected to disown the past without disowning their own selfhood and self-created world.

In that heady, optimistic atmosphere Kapilprasad Bhattacharjee (1904–89) ventured his criticisms of the Damodar Valley Corporation in the late 1950s and early 1960s. He was not the first to do so. K.B. Roy, a Calcutta-based engineer and specialist on rivers, had already openly criticized the DVC, as had a few others. Indeed, for a short while, Bhattacharjee was enthusiastic about the DVC and even wrote a letter to the editor of *The Hindustan Standard* supporting the project. But he soon changed his mind and was one of the first in the world and certainly the first in South Asia to develop a systematic technical and social critique of large dams.

[11]That certitude and self-righteousness persist. Even today, critics of the Tehri and the Narmada Sagar dams in India are seen as traitors in the pay of the enemies of the countries, even when they are respected Gandhians and freedom fighters like Baba Amte and Sundarlal Bahuguna. Some journalists have even popularized the term 'environmental terrorists' for them.

Neither the term environmentalism nor the idea of the social audit of mega-technology was then a part of mainstream public discourse and, during much of his life, though he had a reasonably large readership, few saw him as a pioneering environmental activist. Indeed, for many he was a dangerous and evil presence who, like Professor Moriarty in the Sherlock Holmes stories, knew the science of multi-purpose water-management projects like the DVC but used that knowledge to benefit the enemies of the country.[12] This reading was strengthened by the fact that Bhattacharjee had at one time supported the DVC publicly.

Kapil Bhattacharjee was born in a lower middle-class Brahmin family of Telenipara in the Hooghly district of West Bengal, a place not far from Calcutta or from the banks of the Hooghly, one of the majestic rivers that were to be affected by the DVC. The family originally belonged to Dakshineshwar, another town on the banks of the Hooghly, close to the city of Calcutta. It was a town made famous by the nineteenth-century mystic Ramakrishna Paramhamsa. Kapil was the eldest of four brothers and three sisters. His father was a railway clerk and his grandfather a priest who made his living by taking groups of pilgrims to Gangasagar. Two of Kapil's elder brothers had died soon after birth and he was born after a *manat* made to the ancient sage Kapil. Hence the name Kapilprasad (Kapil's gift/benediction). Thus, for all practical purposes, Kapil was brought up as the first-born. The death of his brothers also ensured him an especially protected, pampered childhood. He never quite acquired, his wife Tilottama believes, the capacity to stand physical hardship. Like his father, he had a nasty temper but an otherwise easygoing manner— a combination that, Tilottama thinks in retrospect, conformed to the family style of the Bhattacharjees.

When Kapil was young, his father was transferred to Katihar, in the

---

[12]The following is from a news item published in India's largest-selling newspaper at the time (*Ananda Bazar Patrika*, 7 November 1961):

> The Central government's attention has been drawn to the propaganda being spread by a group of people that the Farakka Barrage will be harmful for West Bengal. The state government has been instructed by the central government to find out details about the leader of this propaganda. It has been also revealed that Pakistan, taking advantage of this propaganda, is conducting an anti-India propaganda internationally. ...
>
> ... the person [Kapil Bhattacharjee] leading the propaganda [who] touts himself as an experienced engineer has published sometime ago a pamphlet called *The Harmful Effects of the Farrakka Barrage* and a Pakistani spy collected few copies of the booklet and sent them to the Pakistani government.

adjacent state of Bihar. The elder Bhattacharjee liked the town and wanted to stay on there after retirement. His hand was forced when he was sacked from his job—reportedly because he beat up his English boss on being insulted—and the family decided to make Katihar their home. It was from there that Kapil matriculated in 1921. He did his Intermediate Science course (a preparatory course that allowed one to join degree courses) from the TNG College in Bhagalpur, which was close to Katihar, and went to Calcutta to study civil engineering at the Bengal Engineering College, Shibpur, from where he graduated in 1928.

Coming from a family of modest means, Kapil's first priority after graduation was to achieve economic self-sufficiency, and he established a private firm in civil engineering at Bhagalpur. He also got married in 1930. His wife, Alokmayee, belonged to another Bengali Brahmin family settled in Bihar; she was the daughter of an advocate who practised in Patna. Kapil's married life was sad, if eventful. Their first children, twins, died soon after birth. Their third child, a son, was born in 1932. At around this time, Alokmayee began to show signs of mental illness, to be diagnosed later as schizophrenia. Probably in the beginning the illness did not seem serious, for they had a second child, a girl, in 1936. However, soon afterwards Kapil began distancing himself from his wife, for he had in the meanwhile fallen in love with Tilottama who came from a large, well-to-do family of famous writers, some of whom were also well-known public figures. Her father, Surendranath Gangopadhyay, was a writer, her uncle Upendranath a novelist and the editor of the trendy literary journal, *Vichitra*, and her father's cousin, Saratchandra Chattopadhyay, was India's most popular novelist of all times. The young, struggling engineer might have been keen to shed his first wife.

Divorce at the time was not a popular option; in 1937 Kapil simply sent Alokmayee back to her natal family. Unable to take care of her at home, they in turn sent her to the well-known mental hospital at Ranchi, where she spent the rest of her life. Her son and daughter and their families were the only ones to visit her there once in a while. Kapil never visited or met her again and, it seems, tried hard to forget his first brush with marriage. He even kept it a secret from Tilottama that he had a daughter from his first marriage, born after his first wife had fallen ill. Alokmayee died at Ranchi in 1984.

As for his professional life, for about five years after his graduation, Kapil worked on inconsequential projects of various kinds. He then had a break. He got a chance to go to Paris for further studies with financial support from a well-known local patron of education, Dipnarayan Singh of Bhagalpur. Paris must have been a strange experience for the young

engineer brought up in a small railway colony, but Kapil was not over-
awed by it. Within a year he had picked up excellent French and opened
an engineering firm in collaboration with a German friend. He also
came under the influence of a French expert on hydrology and water
management. Those were, however, difficult and unpredictable days in
Europe and a strange set of events ended Bhattacharjee's sojourn at
Paris. In 1935 he was reportedly contacted by Adolf Hitler through an
intermediary. The French police came to know this and informed the
British police, who in turn warned his father. The worried father sent
him a cable saying he was seriously ill. Kapil rushed home, never to return
to Paris. He resumed work as a civil engineer at Bhagalpur.

Kapil and Tilottama got married in 1936. Kapil, despite his odd brush
with politics in Paris, had never really been political, but his second wife
had been exposed to the freedom movement and the Indian National
Congress through her family, mainly her father. It was probably because
of her that Kapil later on began to take some interest in active politics.
Also, Kapil had been reared in a bicultural Bengali–Bihari atmosphere at
the margin of poverty; Tilottama's family, though it belonged to Bhagalpur,
was proudly Bengali and conspicuously bourgeois. But perhaps for that
same reason it lacked, Tilottama herself says, something of the warmth
and kindness of the Bhattacharjees.

Kapil had been a good student throughout and had won a number of
scholarships and awards. Everyone who knew him expected him to be
a successful engineer. Once he returned from an internationally-known
university, he was expected to settle down with a good job or set up a
private practice, especially since he had family responsibilities. At first
he seemed all set to fulfil these expectations. But already other concerns
and interests had begun to occupy his mind. He had always been a serious
reader; now he began to write, too. Some of the translations he did from
French and some stories he published were later put together in two
Bengali books: *Tin Peg Whiskey* and *Ghasetimaler Tabedari*.

Bhattacharjee had a rather complicated career as a professional
engineer. He was in and out of a large number of jobs. Some of his more
important appointments were his tenure at the Calcutta Municipal
Corporation in the late 1930s; his work for Beton Arm as a civil engineer
who pioneered the use of reinforced concrete in India and subsequently
as an army contractor building roads at Ranchi during World War II; his
association with a tea company at Jorhat and Dibrugarh in Assam; and
his work as a ship builder during the 1950s. Many of these were routine
jobs, but some of the experience did not go waste. They helped him
tangentially afterwards, it is said, when he became interested in the

overlapping fields of dams, irrigation, hydrology and water management.

As early as 1939, Bhattacharjee had published an essay in the Bengali newspaper *Jugantar* in which he explored the idea of a network of waterways to relieve traffic congestion in the city of Calcutta. He also wrote, at about the same time, a letter to the editor of *The Statesman*, protesting against the construction of the Hirakud dam in Orissa, probably the first instance of public protest against dams in the modern sector in India. Over the years, such interests pushed him towards science journalism, and his prime interest became the faulty planning and execution of the DVC. This work depended little on any planned empirical research: it was mainly based on his immense reading, his exposure to the French hydrologist in Paris, his early acquaintance with some of the rivers that were later to be dammed, his varied experiences as a civil engineer, and random observations. His intellectual style always remained a Brahminic mix of the amateur and the professional.

It was around this time that Bhattacharjee drifted towards a vague form of radicalism, tinged with nationalism of the kind Subhas Chandra Bose's Forward Block represented. Gradually, given the intellectual atmosphere in Calcutta at the time, he moved closer to Marxism. According to most accounts, it was an uncritical, orthodox, unrepentant form of Leninism, that being the dominant creed in the circles in which he had begun to move. (Though his daughter, herself a part of the Left movement during her student days, now doubts if he ever truly turned a Marxist.) However, Marxism in Bengal, being part of the European cosmopolitanism imported by the Indian literati, carried a Brahminic imprint and Bhattacharjee, given his temperament and upbringing, might not have found it entirely uncongenial. Having been an apolitical person for much of his life, he probably picked up the outlines of his ideology from the group around *Svadhinata*, a Bengali newspaper which served as the official mouthpiece of the Communist Party of India and a newspaper that for a while published his columns. Kapil's son, Pradyumna, was seriously active in the communist movement and played an important role in establishing a relationship between his father and the party newspaper. Kapil himself probably did not have the necessary political background or exposure to critically evaluate the psychological and philosophical structure of the ideology he was opting for. Leninism was in the air in the intellectual circles of Calcutta and that might have been good enough for him. And his remained basically the radicalism of the 1930s—hard, ultra-positivist, subservient to the ideas of universal science, human engineering and linear history, and unrelieved, according to some, by any self-doubt or even any sense of humour. Like many others of his generation, he seemed to have lived happily with his ideal-istic, romantic commitment to historical materialism. His own fiction and the stories he chose to translate from French seem to hint at another informal ideological substratum, but that is beyond the scope of this study.

After more than twenty years of environmental activism and defying his thirty-year-long affair with Leninism, Bhattacharjee spent the last years of his life working mainly for the human rights movement. Though an old-style radical, he had become increasingly aware of the need for such a movement in eastern India where the concern with human rights had been relatively weak. The ruthlessness of law-enforcing agencies in the early 1970s, trying to root out Maoist militancy in urban Bengal, made him aware of the need for such a body, especially as some other prominent citizens, including a few leading lights of the left, had refused to take a public position on the issue. At the age of sixty-eight, Bhattacharjee agreed to chair the Association for Protection of Democratic Rights (APDR). By the time of his death, he had managed in his usual tenacious fashion to give the movement some teeth.

However, by this time, the widespread public rejection of his position on large dams had made Bhattacharjee a disappointed, withdrawn, silent, perhaps somewhat sullen person. He had probably also come to regard his environmental activism as a futile, misconceived project. For the human rights activism of his later years never covered the victims of mega-dams, not even those displaced by the DVC. When he died in 1989, though movements against large dams had already broken out all over South Asia and environmentalism had become globally fashionable, his own environmental activism had become a vague, distant memory even for the younger generation of Greens.

II

'Environmentalists should agitate, but within the defined parameters.'

Kamal Nath, Minister of Environment, Government of India.
Quoted in *India Today*, 15 September 1993.

Bhattacharjee's critique of the DVC was a three-tiered exercise, though it is doubtful if he himself ever saw it as that. There is in it a multi-layered, shadowy fourth tier that he sometimes used to preface his other, 'more serious', scientific criticisms of the project.

At the most manifest plane, the critique offered a bizarre conspiracy theory. He of course did not see it as bizarre; he was confident enough about it to start his famous 1953 lecture, 'Damodar Parikalpanar Samaskar Chai', with a reading of this conspiracy.[13]

Bhattacharjee's argument on this theme is not easy to follow. He starts with the statement that the research of people like the physicist Meghnad Saha and his associates in India spurred the Viceroy, Lord Wavell, to first plan in the mid-1940s a multi-purpose project for the river Damodar that would mainly produce hydroelectricity. Bhattacharjee reminds his readers that Germany had just been defeated in World War II; the secrets of nuclear weaponry and the scientists who knew these secrets in Germany had been captured by the Allies. However, the British empire had no way of 'applying' this knowledge for military purposes. Also, whereas in the United States the TVA had started functioning, Britain herself lay devastated by German wartime bombing.[14] The 'shrewd' British prime minister, Winston Churchill, therefore, had no option but to allow the Americans to build nuclear weapons. Once the atom bombs were dropped on Japan, Churchill's 'faithful disciple' Lord Wavell 'suddenly decided to implement the multi-purpose project planned for the river Damodar'.[15] Within two years of the decision to build the DVC, the pact to transfer British power to the Indian National Congress was signed, and 'Britain's ongoing business continued to flourish' in India.[16] In 1948 work began on the DVC, planned within the framework of imperial self-interest; in the next six years between 440 and 450 million rupees was spent on the project 'of which 210 million was spent reportedly on buying materials from Britain and the United States.'[17] For Bhattacharjee, the clinching piece of evidence was that an obviously happy and satisfied Viscout Swinton, then British Secretary of Commonwealth Relations, had not merely congratulated but 'thanked' the Government of India for the DVC.

Even to the reader overly alert to imperial designs, this might appear to be a tenuous, if not paranoiac theory of conspiracy.[18] But those were

[13]Kapil Bhattacharjee, 'Damodar Parikalpanar Samaskar Chai', in Svadhin Bharate Nadnadi Parikalpana (Calcutta: Kalam, 1986), pp. 14–30; see pp. 17–21, and pp. 23–6.
[14]Ibid., p. 20.
[15]Ibid.
[16]Ibid., pp. 20–1.
[17]Ibid., p. 21.
[18]The DVC did, however, have military significance. The American member of the Central Technical Power Board, Voorduin, did not try to hide this and indeed, as if to spite Bhattacharjee, ended his memorandum to the CTPB by referring to the 'great' role of the DVC as a national defence agency. See W.L. Voorduin, 'The United Development of the Damodar River: Preliminary Memorandum', Preliminary Memorandum on the Unified Development of the Damodar River (1947) (Reprint Calcutta: DVC, 1985), pp. 7–35.

the early years of the cold war and the intellectual climate in modern India, as elsewhere, was filled with suspicion, stereotypes and scapegoating. More complex theories of the complicity of the First World in the sack of the Third, through the global project of development, were to come into vogue later.[19] Bhattacharjee himself was to produce more refined theoretical formulations. However, it must also be admitted that he was ideologically closest to a form of radicalism that thrived on conspiracy theories of all hues; somehow or other, he felt he had to establish evidence of the direct, blatant exploitation of the Third World by the First, even if convincing only the few already proselytized.

At the second plane, Bhattacharjee is a modern, internal critic of the technological dream that sired the DVC, a dream that itself came to be symbolized by the DVC and the Bhakra–Nangal project for nearly four decades.

At this plane, Bhattacharjee argues that before British rule India was never known as primarily an agricultural society ('krishipradhan desh'), though it was famous for its agricultural wealth. Pre-British India was also known as an industrial and trading nation.[20] Bhattacharjee refers to the 'consensus' of historians that to sustain imperial rule and exploitation, Britain reduced India to an agricultural society by making the huge majority of the country's people dependent on agriculture.[21]

Bhattacharjee saw the DVC as the direct continuation of that style of governance. It exploited the fear of the destructive floods of the Damodar to sell the idea of a technological 'marvel' that would bring about dramatic large improvements in the standard of living in East India, even though in reality it was to devastate India's economic future. First, the project reduced valuable fertile land in the name of digging canals to supply water, especially in the three districts of West Bengal—Hooghly, Howrah and Burdwan—where population density at that time was between 200 and 300 per square mile and where three to four crops per year were common.[22] Instead of recovering fallow land or land eroded by river, the new DVC canals led to the loss of large tracts of fertile land. And the people knew it. (See the official figures on land lost due to

---

[19]For a more sophisticated statement of imperial domination through a project like the DVC, see the work of two young environmental activists, Hemant and Ranajiv (eds), *Jab Nadi Bandhi* (Madhupur, Bihar: Jayaprakash Adhyayan ebam Anusandhan Kendra, 1991), pp. 8–11.

[20]Bhattacharjee, 'Damodar Parikalpanar Samaskar Chai', p. 15.

[21]Ibid.

[22]Ibid., p. 16.

TABLE 10.2: *Nature of Land Acquired for Submergence*

Project	Land Acquired (Ha.)	Cultivated land (%)	Wasteland (%)	Total (%)
Tilaiya	6,508	49.14	50.86	100.00
Konar	2,722	31.45	68.55	100.00
Maithon	9,609	66.56	33.44	100.00
Panchet	7,275	54.16	45.84	100.00
Total	26,114	55.10	44.90	100.00

Source: *Statistical Handbook 1980–81*, Table 8.1, ch. 8.

TABLE 10.3: *Nature of Land Acquired for the Power Projects and Hotwar Estate*

Project	Land Acquired (Ha.)	Cultivated Land (%)	Wasteland (%)	Total (%)
Bokaro	424	91.13	18.87	100.00
Chandrapura	490	100.00	0.00	100.00
Transmission & Distribution	101	100.00	0.00	100.00
Hotwar	127	100.00	0.00	100.00
Total	1142	92.99	7.01	100.00

Source: *Statistical Handbook 1980–81*, Table 8.2, ch. 8.

submergence and construction of power stations alone in Tables 10.2 and 10.3. To get a fuller picture, one should add the arable land lost to the new townships and the industrial units. The tables also confirm that more cultivated land was lost to the DVC than wasteland.)

Also, as part of the DVC, a factory was being built at Sindri for 'artificial' chemical fertilizers and things were so arranged that people would be forced to buy these fertilizers at outrageous prices.[23] Bhattacharjee hoped that ordinary citizens would see through such trickery. He expected that the very fact that agriculturists and other affected sectors or targeted beneficiaries were not involved in the planning of the DVC would soon alert people to the destructiveness of such plans, which were actually meant to enrich only a few compradors. These kinds of developmental plans, he felt, were the brainwaves of people who had learnt to parrot imperial ideas and had been nurtured by them.[24] As it happened, like many later environmentalists, Bhattacharjee was to be disappointed:

[23]Ibid., p. 25.
[24]Ibid.

articulate citizens, led by massive propaganda to believe that the DVC would build an earthly paradise through magical technology in eastern India, were to see Bhattacharjee as a maverick critic, sometimes as a traitor.

By this time the reader might have gathered that, unlike many of the recent environmental activists in India, Bhattacharjee was an open votary of the urban–industrial vision. He granted that the DVC would lead to some amount of industrialization and he considered that a positive contribution of the project.[25] He also had no quarrel with the multi-purpose nature of the DVC.[26] To this extent, one might say, he was an internal critic not only of modern technology but also of Indian development, a pioneer of the movement for what would now be called sustainable development. All he wanted were 'alternative' modes of water management for actualizing roughly the same goals that were the stated goals of India's official development policy.

Not surprisingly, Bhattacharjee's sharpest barbs were reserved for experts such as C.A. Bentley, William Wilcocks and C. Addams-William, who had suggested as early as the 1920s and 1930s that something like the DVC was necessary for the good of Indian peasants. Bhattacharjee saw the plea as a prescription for keeping India a backward, agricultural country. He felt that Wilcocks, famous the world over for building a dam on the Nile, had been responsible for reducing Egypt to a backward, underindustrialized country supplying agricultural products to Britain. 'Likewise in 1928–30, the goal of Sir William Wilcocks was to increase the volume of India's agricultural products and the size of her peasant population to serve the military and imperial purposes of the British.'[27]

That is why a major—perhaps the first—concern of Bhattacharjee was the survival of Calcutta port. One of his main criticisms of the DVC was that it would lead to the silting of the Hooghly and ensure the death of Calcutta. 'Before everything else, it is necessary to protect the port of Calcutta,' he repeatedly said. If Calcutta port could not entertain seafaring ships, the city of Calcutta and the industrial area around it were doomed. If Calcutta died, not merely the districts of Burdwan, Hooghly, Howrah and Midnapur but the entire states of West Bengal, Bihar, Assam and Orissa would become the victims of utter misery.[28] He wanted the work on DVC's Maithon and Panchet dams to be stopped for at least five

---

[25]Bhattacharjee, 'Introduction', in *Svadhin Bharate Nadnadi Parikalpana*, pp. 9–13; see p. 13.
[26]Ibid., p. 25.
[27]Ibid., p. 24.
[28]Ibid., p. 29.

TABLE 10.4: *Performance of the DVC at the End of the First Phase of the Project (1956)*

Sector	Estimate	Actual
Irrigation (acre)	10,000,000	3,000,000
Hydro-electricity (KW)	146,000	8,000
Thermal electricity (KW)	150,000	28,000
Expense (million Rs)	550	1,000

Source: Bhattacharjee, *Bangladesher Nadnadi*, pp. 78–9.

years, till an appropriate scientific plan for saving the port of Calcutta had been devised.[29]

Bhattacharjee developed this argument in another well-known essay.[30] He said there that between 1954 and 1959, thanks to the DVC, the maximum discharging capacity of the Bhagirathi-Hooghly had come down from 50,000 cusecs to 20,000 cusecs, a decline of 60 per cent. This he read as the death knell of Calcutta.[31] He believed that the planning authorities, out of 'a false sense of status', hoodwinked the public by 'shrewdly' building the Farakka barrage and diverting between 20,000 and 30,000 cusecs of Ganges water into the Hooghly and the Bhagirathi. This they claimed, dishonestly, would maintain the navigability of the river and its discharging capacity.[32] The building of a new port at Haldia was acknowledgement enough that the port of Calcutta was dead. But Bhattacharjee did not expect the Haldia port to survive either, for it also would die from the silting of river beds.[33]

Despite being a part-time writer of fiction and a translator of Maupassant, Bhattacharjee was not particularly psychologically minded. He had no inkling of the emerging culture of the Indian middle class,

[29]Ibid. The future of the city of Calcutta was a lifelong preoccupation for Bhattacharjee. At different times he toyed with ideas about improving Calcutta's water supply and providing cheap housing for the city's middle class.

[30]Bhattacharjee, 'Damodar Upatakya Parikalpana: Paschim Banger Viparjaya', in *Svadhin Bharate Nadnadi Parikalpana*, pp. 31–7.

[31]Ibid., p. 31.

[32]Ibid., p. 33. This argument did not anticipate that the roots of India's tension with Bangladesh over the sharing of river waters would lie in this project.

[33]Ibid., pp. 33–4. The consistent tendency of the DVC experts to underestimate siltation, despite past experience and data, remains one of the more curious aspects of the whole story. Thus, for two of the older dams, Maithon and Panchet, the annual rates of siltation were expected to be 684 and 1,982 acre feet respectively. The observed rates turned out to be 5,980 and 9,533. Bharat Dogra, 'The Indian Experience with Large Dams', in Goldsmith, Hildyard and Trussell, *The Social and Environmental Effects of Large Dams*, vol. 2, pp. 201–8; see p. 201.

getting increasingly globalized and unable to give up, as unworkable, the progressivist dream that had come to define its vision of India's future. For the self-interest of this expanding middle class intermeshed with the dream. The Leninist crudities in his conspiracy theory of the origins of the DVC could have been more a product of his refusal to acknowledge the primacy of human subjectivity in some areas of public life than of any paranoiac element in his personality. For it was clear by the end of the 1950s, if not by the mid-1950s, that the DVC was not doing well. The data on the performance of the project, released after the completion of the first phase of the project, which Bhattacharjee himself deployed so skilfully, were widely available. The project officials, the dam enthusiasts, and the development community might have had a vested interest in ignoring or underplaying these data (see Table 4), but the newspaper-reading public did not. But they paid scant attention to them. As if the DVC was a crucial part of their self-definition which, if disowned, would bring down an entire worldview and an entire vision of a good society and desirable future. The enchantment of the dominant model of modernization still held in India and many were willing to face self-destruction rather than face any threat to their painfully-constructed self-definition.

At the third plane, Bhattacharjee seemed to defy his own public self and long-term commitment to the urban-industrial vision, his blatant scientism and even his own favourite theory of progress. At this plane he occasionally broke out of his self-created straitjacket of modernism to defend the traditional systems of knowledge in his part of the globe. This respect for the increasingly marginalized systems of knowledge in his community was probably, to Bhattacharjee, the least accessible area of his own personality, where his diagnosis of the DVC, stripped of its ideological moorings, converged with the shared knowledge of his community, transmitted over generations, outside the range of vision of technocrats and development experts. And he certainly was not alert to the sacralized concepts of water and river that framed these alternative knowledge systems.[34]

According to Bhattacharjee, in pre-colonial days, that is, till the first half on the eighteenth century, those who stayed near the banks of the

---

[34]I have in mind especially the kinds of sensitivity that is sought to be captured in the West, successfully or otherwise, in works such as Theodor Schwenk, *Sensitive Chaos* (London: Rudolph Steiner, 1976); and Theodor Schwenk and Wolfram Schwenk, *Water—The Element of Life*, tr. Marjorie Spock (New York: Anthroposophic Press, 1989).

last hundred miles of the Damodar, from *puranic* or epic times onwards, used the floods to supply fertilizers to their land, mainly in the form *pali* (alluvial soil).[35] The practice had been in use for at least 400 years. Also, the region did not suffer from any shortage of rainfall and, according to experts such as William Wilcocks and C. Addams-Williams, the monsoon floods brought in billions of fish eggs and tadpoles to the rice fields, which survived on mosquito eggs. This not merely helped control malaria, but the inhabitants had a plentiful, cheap supply of protein in the form of fish.[36] The experts admitted that the partial damming of the Damodar and subsequent check on floods had already reduced the fertility of land and easy availability of fish.[37]

Bhattacharjee granted that the practice of building embankments/ bunds for the Damodar was nearly 4000 years old. These structures were never high and, in any case, the peasants cut them occasionally for reasons of agriculture at times of floods. (Bhattacharjee usually used the Bengali term *bandh* which, depending on the context, could mean dam, barrage, embankment or dyke and even subsumes under it the Anglo-Indian *bund*, derived from the same source as *bandh*, and the southern Bengali *bhedi*; one has sometimes to guess the specific meaning from the context and by comparing his English and Bengali writings.) That controlled use of floods—and dams—was managed by the peasants collectively; the state did not play much part in it. So the peasants did not even have to pay any tax or levy for their privilege; their gains were seen as part of nature's bounty.[38] Wilcocks guessed, Bhattacharjee says, that the ancient kings of the region had taken the help of Babylonian experts to build some of the embankments and canals of the region.

The maintenance of these structures stopped in the eighteenth century, when Maratha raids became frequent in Bengal. Afterwards, when the Raj was established, the British did not understand the importance of

---

[35] Bhattacharjee, '*Damodar Parikalpanar Samaskar Chai*', p. 21.

[36] Ibid.

[37] Strangely, not only in this instance but in many others, Bhattacharjee depended heavily on these much maligned writers for his understanding of the hydrological regime of eastern India, especially on C.A. Bentley, *Malaria and Agriculture in Bengal* (1925); William Wilcocks, *Ancient System of Irrigation in Bengal* (1938); *Report of the Damodar Flood Enquiry Committee*, Vols. 1 and 2 (1944).

[38] Bhattacharjee, '*Damodar Parikalpanar Samaskar Chai*', p. 22. Bhattacharjee did not take into account and probably did not want to take into account, traditional cultrual means of coping with floods as a natural calamity. There are clues to them in M.Q. Zaman, 'Ethnography of Disasters: Flood and Erosion in Bangladesh', *Eastern Anthropologist*, 1994, 47(2), pp. 129–55.

maintaining these *bunds* and their proper use. They presumed they were only checks against floods, and that the canals were only a means of water supply.[39] The situation worsened when Lord Cornwallis introduced the Permanent Settlement System in eastern India in 1793.[40] The *bunds* that had been under the control of the peasants came under the control of the new landlords created by the system (who had no idea of the traditional water management system). Bhattacharjee does not add that they were often the upper-caste urban rich investing in land the new wealth they had acquired through their connection with the colonial political economy. These new landlords had no deep or time-tested relationships with their own land, the peasants in their domain or, for that matter, with agriculture as a way of life; they were mainly moved by ideas of safe investments and social status.

Though peasants discontented with the new system tried to affirm their traditional rights by often cutting open the *bunds* secretly at night, the image of the Damodar as a destructive river that annually flooded large areas gradually consolidated itself, thanks to the misuse or non-use of traditional flood-management techiques.[41] Malaria too established itself as an annual epidemic in eastern India at around the same time.[42]

The DVC was shaped by this distorted perception of an established agro-ecological system. Instead of an elaborate, costly affair like the DVC, Bhattacharjee therefore suggested the proper maintenance of old canals, tanks, lakes and other storage systems and waterways. They were more than adequate, he felt, for irrigational purposes. Even some small, troublesome sections of the Damodar could be turned into lakes by changing the nature of the embankments already built.[43] Nothing more needed to be done by way of flood-control. Here Bhattacharjee comes dangerously close to contemporary ideas of limits to modern science and technology, and in his 'saner' moments he may not have been very happy about it.

I must hasten to re-emphasize that this aspect of Bhattacharjee—respect for the traditional systems of knowledge and for the life-support systems that backed that knowledge—was less accessible to him and somewhat incongruent with his public self. That self was essentially one of a counter-

[39]Bhattacharjee, *Damodarn Parikalpanar Samaskar Chai'*, p. 22.
[40]Ibid., pp. 22–3.
[41]Ibid., p. 23.
[42]Ibid.
[43]Ibid., p. 28.

expert who offered an alternative technological solution rather than an alternative worldview. For a clue to this public and dominant self, one has to see only the one-page summary of his well-considered suggestions in 'Damodar Upatakya Parikalpana.'[44] They are all basically technocratic, harsh though the term may sound when applied to a person as far-sighted and ecologically sensitive as him. In practice, Bhattacharjee was like a modern medical doctor, alert enough to hit upon the incidence and causes of iatrogenic ailments but who, driven by his own inner needs, has constantly to look for new drugs and surgical procedures to cure the new ailments. There are not many hints in his works, voluminous though they are, that he believed in the limits of human intervention in nature. As I have said, in retrospect, it is easier to read him as a pioneer of the movement for sustainable development than as a radical critic of the idea of development itself.

Nothing reveals this more clearly that the missing or, rather disowned, fourth and fifth levels in his critique of the DVC (see Figure 1). I have mentioned that Kapil Bhattacharjee was not a typical product of urban India. He had spent some of his formative years in semi-rural small towns of Bihar. Also, part of his practical training as a student of engineering was a stay in Ranchi where Kapil developed warm relationships with a number of families belonging to the Munda tribe. So there is at least a good chance that he had seen first-hand or heard of tribal communities ousted from their traditional abodes for the sake of various development projects—the forests cleared, the villages relocated, and little cultures destroyed. At least 150,000 refugees had been created by the DVC who,

FIGURE 1: *Layers of Critical Awareness in Kapil Bhattacharjee*

Critique of western imperialism and the West's neocolonial designs	
Critique of the scientific basis of the DVC, its faulty planning and threats to the survival of Calcutta port	
Critique of mindless destruction of established traditional technology of the region	
Critique of attacks on the little cultures of communities, their technological traditions, micro-ecologies and micro-economics	Critique of modern science and technology, the totalism of urban-industrialism and developmentalism
Critique of desacralization of nature; accepting rivers as 'civilizational boons'	

[44]Bhattacharjee, *'Damodar Upatakya Parikalpana'*, pp. 36–7.

TABLE 10.5: *Internal Refugees Created by Indian Development*

Project	Displaced	Rehabilitated	Remaindered
Coal/Other mining	17,40,000	4,40,000	13,00,000
Dams	1,00,00,000	30,00,000	70,00,000
Industry	20,00,000	6,50,000	13,50,0000
Sanctuaries/National Parks	6,00,000	2,00,000	4,00,000
Other	20,00,000	6,50,000	13,50,000
Total	1,63,40,000	49,40,000	1,14,00,000

Source: *Social Action*, July–September, 1988. Quoted in Hemant and Ranajiv, *Jab Nadi Bandhi*, p. 97. Note the entry of environmentalism into the picture—a case of environmentalism itself creating new iatrogenic environmental problems. Most of the 600,000 displaced by the creation of sanctuaries and national parks are recent cases of internal refugees. So they constitute a small but more significant proportion of the total today than the figures suggest.

being unorganized and lacking political clout, had received less than adequate compensation for the land they had lost.[45] Most of them were tribals. They were a part of the more than 15 million internal refugees created by Indian development, of whom only about 5 million were to be rehabilitated; the rest being considered fit for remaindering (see Table 10.5).[46] Bhattacharjee, though a pioneer in human-rights activism in his later years had almost nothing to say about that part of the story.

Likewise, Bhattacharjee must have seen something of the cultures of the tribes disappearing before the advancing juggernaut of the DVC.

[45]ECAFE figures on a typical case suggest that the purchase price of land then was a little less than Rs 900 per acre (U.S. $ 42.60) and compensation was calculated on that basis. United Nations Economic Commission for Asia and the Far East, *A Case Study of the Damodar Valley Corporation and Its Projects* (Bangkok: ECAFE, 1960), Flood Control Series No. 16, p. 62. According to Social anthropologist B.K. Roy Burman, the compensations were higher at the beginning; they declined later in response to advice from the World Bank.

At first, the DVC authorites built houses for the displaced, but the houses had little to do with the concept of housing of the displaced, who in many cases tore them down 'to better accommodate their way of life' (ibid., p. 64). Later on, the DVC ascertained in advance what the displaced wanted, cash settlement or compensation in the form of a house or land; 92 per cent chose cash and 'the remaining families took cash compensation to build houses for themselves and some even elected to do their own reclaiming' (Ibid.). It is said that a large proportion of the displaced families, with little familiarity with the market economy, quickly burnt up their money without being able to build any tangible vocation or asset.

One indicator of the poor bargaining power of the displaced and the social ambience of the time was DVC's ability to acquire 96 per cent of the targeted land without much problem. See Table 10.1.

[46]This figure could be a gross underestimation and may represent the number of people on whom rehabilitation data are available. According to another estimate, 21.6

He must have seen the traditional artisan skills, healing systems, and the art of forest management implicit in the lifestyle of many forest-dwelling communities, and even the environmental, awareness that characterized peoples such as the Santhal, Munda, Oraon and Kol.[47] Yet, there is no hint in his works that he recognized the range of the pain and suffering of the tribals. One might say that he was never as alert to the cultural and communal fate of the communities uprooted and decultured by the DVC as he was to the fate of Calcutta and the urban–industrial future of West Bengal.

The reasons for this partiality are not hard to guess. Like many Bhadraloks of his generation, Bhattacharjee thought himself to be a stepson of the modern West and the European Enlightenment. He shared the anxieties of a class that had been sired by the West and had always felt that it had been infantilized and exiled from its natural and rightful inheritance by an exploiting, scheming, jealous father, imperial in goals and style. The class therefore spent its creative life trying to separate the 'true' modern West with its 'true' heritage of the Enlightenment from the false West, violent and expropriatory. The former they wanted to own up; the latter they rejected. Within such a framework there could be no harm in mimicking Europe and North America, for that represented a step towards equality, adulthood and the universal principles the West had discovered earlier than other civilizations.

For Bhattacharjee, the moral rejection of the West's record outside the West, therefore, had to go hand in hand with efforts to internalize the 'technology' of dominance the West had developed, so that one would not be hoodwinked once again or caught in the imperial game as a hapless victim. This technology of dominance was seen to include a sharp scepticism towards the pre-industrial and non-industrial worlds,

---

people—roughly the population of all the Scandinavian countries put together—have been displaced only by the construction of dams in India. Gayatri Singh, 'Displacement and Limits to Legislation', in Singh, *Dams and Other Major Projects*, pp. 91–7; see p. 91.

According to another study, of the 70 million tribals in India belonging to some 212 tribes, 15 per cent have been displaced by development projects, so that they could themselves be developed and turned into 'skilled human resources'. Smithu Kothari, 'Theorizing Culture, Nature and Democracy in India' (Delhi: Lokayan, 1993), mimeo. A little less than half of all the invisible refugees created by Indian development are tribals.

[47] Most of the displaced were Santhals, a tribe that has probably paid the most heavily for he development and modernization of India. The tragedy of the Santhals, as it has unfolded over the last two centuries thorugh western colonialism and the growth of a modern political economy in India, is fit subject for an epic. The DVC has reportedly displaced at least 50,000 Santhals. Other tribes that have suffered include the Kols, one of the oldest in India.

viewed as expendable luxuries or artificially-promoted pastoral utopias, and a clear rejection of social visions that did not accept the western-style modern, urban–industrial society as the ultimate goal of all southern societies. All other visions were bound to look dangerous to Bhattacharjee, for they could be shown to be incapable of withstanding the masculine, technicized, this-worldly rationalism that powered the imperial West.

There was another aspect to the disowned self of Bhattacharjee. The revised version of his Bengali collection of essays, *Bangladesher Nadnadi o Parikalpana* (1955), begins with two elegant comments on the millennia-old place of the river Rupnarayan in the life of eastern India, and his unpublished MS, 'Hydrological Regime in Eastern India', begins with a hand-some acknowledgement of the role of rivers in the cultural self-definitions of Bihar, Orissa, West Bengal, Bangladesh, Nepal and Assam. Yet Bhattacharjee probably saw such comments and acknowledgement as indulgences he was entitled to.[48] Usually he defined the civilizational role of rivers on stark, secular lines that had little to do with the tradi-tional categories and meanings of river in the region. Though he always chose to speak on behalf of the people, 'the idea of preserving the sanc-tity of environment, and especially of the great rivers that since almost the beginning of mankind have been defining features of certain civili-zations' was beyond his worldview.[49] He saw himself as a secular ratio-nalist and a progressive and could never take the position that rivers like the Ganga were a 'civilizational boon' that could be left out of cost–benefit analyses and large-scale techno-social interventions, and consid-ered inviolable. Nor could he, even when he talked of the loss of cultivable land and top soil, mobilize from within himself a sensitivity to the life of the soil akin to that of someone like Daniel Hillel.[50]

Central to this secular rationalist view of the world was Afro-Asian Marxism. A devoted child of the Enlightenment and committed to a full-blown theory of progress, Marx when invited into the savage world did not remain merely a bearded prophet of equality and justice. He was turned into a symbol of transcending that part of one's own cultural self that had become associated with humiliation, victimization and self-contempt. The savage Marx was not only a protest against inequality,

---

[48]Kapil Bhattacharjee, *'Paschim Banger Jivane Rupnarayan Nader Bhumika'* and *'Bangladesher Nadnadi Sambandhe Sadharan Katha'* in *Bangladesher Nadnadi o Parikalpana* (1955) (expanded 2nd ed., Calcutta: Vidyodaya Library, 1959), pp. iii–ix, 1–9; and 'Hydrological Regime in Eastern India', mimeo.

[49]Mukundan, 'The Dams on Narmada and Bhagirathi'.

[50]Daniel J. Hillel, *Out of the Earth: Civilization and the Life of the Soil* (New York: The Free Press, 1991).

exploitation and the bourgeois sham in which they were packaged, but a philosopher–activist who allowed one to exteriorize one's anger and project on to others the unacceptable parts of one's own self—expropriatory, greedy, hyper-competitive, ruthlessly materialistic and open to the enticements of bourgeois hedonism.[51] (That rejected self could then find expression in a distorted or pathological form under propitious circumstances. Perhaps the discovery of pathetic collections of French wines, Russian caviar, designer clothes, and American currency in the secret basements and vaults of the puritanic, orthodox-Marxist leaders of East Europe's collapsing communist regimes is part of the same story of self-hatred coated in self-righteousness.)

Marx in the southern world also legitimised an Europe that had already been internalized by a significant section of the southern élite, on grounds other than those Lord Macaulay had so thoughtfully spelt out in colonial India in the early nineteenth century. Macaulay dreamt of natives who would inherit the earth in the tropics by virtue of being European in thought and emotions beneath their darker skins. Marx suggested that another internalized Europe, brought about by colonial conquest, would supply the principles and frames of dissent to help contain or counter the depredations of imperial Europe. The only concession that second Europe demanded in return was that all other forms of resistance, rooted in the worldview of the violated, be jettisoned as ineffective, effeminate, superstitious or romantic. Marx in the tropics might have fought for the dispossessed and exiled, but he also decultured and alienated. To this positivist Marx, the cultural inheritance and the ecological niche of the tribal communities submerged by the rising waters of the newly-built dams of the DVC were nothing more than embarrassingly humble artifacts and practices. They could be easily preserved as curios in the interstices of the modern world for the sake of the scholarly and the curious. In the meanwhile, the tribes themselves were expected to dutifully merge themselves in the mainstream culture of resistance defined by the industrial trade unions.

During the first half of this century, two persons pioneered environmentalism in South Asia. They may not have been the only environmentalists in a country where ecological concerns were often a cultural inheritance or, as in the case of some forms of Gandhism, an implicit component

---

[51]This awareness is reflected in a rudimentary form in Daniel Bell, 'After the Age of Sinfulness: Lukacs and the Mystical Roots of Revolution', *The Times Literary Supplement*, 26 July 1991, pp. 5–7.

of a political ideology that did not even use the term environment. But the two I have in mind were the eponymic figures who mounted a lonely struggle to rediscover nature and the biosphere for modern Indians, awed by the dazzling achievements and power of an industrialized, arrogantly imperial West. The first of the two, Radhakamal Mukherji (1889–1968), was primarily an academic; he 'found' environmentalism as part of a lonely intellectual journey. That part of the story has been well-told by Mamkootam Kuriakose in his unpublished essay on Mukherji.[52] The other, Kapil Bhattacharjee, as I hope I have shown here, came to environmentalism through his practical concern for the survival of modern Bengal as represented by the cultural and socioeconomic fate of the port city of Calcutta and its industrial suburbs.

India is not only its villages; it has a tradition of some 4,000 years of urban living and Bhattacharjee's broad concerns did enjoy substantial cultural legitimacy. But he was not able to see, despite his obvious moral passion, that this heritage of urban living intermeshed intricately with a kaleidoscopic maze of lifestyles ranging from the better-known peasant cultures of India to the lesser known micro-cosmos of a myriad of interdependent communities, castes, and tribes. Not only did Bhattacharjee belong to a class that considered itself the wronged stepchild of Enlightenment Europe, but a class that had, through deliberate choice, disavowed its cultural parents and kinsfolk within India. To him, Indian modernity, as represented by Calcutta and its industrial suburbs, was not merely a part of a larger civilizational mosaic that also had a place for the small, the humble and the less vocal. To him, that modernity deserved a place at the centre of the Indic civilization and was being unjustly denied its right by a conspiratorial West and its accomplices in India.

This disavowal of important aspects of one's cultural self brings me to one particular form of the politics of dams that a 'progressivist' ideology has to be blind to. This is the massive use of the idea of modern science to legitimize large dams by politicians, technocrats, contractors, and development experts. The use of the idea of Baconian science as the ultimate court of appeal helps identify all scepticism of technology as obscurantist and romantic, even in situations where available data seem inconsistent with large-scale intervention in nature.

This scientism of the protagonists of mega-technology is not a disease that can be cured by empirical data, however voluminous and rich. The real interests of politicians and developmentalists, Kapil Bhattacharjee

---

[52]M. Kuriakose, 'Radhakamal Mukherji: Pioneer in Ecological Studies' (Delhi: Department of Sociology, Delhi School of Economics, 1980) mimeo.

came very close to acknowledging, are not vested in the right kind of dam but in the idea of the dam itself. A mega-technological project is a major political-economic and psychotherapeutic intervention in a community's life and self-definition. It is often a major source of distributing patronage through contracts, political financing, building new networks of political obligations, generating politically powerful blue- and white-collar specialist jobs.[53] It is also often a technology of electoral mobilization and a means through which an impression of grand political performance can be created. Such a project gradually becomes an end in itself and cultivates a certain forgetfulness about its effects on the life-support systems of the community. Hence the addictive appeal of the bonding of science, development and state intervention in progressivist ideologies. These ideologies try to see through, demystify or deconstruct all ideologies except the ones that will, if successfully demystified, destroy the ideational basis and the certitudes of progressivism itself.

---

[53]This is indirectly acknowledged in 'The Politics of Damming', in Goldsmith, Hildyard and Trussell, *The Social and Environemntal Effects of Large Dams*, Vol. 1, ch. 19.

Index

Abdullah, Farooq, 146
achievement motive, 17, 126, 165n, 177
Addams-William, C., 196, 199
Adorno, Theodor, xi
Advani, Lal Krishna, 65n, 67, 103
affirmative action, religion-based, 36
Ahmed, Durré Sameen, 11n
Aichorn, August, 101
Akbar, 45, 50
Alberuni, 100
Ali, Bade Ghulam Ali, 51-2
Althusser, Louis, 89
Alvares, Claude, 9n, 11n, 25n, 27n, 128n, 158n, 159n, 171n, 177n, 185n
Amte, Baba, 187n
Anandpur Sahib Resolution, 58
anarchism, 13
Andreski, Stanislav, 91
Annadurai, C.N., 146
Anushilan Samiti, 134
Apffel-Marglin, Frederique, 68n, 69n, 128n, 155n, 172n
Arendt, Hannah, 74n, 97, 120, 124, 174
Arora, Satish, 6n, 177n
Arthashastra, 16n, 111
Aseniero, George, 160

Ashoka, 45, 50, 111
Ataturk, Kemal, 5
Attenborough, Richard, 24n
authoritarianism, xii, 9, 10, 29n, 56, 164, 172, 175-6, 177-8, 179-80
and development, 176-9
see also zealotry, Nazism
Ayodhya, riots in, 67

Babri Mosque, demolition of, 67, 102, 105
Bacon, Francis, 88
Badrinath, Chaturvedi, 79n
Bahuguna, Sunderlal, 155n, 187n
Bailey, C.A., 70n
Bains, Ajit Singh, 148n
Bajaj, J.K., 184
Bajpai, Kanti, 132-3n
Bakunin, Mikhail, xi, 5
Bali, Yogendra, 136n
Bandopadhyay, Jayanta, 155n
Banerjea, Krishna Mohun, 108
Banerjea, Surendranath, 101
Bannerji, Sumanta, 70n
Banuri, Tariq, 6n, 10n, 11n, 72, 75, 76, 90n
Bauman, Zygmunt, 74n
Bell, Daniel, 205n
Bentley, C.A., 196, 199n

Berry, N.O., 144n
Bharati Agehananda, 47
Bharatiya Janata Party (BJP), 64, 65n, 78n, 142, 145n
Bhashani, Maulana, 17, 36
Bhat, Maqbool, 134
Bhatia, Gautam, 125n
Bhattacharjee, Kapilprasad, 187–207
    and human rights movement, 192, 202
    and Leninism, 191–2
    and traditional knowledge systems, 198–201
    childhood, 188–9
    education, 189–90
    levels of awarenss, 201
    marriages, 189–90
    public self of, 198–203
    radicalism of, 191–2, 204–5
Bhave, Vinoba, 48
Bhindranwale, Jarnail Singh, 17, 48, 58
Bhutto, Zulfikar Ali, 42
Bilgrami, Akeel, 73n
Billorey, Ramesh, 185n
bin Laden, Osama, 133n
Binder, Leonard, 165n
Birnbaum, Pierre, 113n6
Blake, William, xi, 7
Banerjea, Krishna Mohan, 100, 108
Bose, Ajay, 150n
Bose, Girindrasekhar, 99–102
Bose, Subhas Chandra, 42, 191
Brahminism, 44–5
Brecht, Bertolt, 109

Cabral, Amilcar, 17n, 155
Campbell, Joseph, 106
Camus, Albert, 123
capitalism, 3, 127, 161
Caudwell, Christopher, 114
Césaire, Aimé, 17n2
Cetron, Marvin J., 133
Chakravarty, Dipesh, 93, 117n
Chandler, William U., 184n
Chandra, Bipan, 104, 105n

Chattopadhyay, Bankimchandra, 19n
Chattopadhyay, D.P., 17n
Chattopadhyay, Deviprasad, 114n, 167n
Chattopadhyay, Saratchandra, 20n, 153, 189
Chattopadhyaya, Kamakshiprasad, 183
Chiu, Fred, 131
Chowdhary, Raj, 136n
Chowdhury, Aditi, 25–6n
Chowdhury, Sumit, 25–6n
Christianity, and the primacy of the state, 19
Churchill, Winston, 193
Citizens for Democracy, 30n
citizens, hierarchy of, 37
citizenship, 70, 72
civil society, 6, 13, 140
civilizing mission, 158
    concept of, 4
    native version of, 8
Cohn, Bernard S., 4n, 112
Cohn, Norman, 64n
Collingwood, R.G., 107
colonialism, 4, 8, 18–9, 22, 95, 107, 129, 153, 158, 159, 164, 171, 178
    internal, 27, 30
    see also imperialism
communalism, 61, 75
    communal violence, see riots
communism, 107
    Communist Party of India (Marxist), 48
    Communist Party of India, 191
community, extinction of, 129
competition, 167
Congress (I), 58, 146, 148; see also Indian National Congress
consumerism, 162, 167
continuity, metaphor of, 120, 121
Coomaraswamy, Ananda, 21n, 92, 107
Cornforth, Maurice, 114
Cornwallis, Lord, 200

corruption, 41, 142, 143
cosmopolitanism, 128
counter-terrorism, 133, 135, 136, 137,
    138, 139
    faith in professional, 142–4
    vote-bank for, 148
    see also under terrorism
creativity, 51, 52
Croce, Benedetto, 99
crusades, 74n
cultural integration, 59, 108
cultural intervention, 83
    cultural engineering, 19, 20, 161,
        171
    cultural reform, 24
    cultural revolution, 24
cultural relativism, 26, 154
cultural self-affirmation, politics of,
    131
culture, 22–3, 25–33, 128, 151–7
    and economic growth, 17
    and emic/etic categories, 154
    and modernity, 22, 128, 157,
        156–60
    and science, 17–8, 158–9
    and state, 15–6, 18–21
    and territoriality, 3
    as a language, 155–6, 157–8
    as lifestyle, 154
    as resistance, 25, 32, 155–6, 157
    as resource, 26, 152–3, 156
    civic, 31
    hierarchies of, 26, 38
    museumization of, 26
    survival of, 26, 163

D'Monte, Darryl, 185n
Damodar Valley Corporation (DVC),
    182–202
    acquisition of land for, 185–6, 195
    and displacement, 203n
    critique of, 187, 191, 192–205
    performance of, 194–8
    siltation rates in, 193n
Dang, Satyapal, 136n

dar'ul Islam, 53
Darwinism, 107
Davids, Anthony, 88n
Davies, Merryl Wyn, 63n
Davis, Owen, 133
deculturation, 121, 123, 179, 186
democratization, 12, 30, 39, 41
demythologization, 87
depoliticization, 30, 30–1n
deracination, 63
Deshingkar, Giri, 9n, 27n
Deutsch, Karl, 17, 177
development, 25, 27, 80, 107, 116,
        129, 130, 156, 157, 164, 177
    alternative, 162–3, 165–6, 177
    and colonialism, 158, 159
    and mega-technology, 168, 174n
    and modern science, 158, 159
    and tolerance of cultures, 165–7,
        174–5
    and violence, 175–6, 177–9, 180–1
    costs of, 161, 162, 164
    critiques of, 130, 165–70, 173–4,
        201
    displacement by, 121, 174
    ideology of, 158, 159, 160–2, 166–
        7, 169, 171, 173, 174, 175
    modernism as, 80, 173
    state-sponsored, 25
    sustainable, 196, 201
Dharampal, 25n, 155n
dharma yuddha, 75
dharmashastras, 105
diaspora, culture of, 9
displacement, 120, 122, 174n, 179,
        186–7, 101–2, 121–2, 201–2; *see
        also* exile, refugees, uprooting
dissent, 32, 70, 118n, 129
    against development, 173
    against DVC, 187, 191, 192–203
    secularism as, 63
    Enlightenment values as symbols
        of, 100
Dogan, Mattei, 62n
Dostoevsky, Fiodor, 154

Dravida Kazgham (DK), 145
Dravida Munnetra Kazgham (DMK), 145
Dubashi, Jay, 105n
Dutt, Rajni Palme, 114

Easton, David, 17, 177
economism, bondage of, 17
Eghbal, Afsaneh, 10n, 27n
Elliot, H.M., 100
Else, Koenraad, 105n
Emergency (in India), 8, 142, 179n
Engels, F., 85
Enlightenment, xi, 7, 26, 45, 46, 50, 76, 83, 88, 94, 100, 101, 106, 115, 128, 159, 203, 204, 206
environmentalism, 13, 155, 166, 188, 192, 205–6; see also under movements
Erikson, Erik H., 98–9, 106
Escobar, Arturo, 10n, 25n, 173, 175n, 176
Esteva, Gustavo, 10n, 61, 155n, 163
ethnicity, 3, 27n, 38, 39, 43, 46, 48, 97
    ethnic cleansing, 74n
    ethnic diversity, 11
    ethnic separation, 139
ethnocentrism, 34
exile, culture of, 95–7, 119–23
    and chauvinism, 123–5
    and myth of return, 126
    metaphor of, 120
    psychology of, 95, 96–7, 119, 120, 125–6
    see also displacement, refugees, uprooting

faith, decline of, 62, 63
    and ideology, 73
    marginalization of, 38
    public and private, 36, 48
    see also religion, fanaticism
Falk, Richard, 10n
fanaticism, 34, 56, 57, 59, 72, 77; see also zealotry

Fasano, Enrico, 19n
Feith, Herb, 9n, 164, 172n
Fernandes, Walter, 174n
feudalism, 18
Feyerabend, Paul, 89
Fogelman, Eva, 66n
Forward Block, 191
French Revolution, 2
Freud, S., 2, 10, 76, 87, 90, 101
Fukuyama, Francis, 92
fundamentalism, 75, 123, 172

Gadamer, Hans-Georg, 75
Gadgil, N.V., 183
Galtung, Johan, 85, 162n
Gandhi, Indira, 8, 36, 39, 42, 48, 58, 141, 145n
Gandhi, M.K., xi, 5n, 13, 17, 23, 26n, 32, 34, 36, 37, 41, 47, 48, 50, 51, 54, 62, 134, 149, 155
Gandhi, Rajiv, 143, 149, 150
Gandhi, Ramachandra, 106–7, 128n
Gandhism, 13, 24n, 144, 205
Gangopadhyay, Surendranath, 189
Gardiner, W. Lambert, 165n
Garewal, Naveen S., 136n, 147n, 148n
Gautam, Akhil, 147n, 148n
Gellner, Ernest, 141
Georgescu-Roegen, N., 91
Ghising, Subhas, 134
Gibbons, S., 100
Giddens, Anthony, 92
Gill, K.P.S., 148
globalization, 12, 110, 127, 131
Godse, Nathuram V., 23, 48
Goel, Sita Ram, 105n
Gokhale, Gopal Krishna, 22
Goldsmith, Edward, 185n, 197n, 207n
Gopal, Ajit S., 136n
Gopal, S., 104
Gouldner, Alvin, 91
Gregor, James, 178
Gregorios, Paulos Mar, 63n
Guenon, René, 92
Guha, Seema, 147n

Gupta, S.P., 104, 105n

Hagen, Everett E., 126n, 165n, 177
Haksar, Nandita, 135
Hall, Stuart, 125n
Hamsun, Knut, 4
Haq, Zia-ul, 140n
Harrison, Selig, 145–6
Hartnack, Christiane, 99
Hasan, Tariq, 66n
Hedgewar, Keshav, 67, 103
Heidegger, Martin, 4
Herzog, Werner, 128–30, 131, 169n
Hettne, Bjorn, 165n
Hildyard, Nicholas, 185n, 197n,
    207n
Hillel, Daniel, 204
Himmler, Heinrich, 97
Hindu Mahasabha, 114
Hindu nationalism, 2, 23, 29, 36, 45,
    46, 49, 61, 67, 70, 71, 79–82,
    103–8, 111, 114
    and the fear of people, 113
Hinduism, 35, 51, 105
    and Hindutva, 79–82
    and the nation-state system, 19
    apologists of, 37
    attempts to masculinize, 108
    formation of a self-defensive, 18
    Islam as a part of, 52
    Muslim construction of, 51
    traditions of, 29
Hindutva, 79–82, 108
    and history, 111, 102–7
history, 49, 83–84, 90, 94–5, 109, 116,
    118
    ahistorical societies, 85–6, 90–1,
        110–1, 118–9
    alternative history, 76–7, 83–4, 88–
        9, 93, 102
    alternatives to, 83, 93, 102
    and development, 172
    and ambiguity, 88–9
    and anthropology, 104
    and forgetfulness, 86–104

and myth, 84, 99–102, 106, 116,
    117–8
and the past, 94, 95, 97
and psychology, 97–9
and self, see self
and violence, 66, 96–7, 102–7, 108
as theory of future, 97–8
building ethics on, 40, 106–7
European connection of, 36, 39,
    108, 109, 115–6
historicization of, 90, 91–4, 97–8,
    118
historical self, 116–8
imperialism of, 84, 95, 97
objective, 40, 70, 88, 89, 104, 106,
    118
scientific, 40, 88, 108
self-reflexivity in, 95–
Hitler, Adolf, 190
Hobsbawm, E., 117n
Hodgson, Marshall, 112n
Home, Amal, 183
Huntington, Samuel, 17, 30

Ibrahim, Dawood, 65n
Illich, Ivan, 102
imperialism, 80, 82, 95, 177; see also
    colonialism
impersonality, 90n
Indian National Congress, 48, 145n,
    190, 193; see also Congress (I)
individualism, 167, 173
industrialization, 54, 96, 121, 122,
    173, 196
    industrialism, 7
Inglehart, Ronald, 62n
Inkeles, Alex, 165n
irrationality, 159
Islam, 35, 51
    folk, 49
    Hindu construction of, 51
    Hinduism as part of Indian Islam,
        52
    primacy of state in, 19
    West Asian Islam as ideal, 21, 52

itihas, 106; see also history

Jagmohan, 142
Jammu and Kashmir Liberation Front, 139
Janata Dal (S), 148
Janata Dal, 148
Jenkins, Brian M., 133, 137n
Jenkins, Keith, 92
jihad, 74n, 75
Jinnah, M.A., 36, 41, 42, 48
Joshi, Murli Manohar, 67, 103
Jugantar Samiti, 134

Kakar, Sudhir, 99
Kapp, K.W., 177
Kapur, Rajiv A., 137n
Kautilya, 53, 111
Kaviraj, Sudipto, 19n
Keer, Dhananjay, 80
Keller, Stephen, 125n
Kesavan, Mukul, 112n
Khan, Allauddin, 51
Khan, Ayub, 8, 172n
Khan, Khan Abdul Ghaffar, 36, 155n
Khan, Syed Ahmed, 115
Khanna, K.C., 149n
Khomeini, Ayatollah, 17, 31, 39
Khudai Khidmatgars, 155
King, Martin Luther, 48
Klein, Kerwin Lee, 115
knowledge, systems of, 31–33, 168, 176, 203–7
    alternative paradigms of, 31, 198
    and development, 167–8, 174–5
    culture as, 25, 26, 152–3, 156, 167–8
    indigenous, 26, 198–202
Kosambi, D.D., 17n, 167n
Kothari, Rajni, 27n
Kothari, Smitu, 121n, 174n, 177n
Krishna Iyer, V.K., 144
Kropotkin, Piotr, xi, 6
Kumar, Ravinder, 12n
Kuriakose, Mamkootam, 206

Lacqueur, Walter, 134n
Laing, Ronald, 91
Lal, B.B., 104
Lal, Vinay, 93
Laldenga, 134, 145, 146
Laski, Harold, 114
Lenin, V.I., 177
Levine, Donald N., 88n
Lifton, Robert J., 74n, 96, 123
Lipner, Julius J., 74n
lokachara, 16n
lokniti, 30
Lowenthal, David, 94
Luithuli, Luingam, 135

Macaulay, Thomas, 79, 205
Madina Begum, 51
Mahadevan, T.K., 47
majoritarianism, 73
Manu, 53
Marcos, Ferdinand, 8
Marglin, Stephen, 172n
Martin, David C., 132
Marwah, Ved, 133n, 147
Marx, Karl, 5, 6, 17, 22, 24n, 25, 40, 85, 87, 92, 204–5
Maslow, Abraham, 44, 89, 91
mass culture, global, 139, 175
    as middle-class culture, 162
    symbols of, 139n
materialism, 157, 166, 170
mathematization, 32, 88
May, Rollo, 91
Mayaram, Shail, 11n, 66n, 69n, 84n, 103n, 124n
Mazrui, Ali, 82
Mazzini, Giuseppe, 113
McClelland, David, 17, 126, 165n, 177
Mehta, Vinod, 147n
memories, 117–8, 180
Mill, James, 100
Mishra, Pankaj, 125n
Mitra, Chandan, 146n, 147n
modernity, 28, 31, 33, 37, 38–9, 43,

50–1, 52, 80, 90n, 118, 123, 128, 130, 131, 154, 156, 158, 166, 172, 173, 176, 206
modernization, 8, 27, 39, 54, 67, 90n, 114, 160, 165, 172, 198
political, 29
Mody, Nawaz B., 137n
Mohan, Sadhna, 141n
morality, 40, 45, 63, 86
movements, 131
alternative science, 13
anti-imperial, 13
anti-imperial terrorist, 21
human rights, 30, 192, 202
Naxalite, 134
Ramjanmabhumi, 93n, 102–7
Morgan, E., 5n
Mukherji, Radhakamal, 206
Mukhia, Harbans, 104, 105n
Mukhopadhyay, Ashutosh, 183
Mukhopadhyaya, Bhudev, 19n
multiculturalism, 69n, 128
Munje, Balkrishna, 67
Muslim fundamentalists, 45, 49
Muslim nationalism, 115
Myths, 84, 86, 99–102, 106, 116, 117–8, 126–31

Nabokov, Vladimir, 126
Naqvi, Saeed, 77n
Narain, Harish, 105n
Narain, Jayaprakash, 29n, 58, 134, 135
Narmada Sagar project, 185n
Nasr, Seyyed Hossein, 92
nation-building, x, 1, 2, 41, 44, 95
nation-state, 1, 8, 12,
and civil society, 6, 13
and colonialism, 8
and culture, 2, 5, 19, 36
and Hindu nationalism, 20, 23; See also Hinduism
and progress, 1, 8
and religion, 43
as clue to the West's success, 5

Brahminic idiom of, 19, 20
crisis in, 38
cultural traits necessary for, 1
ideal counter-terrorist, 140, 141
nationalism, 2, 19, 38, 81, 116, 123, 125, 126, 137, 138, 141, 142, 149, 153, 163, 176, 183, 187
Nayar, Kuldip, 146n
Nazism, 107
Nehru, Jawaharlal, 18, 23, 36, 41, 42, 45, 48, 50, 177, 183
nepotism, 40, 142
Nivedita, Sister, 21n
Norberg-Hodge, Helena, 181n

O'Neill, Michael, 137n
O'Rourke, Dennis, 167
Oak, P.N., 52
Oakeshott, M., 5n
Obeyesekere, Gananath, 83–4n
objectivity, 56, 116, 118, 159
Operation Bluestar, 143
Organski, A.F.K., 179
'Oriental Despotism', xii, 6, 10, 158, 172, 177
Orientalism, 110
Orientalists, 26
Orwell, George, 39, 95

Pachauri, Pankaj, 150n
Pandey, Bhola, 145n
Pandey, Devender, 145n
Pandey, Gyanendra, 87n, 108n
Panikkar, Raimundo, 62
Pant, Pitambar, 186
Papastergiadis, Nikos, 169
Parsons, Talcott, 17, 177
participatory politics, 20, 40–1, 48, 50, 71, 164
Partition, 87n, 125
Partition riots, see under riots
Patel, Gieve, 34
Patel, Vallbhbhai, 18, 36, 48
patriotism, 32
Pawar, Sharad, 140n

People's Union of Civil Liberties, 30n
People's Union of Democratic Rights,
    30n
peripherality, 47, 49–56
Permanent Settlement system, 200
Picasso, Pablo, 123
Pipes, Richard, 97
Polanyi, Karl, 120n
political engineering, 154, 161
politicization, 39
Popkins, Richard, 92
Popper, Karl, 32
Pound, Ezra, 4
Prakash, Gyan, 93
Prakash, Madhu Suri, 155n
Prebisch, Raul, 176
prejudices, 56
progressivism, 1–2, 198–9
puranas, 16n, 99–102, 106
Puri, Balraj, 136n, 139
Pye, Lucian, 17

racism, 38
Raina, Vinod, 25–6n
rajadharma, 40
rajniti, 30
Ramjanmabhumi movement, see under
    movements
Rana Pratap, 111
Rao, Parsa Venkateshwar, 80
Rashtriya Swayamsevak Sangh (RSS),
    57, 80, 114
rationality, x, 32, 39, 40, 56, 59, 70, 72,
    74, 76, 114, 129, 157, 158, 159,
    169, 180;
    critical, 63
    pathology of, 80
Ray, Satyajit, 110–1, 130–1
realpolitik, ix, 11, 39, 40, 46, 91, 113
Rebeiro, J., 146–7
refugees, 119–21, 125, 126, 201–2;
    see also displacement, exile,
    uprooting
religion, 36–7, 40–2, 79
    and self-interest, 41, 74
    as cultural resource for the defence-
        less, 75, 77
    fear of, 75, 78
    'irrationality' of, 76
    marginalization of, 38–9
    pathologies of, 39, 43
    'peripheral believers', 47–8, 50–4
    political use of, 41, 56, 74
    separatation from politics, 34, 36
Reynolds, Henry, 155n
riots, 54, 65, 67
    anti-Sikh riots, 60, 65
    as largely urban, 66
    as secularized, 56, 58–60, 64–5,
        73, 74–5
    Partition, 40, 57, 66, 121
    resistance to, 57, 65–7
Rorty, Richard, 91n
Roy, K.B., 187
Roy, M.N., 29n, 36, 37, 48
Roy, Ramashray, 162n
Roy, Rammohun, 5, 20n, 22, 44–5, 110
rumours, 66, 118
Rushdie, Salman, 126
Ruskin, John, 7
Russell, Bertrand, 114
Rustomji, K.F., 133n, 138

Sachs, Wolfgang, 171–72n
'sacred', 34
Saha, Meghnad, 193
Sahasrabudhey, Sunil, 24
Sahi, Jyoti, 71–2n
Santhal rebellions, 155
Sardar, Ziauddin, 63n, 89n
Sarkar, Tanika, 155n
satyagraha, 75
Savarkar, V.D., 19, 36, 41, 42, 48, 67,
    79
savarna purana, 80
Saxena, N.K., 143n
Schapiro, Barbara, 65n
Schmid, Alex, 145n
Schrijvers, Joke, 181n
Schumacher, Joseph, 91

Schuon, Fritjof, 92
Schweitzer, Albert, 159
Schwenk, Theodor, 198n
Schwenk, Wolfram, 198n
science, 40
  and the state, 25, 27
  hegemony of modern science, 27, 95
  indigenous theories of, 26
  as language of global communication, 157
scientific rationality, 10, 28, 40, 45, 76, 107, 117, 156
scientism, 7, 206
scientization, 88, 163
secularisation, 41–3, 54, 62–3, 64; see also under riots
secularism, 34–5, 36–7, 39, 40–3, 59, 60, 67, 68, 69, 71, 73, 75–7, 79, 114,
  and class affiliations, 72
  and secularisation, 62–5
  and tolerance, 77
  as counterpoint of religious chauvinism, 77
  as the double of communalism, 61
  European associations of, 72, 76
  and Gandhi, 34, 36, 41, 42, 43
  ideology of, 61, 62–4, 70–2, 74, 78
  'official', 11, 37–8, 63, 70–1, 78
  politics of, 65–71
  as a principle of exclusion, 70
  private and public, 36–7, 42
  pseudo-, 70, 77, 78n, 80, 105, 108
self, 110
  historical, 128
  dialogue with, 110–1, 126–7
  engineering of, 110
  modern, 110–1, 123, 127–8
  partitioned, 131
  public, 198–203
  representation of, 110
Sen, Amartya, 73n
Sen, Anikendra Nath, 136n

Sen, Asit, 183
Sen, Sankar, 136n
Sen, Sunrita, 148n
Senghor, Leopold, 17n
separatism, idiom of, 145
Shariati, Ali, 48
Sharma, Suresh, 178n
Sharma, Suresh, 19
Sheth, D.L., 29n, 138
Shils, Edward, 17, 177
Shiv Sena, 64, 141
Shiva, Vandana, 11n, 25n, 128n, 155n, 181n
Shourie, Arun, 105n
Singh, Avinash, 147n, 198n
Singh, Brijbhushan Sharan, 65n
Singh, Dipnarayan, 189
Singh, Gayatri, 96n, 174n, 202–3n
Singh, Guru Gobind, 111
Singh, Kumar Suresh, 69n
Singh, Paramjit, 149–50
Singh, Raajen, 185n
Singha, Radhika, 4n
Sinsheimer, Robert, 96n
Sivaraksa, Sulak, 165n
Skolimowsky, Henryk, 162n
slavery, 95
Smith, D.H., 165n
Snow, C.P., 94
social engineering, 19, 25, 44, 71, 154, 160
Sorel, George, 6
Soroush, Abdolkarim, 73n
Srivastava, R.K., 162n
Stalin, Joseph, 88
state, 1–14, 15–6, 21–4, 35–6, 38, 40
  ancien regime, 3, 6
  and culture, 1–4, 23–4, 27–33, 110–4
  and development, 5, 9–10, 25
  and military research, 10
  and national security, 8, 9, 10, 26, 27
  and nationalism, 2
  and religious tolerance, 35

and scientific rationality, 10
and secularisation, 3, 35, 37, 40,
    41, 42
and society, 8–14
as arbiter, 3
civilizational, 12–3, 24
concept of, 3, 4, 5n, 12, 36, 113,
    114, 117, 145
crisis of the, 12
critique of, 7, 11–2n, 23–5
Hindu, 110–1, 113
ideology of, x, 3, 9–10, 36, 79, 84,
    114, 126, 127
imperial culture of, 4, 111–2, 113–5
moderate, 13
new reasons of state, 27
popular ideology of, 3
postmodern, 12
pre-modern, 5–6
'repressive-developmentalist', 9–
    10n, 164, 172n
as nation-state, 5–6
theocratic, 44
violence by, 9, 11, 13
state-formation, 95
statism, 16, 18–20, 22, 30, 31–3, 71,
    78, 138
advent in India of, 18–9
and democratic institutions, 29n
and exile, 138–9
and terrorism; see under terrorism
see also state, ideology of
stereotypes, 56, 118, 140, 141, 194
Suleri, Sarah, 62, 94
Sunil, K.P., 147n
Swain, Ashok, 122n
Swarup, Ram, 105n
Swinton, Viscount, 193
syncretism, 49, 77
Szasz, Thomas, 91

Tagore, Rabindranath, 11–12n, 20n,
    22, 117n, 128n, 134
Tarkovsky, Andre, 130
Tarkunde, V.M., 144

Tennessee Valley Authority (TVA), 183,
    184, 193
terrorism, 132–3, 139
and counter-terrorism, 139, 142–
    3, 146–8
and cultural codes, 148
and democracy, 144–6, 148–9
and fear of people, 141–2
appearance in modern India, 134–
    7
as an alternative form of negotia-
    tion, 144–5
as commodity, 137
as politics, 132, 133, 135, 139–40
efficacy of, 144
limits of, 135
state-oriented theory of, 138, 140–
    1, 142–4, 149–50
trend worldwide, 132–3
Thapar, Romila, 104, 105n
Thatcher, Margaret, 137
Thompson, William, 92
Thoreau, Henry David, xi, 5n, 7
Thukral, Enakshi Ganguly, 185n
tolerance, 39, 77
ethnic, 52, 53, 77
religious, 61, 70, 71, 77
Tolstoy, Leo, 6
traditions, ix, 37–8, 40, 50, 52, 53, 64,
    68, 71, 75, 78, 93, 95, 106, 114,
    115, 127, 131, 140, 157, 164,
    165, 172n, 174–5, 206
and riots, 54
Brahminic, 47
family, 78
of constructing the past, 101, 106
of self-censorship, 135
transcendence, theory of, 74, 89, 90
Treaty of Westphalia, 2
Trevor-Roper, H.R., 64n, 81
'trickle-down effect', 180
Trivedi, Shikha, 11n, 66n, 103n, 124n
Truman, Harry S., 180
Trussell, Denys, 185n, 197n, 207n
Tucker, Aviezer, 120n

Turnbull, Collin M., 157n

underdevelopment, 159, 177
universal civil code, 36, 60
universalism, 128
Upadhyay, Brahmabandhav, 134
uprooting, 60, 96–7, 119, 120–6, 178,
    179, 201–2
    and achievement motivation, 126
    and fundamentalism, 124n
    and language of continuity, 123–4
    and ultra-nationalism, 123–5142
    by DVC, 186
    memories of, 122
    psychology of, 122, 123–4, 125–6
urbanization, 96, 121–2, 173

Vajpayee, Atal Behari, 145n
Vico, Giambattista, 88
violence, 74, 123–5
    and development, 163–4, 172–80
    religious, 54, 59
    see also authoritarianism, riots,
        terrorism
Vishwa Hindu Parishad, 105n
Vishwanathan, Shiv, 9n, 25n, 159n,
    171n, 187
Visvesvaraya, M., 187
Vivekanand, Swami, 21, 106–7
von Herder, Johan Gottfried, 113
von Humboldt, W., 5n
Voorduin, W.L., 183n, 193n

Walcott, John, 132
Wariavwallah, Bharat, 27n
Wavell, Lord, 193

Weber, Max, 6, 10
Wells, H.G., 114, 117n
West Asian Islam, as an ideal for
    'revivalists', 21
Western Christianity, as an ideal for
    'revivalists', 21
Wilcocks, William, 196, 199
Wittfogel, Karl, 6
Wittgenstein, L., 91n
worldviews, 31–33, 38, 49, 50, 59, 180
    Baconian, 107
    colonial, 158
    Enlightenment, 90, 156
    historical, 85
    Judaeo-Christian, 71n, 158
    of the violated, 86, 205
    Parsonian, 165
    religious, 35
    secularist, 78, 80
Worsley, Peter, 155n

xenophobia, 34, 75; see also zealotry,
    'fanaticism'
Xenos, Nicholas, 120n

Yagnik, Achyut, 11n, 66n, 103n, 124n
Yajnavalkya, 53
Yaseen, Ghulam, 53, 54
Yat-Sen, Sun, 5
Yew, Lee Kuan, 8

Zealotry, 34, 45–6, 49, 55, 56, 57, 72,
    77
Zia-ur-Rahman, 42
Zimmerman, Francis, 168